W9-BHY-558

06/24

STAND PRICE
$ 5.00

The *American Men of Letters Series*

From an engraving by J. C. Buttre, after the Brady daguerreotype

James Fenimore Cooper

James Fenimore Cooper

James Grossman

The American Men of Letters Series

WILLIAM SLOANE ASSOCIATES

To ELSA

Acknowledgments

IN ADDITION to my incalculable debt to all of those who have worked in the same field before me, I have incurred many other obligations in the course of writing this book. I wish to thank the following institutions and their staffs not only for ready access to and use of material but for their cooperative and courteous aid to my wife and me: New York Public Library—Berg Collection, Information Division, Manuscript Collection, Newspaper Division, and Reserve Room; New-York Historical Society; Mechanics Institute Library, New York City; Columbia University Library; Sterling Memorial Library of Yale University; Houghton Library and Widener Library of Harvard University; New York State Historical Association, Cooperstown, N. Y. Mr. Robert C. Gooch, Chief of the General Reference and Bibliography Division of The Library of Congress, gave me the benefit of considerable research on the authorship of *The Cruise of the Somers*. My friend Quentin Anderson made available to me an admirable unpublished essay on *The Spy*. Margaret F. Sloss, with that kindly wisdom which is always at the service of her friends, made most valuable suggestions and comments on the manuscript. I am also deeply grateful to my friends Diana and Lionel Trilling for their invariably generous and helpful detailed criticism of each chapter and for their affectionate encouragement and guidance. In every phase of the work I have been aided inestimably by my wife, Elsa Neuberger Grossman, who has done much independent research on Cooper to make this book more accurate and has made many improvements in its text; she has performed so cheerfully such dreary chores as checking quotations and facts and has listened with such endless tender patience through the years to every variant of every phrase that in lightening my task she has made it, from the beginning to the end, a happy one.

Contents

James Fenimore Cooper

Chapter I

IN 1850, at the end of a writing career of thirty years in which he had published thirty-two novels and a dozen other books, Cooper wrote: "If any thing from the pen of the writer . . . is at all to outlive himself, it is, unquestionably, the series of 'The Leather-Stocking Tales.' To say this, is not to predict a very lasting reputation for the series itself, but simply to express the belief it will outlast any, or all, of the works from the same hand."

Almost every book about Cooper has indicated in one way or another that it is unfortunate, or at least a source of embarrassment, that his prediction has come true and that Cooper is known generally only by his best work. For these five novels about Natty Bumppo—their very titles, *The Deerslayer, The Last of the Mohicans, The Pathfinder, The Pioneers, The Prairie*, betray it—are adventure stories. They are read by boys. A reviewer in 1883 urged this as proof that Lounsbury's book on Cooper, for all its own merits, greatly overestimated its subject's; and in the 1920's the same point was made with indulgent superiority to Marcel Clavel by his intellectual American friends when they

heard he was undertaking a monumental work on the author
of *The Last of the Mohicans.*

It is difficult to defend the adventure story today, for we
often refuse to recognize it when we read it at its very best.
To refer to Joseph Conrad or Ernest Hemingway as adventure writers would seem absurdly unfair, but their connection with Cooper is real. Conrad himself in an appreciative
essay has indicated his indebtedness to Cooper's sea tales.
Hemingway's relation has been noted by Philip Rahv in a
way that illustrates neatly our belief in the inherent imma-
turity of the adventure writer: ". . . one suspects that
Hemingway, that perennial boy-man, is more accurately understood as a descendant of Natty Bumppo . . . than as
the portentously disillusioned character his legend makes
him out to be."

This use of the hero of the Leather-Stocking Tales as a
convenient symbol of "pure" adventure and freedom from
civilized complication is fully justified in its context, which
is really our own simple-minded recollection of boyhood
reading. Yet it is something of a paradox that in his own
time and context Leather-Stocking was at the very center
of a dilemma of civilization: he burst on the world in *The
Pioneers* (1823)—the first of the series in order of writing
—as a quarrelsome garrulous old hunter, driven from his
hills by the kindly new settlement that has been made among
them, and broken by its civilized laws. When in the last
written of the series (1841), he is the romantic ingenuous
youth, Deerslayer, on his first war path, the flight backward
into time is not an escape from civilization, for civilization
is embodied in its harshest form in the two murderous white
men in the story.

The novel of adventure ruined Cooper's posthumous reputation, but in his own lifetime it was the novel of ideas that undid him. His reputation never recovered from the hatred aroused by *Home as Found* (1838), that ferociously extravagant forerunner of *Main Street* and *Babbitt*. This strange book about the provincial cringing of the inhabitants of New York City before foreign opinion and the provincial lawlessness of opinion in the village of Cooperstown is not an accident in Cooper's career but the climax of a decade of conscious political thought. In part his downfall was due to public dismay at a romancer's thinking at all about politics; even the exposition in works of nonfiction and in his novels about Europe of his first important idea, the superiority of American democracy to European aristocracy, had caused some diminution in his great popularity. This idea, explored by so fresh a mind as Cooper's, was only superficially a safe one; it led to another, the actual failure of democracy in America to create a free life. Personal experience, perhaps even some personal need to be disliked, as well as honest thinking, had drawn him to this unpopular conclusion. Cooper has himself insisted that the violent *Home as Found*—and it seems true to some extent also of his abstract political treatise, *The American Democrat* (1838)—was written to give universal meaning to a petty quarrel with his neighbors about their right to picnic on a small unprofitable piece of land.

The subject may seem a trivial one, but to Cooper "Vive la bagatelle" had become the grim battle-cry of freedom. He saw in the mean spitefulness of his neighbors' opinions, and in the silly newspaper comment in their favor, a despotism as ruthless and crushing as that of the terrible Venetian oligarchy whose efficient organization for evil he had pictured so brilliantly in his first novel of ideas, *The Bravo*. The new tyranny of the majority and of the manufactured public opinion that acted in its name, like the old police-state of Venice, was absolute in its demand for uniformity.

The frenzied vilification of Cooper after *Home as Found* only confirmed him in his gloomy view; and he regarded the libel suits he brought against the most powerful newspapers in the country not as retaliation but as the further performance of the duty of a good democrat to resist tendencies dangerous to democracy. His sales went down considerably. The practical question of how he was to live as a writer was closely connected with the question of principle: if he was to lose his audience, how was he to enlighten it? The momentum of the writer's courage in opposing a monolithic society constantly drives him further from it; but when his alienation from his world is complete, it is difficult for him to speak to it at all. Some of Cooper's later novels of direct propaganda were often wildly hysterical in their appeal for a life of reason and restraint.

To his quarrel with his country he owes his failures and also some of his greatest aesthetic successes. The spirit of opposition entered into much of his work in the last dozen years of his life and gave to the novel of adventure a subtlety and variety it had frequently lacked. He could do to the life worlds he had never known—the British fleet in *The Two Admirals*, the old colony of New York in *Satanstoe*, so cozily and smugly dependent on England. Never losing hold of moral values, he could in *Wing-and-Wing* exploit to the full the decency possible in men who live by a code that is wrong and the malevolence that may motivate the men who are right; and in a chauvinistic age could present sympathetically a legalistic British martinet, an atheistic Jacobin, and make the one American in the story—the impressed seaman with a just grievance—the most villainous character in it. He could mock himself, tenderly enough it is true, by giving his own crotchetiness to the narrator of *Miles Wallingford*, who makes his adventures the more real and exciting by interrupting them at their tensest moments to comment unfavorably on the manners and political problems of the day.

The right to be different from one's neighbors, unless it is to become a mere crotchet, forces men inevitably into homogeneous groups of their own. For all that he felt the need for group support, Cooper did not fit easily into any one minority. He was not in sympathy with the radical reformers, despite his understanding that the commercial classes acted systematically and inexorably in the interests of money regardless of any other interest of society. His liberalism was genuine, but he held a number of views unconventional in the liberal of his or our day. He liked big navies, disliked a free press, saw dangers in trial by jury. His experience had led him to his own conclusions on matters about which liberalism was rigid. In the last years of his life he identified himself fairly closely with a small group which did not seem to demand the surrender of his own notions. He took the side of the landlords of New York in the Anti-Rent War waged against them by their farmer-tenants.

He saw in the manorial landlords a small group of distinguished individuals who could set a high tone for society. The democratic gentleman, he had always said, was a person not necessarily of wealth but of distinction; and the mere wealth of the landed gentry was significant to him only as the cause of the demagoguery and envy of their opponents. Once more he was defending a minority against the attacks of the majority; he failed to recognize the difference: the few were the very rich and the many the poor. It was impossible to support the men and continue to ignore their wealth. Just as the tenants' war spread from the perpetual leases with their "feudal" requirements of fat fowls and days' work, to all long-term agricultural leases including those that called merely for modern hard cash, so Cooper's defense took in more than the worth of the picturesque old ways; it came to take in money itself. He had to tie in commercial with landed wealth to show that an attack on the one was an attack on the other. Having undertaken the defense of landholding for its humane values, he came to accept the inhuman impersonality he had once found in commerce. He had begun his career as a conscious critic of society with the fine assertion: "In America man had early discovered that the social machine was invented for his use"; and ended it on the side of the machine itself, and the abstract rights of property.

In a work on New York unfinished at the time of his death, he took a rather sour joy in anticipating the absolute triumph of commerce. It was a delusion to talk of "the irresistible power of popular sway," for "men in political matters become the servants of money as certainly and almost as actively as the spirits of the lamps were made to do the bidding of Aladdin"; and whether the government remained democratic in form or became a frank despotism nothing was more certain than that "associated wealth will take care of itself." He had abandoned the democracy of his middle years for a belief in the power of wealth. Could he have believed equally in its virtue, his return to the faith which had surrounded the first years of his life and which was rightfully his by the circumstances of his birth and early environment would have been perfect, for his father and his father's friends had believed simply and wholeheartedly in the men of property as the rightful masters of the country.

William Cooper, the novelist's father, who was to become one of the most successful founders of new settlements in the early republic, was descended from English Quakers who had come to West Jersey around the year 1680 and had prospered. In 1775 William married an heiress, Elizabeth Fenimore, also of English descent. During the Revolution and shortly after, he and a partner bought up the rights to an unsuccessful colonial grant of land on Otsego Lake in central New York. After an autumn visit to survey the lonely new country, he opened up the sale of land early in 1786 and was so successful that many settlers came even before the snow had melted.

After several years of traveling back and forth between his comfortable New Jersey home and the wilderness, he decided to settle permanently in Cooperstown, the new village he had laid out on the southern shore of Otsego Lake, at the source of the Susquehanna. There is a tradition that at the last minute his wife refused to stir from her armchair, and he had to carry her out in it before the great wagon-train could start with its load of household goods, servants, and seven children.

The youngest child on the journey was only fourteen

months old when they arrived at Cooperstown in November 1790. He had been born in Burlington, New Jersey on September 15, 1789, the twelfth of thirteen children—five had already died, and one was to be born in the new home—and had been named simply James Cooper. (It was not until 1826 that as an act of family piety he was to add the "Fenimore" to his name.)

The risks of life in the new settlement were not those we usually associate with pioneering. Just the year before, the settlers had starved almost to death because the high price of grain in Europe had irresistibly drawn to the Albany market the local crops they had expected to buy; only William Cooper's influence with the legislature enabled him to get a supply for them. The Indians, the traditional frontier enemy, were not a danger. They had been severely beaten in the Revolution; only a few came occasionally to hunt and fish or to sell the townspeople brooms and baskets they had made. The memory of their earlier massacres was still potent, and when James was five a great Indian alarm brought the men out on picket duty "watching intently for the descent of the savages with scalping knives and tomahawks." This false alarm was his nearest experience to Indian warfare, and from the safe distance of forty years Cooper was to find the whole incident ludicrous.

In a few years William Cooper acquired a judgeship, a seat in Congress as a Federalist, and, as the objective proof of his great wealth, a fine brick mansion, Otsego Hall, modeled after the Van Rensselaer manor-house. According to his own account, in his charming pamphlet, *A Guide in the Wilderness*, his success was the reward of his system of shrewd kindness in dealing with settlers. He sold land outright, taking back mortagages, and not pressing hard for payment. Settlers might have a lighter annual burden under a Van Rensselaer perpetual lease, but they wanted ownership, not tenancy; their land-hunger could be appeased only by the mystic notion of title. As owners the whole community worked freely on community projects. "A few quarts of liquor cheerfully bestowed," Judge Cooper observed, "will open a road or build a bridge, which would cost if done by contract, hundreds of dollars." His electioneering was an extension of his cheerfulness. Report had it that for votes he was very civil to the young and handsome, flattered the old and ugly, and even embraced the toothless and decrepit.

His kindness did not take in his political opponents. According to them, he bullied the young ("You are a fool, young man," they quote him as saying, "for you cannot know how to vote as well as I can direct you.") and threatened his debtors with ruin if they didn't vote the Federalist ticket. His shrewdness deserted him completely under the strain of principle. He had an old Revolutionary veteran arrested and sent off to jail in irons for circulating petitions against the Alien and Sedition Laws. This instance of Federalist tyranny is supposed to have caused the downfall of the party in New York.

Judge Cooper's connection with the Society of Friends was soon to be formally severed, and after James had gone a few years to the local Academy, "one of those tasteless buildings that afflict all new countries," he was put under the care of an Episcopal clergyman in Albany. The Reverend William Ellison's small school offered all of the advantages to which the son of a wealthy Federalist was entitled. Two Van Rensselaers, a Livingston, and a Jay were pupils. The master was an Englishman and the epitome of national prejudices; he entertained, Cooper remembered, "a most profound reverence for the king and the nobility . . . contempt for . . . dissenters and . . . ungentlemanly sects, . . . was particularly tenacious of the ritual, and of all the decencies of the church, detested a democrat as he did the devil; cracked his jokes daily about Mr. Jefferson and Black Sal . . . prayed fervently of Sundays . . . and, as it subsequently became known, was living every day in the week . . . with another man's wife."

In 1803, after Ellison's death, Cooper entered Yale College. He was thirteen, "a fine sparkling beautiful boy of alluring person & interesting manners," so one of his teachers, the scientist Benjamin Silliman, wrote him with startling directness a quarter of a century later. His charm never ceased for those who loved him and never stood him in good stead with those who didn't. He was expelled from Yale for traditional undergraduate misconduct in his junior year —there is a story of an explosion (apparently of gunpowder) in a college room and of a donkey placed in a professor's chair. The expulsion may have been the more disturbing for the family because his brother William had already had his career at Princeton cut short by what was either a prank or an attempt to burn down the college.

We can expect Cooper to be bitter about Yale; he was always an extravagant mixture of the gay and the bitter. But we have no clue to the meaning of his one serious comment on his college experience. In a travel book, after some discussion of puritan folly and vice ("there is nothing more vicious," he writes, "than self-righteousness, and the want of charity it engenders") he breaks out: "I can safely say that the lowest, the most degraded, and the most vulgar wickedness, both as to tone and deed, and the most disordered imaginations, that it has ever been my evil fortune to witness, or to associate with, was met with at school, among the sons of those pious forefathers. . . ." Like so much that Cooper has written about himself there is a mysteriousness and vagueness about this that may mean anything. The reader is inflamed with the most lurid notions, and at the same time worried that he is being a bit of a fool and misinterpreting a description of some form of spiritual vice. Cooper was always torn between a gentlemanly ideal of personal reticence and a simple desire to talk about himself. He compromised by generalized statements from which all specific facts have been removed. We know his ideas and his feelings about them; he made it his business that we should, and created a literary personality—an awkward and unpleasant one—to go with his work. On his deathbed he requested that no biography should be authorized, and a pious daughter destroyed many of his papers. But Cooper himself had not adequately respected his right to privacy. Every account of his life reveals this dilemma: too much is known about him to accept the literary personality at face value, too little to create a man independently of it; the result is a certain vagueness, having its sources not in his silence but in what he has written.

In October 1806 Judge Cooper sent James to sea as a common sailor before the mast. He was to enter the Navy, and a voyage or two in a merchantman, there being no naval academy, was the usual training before a young man was placed on the quarter-deck of a man-of-war. Cooper enjoyed his year on the *Sterling;* but the assembling of the crew still suffering the effects of life on shore, some listless and stupid with drink, some in the "horrors," must have been an ugly beginning for a seventeen-year-old boy, even one fresh from "those abominations" at Yale.

The passage to England was long and stormy. Off Portugal an armed felucca gave chase; the crew hid a bag of guineas so well that they only found it weeks later in a bread-locker after they had eaten their way down to it. Impressment by the English was their greatest danger. They were mustered on deck for formal seizure by a naval officer; some were stolen informally by the press-gangs on shore. The captain, when he went ashore, used to dress in blue long-tog, drab breeches, and top-boots, so that he could pass for a country gentleman; but he was picked up. "Them press-gang chaps," the mate said, "smelt the tar in his very boots."

Cooper had absorbed from birth the pious Anglomania of the Americans "who looked up to England as to the idol of their political, moral, and literary adoration." He had been accustomed to see an Englishman welcomed to an American home like a brother. England's welcome to the ardent boy—"twenty-two years before, an ardent boy, I had leaped ashore . . . with . . . love"—was more restrained. In his sailor rig and with his nautical air he couldn't be told from his shipmates of the forecastle, and the only acquaintance he made was with a customs officer, a former gentleman's servant full of the lore of the servants' hall, who reverently pointed out an earl in a West End street.

Mostly Cooper drifted around London alone or with his shipmates, taking in the sights. They didn't dare enter Green Park until a citizen told them it was a free country and they had as much right there as the king. The boy perceived on the spot "the broad distinction that exists between political *franchises* and political *liberty*." For the date of this tremendous perception we have only the word of the mature Cooper who delighted perversely in assigning just such disconcertingly slight origins to his most ponderous social ideas. Still, although he did not exploit this idea until he was again a stranger in Europe a quarter of a century later, he was perhaps right about its source: the lonely young outsider's resentment at well-intentioned kindness might have made him see the wrongness of a system in which he was merely tolerated.

After his return to America Cooper was commissioned a midshipman on January 1, 1808. His three years in the Navy, which were to make him an authority on naval warfare all his life, were spent peacefully. He served for a few months on board the *Vesuvius* and the *Wasp*, and was one of a party sent to Oswego on Lake Ontario to supervise the building of a brig. The stay at the primitive frontier village was enlivened by the threat of war with England and by the determined gaiety of the young officers. When the brig was launched the war scare was over, and the launching was celebrated by a grand military ball to which some of the ladies came barefoot.

In December 1809 as Judge Cooper was leaving a political meeting in Albany, he was struck from behind by an opponent and died of the blow. Cooper's worldly position was much improved. He was to inherit $50,000 immediately and had a remainder interest with his brothers in the $700,000 estate. Less than half a year later he was engaged to marry Susan Augusta De Lancey, an amiable young lady of the finest family and with the reversion of an estate in West-chester from an aunt who was already seventy-two.

Susan's grandfather had been a Royal lieutenant-governor of New York, so naturally most of the De Lanceys fought on the King's side in the Revolution, some with such ruthless vigor that by the end of the war De Lancey, as Governor George Clinton said, was a very bad name. But the feeling against the loyalists died down quickly, and many of those whom Washington had once called detestable parricides became respectable members of his own Federalist party. Susan's father, John Peter De Lancey, although an officer in the British Army during the war, returned to live comfortably among his Westchester neighbors at Heathcote Hill, a family place at Mamaroneck.

The marriage took place on January 1, 1811, and Cooper resigned from the Navy. In the next few years the Coopers moved back and forth between Cooperstown and Westchester, meaning to settle in the former but ending up in the latter in 1817. The old De Lancey family nurse had been seduced at Cooperstown into marrying a wayward Methodist for the good of his soul; Susan's grief at the desertion could be assuaged only by a long visit to her parents, at the end of which the Coopers built a new home on De Lancey land in Scarsdale. They had one of those thoroughly happy old-fashioned marriages in which the husband's formal rights of mastery were rigidly respected and the wife, through her delicate sensibilities and the other arts of love, had her way. Susan's way was always in her husband's interest, and the gracefulness of her management left full room for the play of his independent vigor. He busied himself with gentleman farming, belonged to the county agricultural society and the county Bible society, was a vestryman of the church, a colonel in the militia, and part owner of a whaler on which he occasionally sailed in local waters. In these early years five daughters were born and one of them died. Of the two sons born later, one also was to die in infancy.

Between 1813 and 1819 Cooper's five brothers all died. They were fine young men who had lived well. Either through their extravagance or speculations or because its own foundation was speculative, the fortune that had been left them was gone. Otsego Hall was sold. Some of the brothers died insolvent and the burden of making good on their debts and of contributing to the support of their widows and children fell on Cooper.

Around the time of the last of these deaths Cooper began to write. One evening when his wife was unwell he was reading aloud the latest English novel of family life. After a chapter or two he threw it aside in disgust, saying, "I could write you a better book than that myself." Susan turned what could have been merely conventional and inherently modest criticism into a challenge: it was absurd, he hated writing even a letter. He set to work almost immediately, started a moral tale which grew to unwieldy size, tore up his manuscript, and changed his story to a full-length novel about English life, which he finished in June 1820. Cooper had a model before him, and luckily it is improbable that it was the trashy unread book; for Cooper's novel *Precaution*, as George E. Hastings has ingeniously discovered, is an imitation of Jane Austen's *Persuasion*, and to a lesser extent, so others have noted, of *Pride and Prejudice*.

While he was still writing, Susan and his friend William

Jay urged him to have the book printed. Money could not have been one of the admitted reasons. Despite Washington Irving's recent success with *The Sketch Book*, it was improbable that an American would make money writing and questionable whether he ought to. Just a few years before, De Witt Clinton, in expressing his horror of two writers who were his enemies, had said, "Almost in every other place men write for amusement or for fame—but here there are authors by profession, who make it a business and a living." Perhaps out of deference to this prejudice Cooper in his first letter to his publisher carefully pointed out that he had written the book merely to give himself employment and for the amusement of his wife who was in low spirits. But if money could not be a motive, it was still a subject of discussion; publication was to be at his own risk, and Cooper asked a number of naïv. and sensible questions about printing costs and probable sales. He insisted on secrecy; it would go much better as an English book and was sure to fail if its authorship were known.

The last dozen chapters were written in great haste; he hoped to get the work off his hands before his whaler came in, but the printing took months. Stupid printers botched the careless manuscript, turning the lazy dashes he used for breaks into indiscriminate semicolons, and misreading his difficult handwriting creatively. Their mistakes made an author of him, or at least taught him to complain like one: they ought to give him a fair chance, the work was his own; "if they wish to write—let them begin de novo." He threatened a law-suit and settled for a list of errata. At last on November 10, 1820, *Precaution* was published in New York City, anonymously of course, even with a hint of foreign origin

—the publisher blaming the errors on "a great distance inter-vening between him and the author." There is a critical fiction that the first novel of a great writer must be either very good or very bad; Cooper's was very bad, regardless of the printers' faults.

Chapter II

TO AN AMERICAN setting out to imitate an English novel in the second decade of the nineteenth century the choice, roughly, was between Scott and the women, between the novel of adventure in which the hero's marriage was generally only a convenient device to bring the story to an end and the domestic novel in which the heroine's getting married was the story's true reason for existence. Although we shy away from the notion of accident in history, nothing can adequately explain how the American Scott made the mistake of beginning his career as the American Austen. In his forthright handling of the theme of the managed marriage Cooper is as clumsy as Achilles among the women. *Precaution* is throughout an overloaded overtold tale; one is surprised it achieved even a modest success.

Like other stories of its kind, *Precaution* has the usual incident of a lover frightened off when he sees he is being managed by the mother of his beloved. But Cooper with a male logic that is much too clear makes explicit the inarticulate major premise of the domestic novel—that parents have a moral duty to find husbands for their daughters; the care parents should take is the announced theme of the story. The duty to manage having been made as clear as the desire to escape management, the story forces on us a conclusion which Cooper does not dare draw: skill in intrigue is also a moral duty of parents. Jane Austen could at least hint at this conclusion by dramatically presenting its opposite; Mr. Bennet's philosophical indifference is shown to be as much a wrong to his daughters as his wife's inept zeal on their behalf.

Cooper sees so clearly that love and marriage are the intense business of a household that he lets his characters talk openly about them all the time, a violation of the decencies he is purporting to uphold. This is in part the sheer technical incompetence of a beginner; but it is also part of his general failure to understand that thorough discussion of conventions is a means of overthrowing them. In his first novel he went so far in crudeness that, had he accepted its intellectual implications, *Precaution* would have been of the same school as *Man and Superman*, a manifesto of the right to arrive openly at sexual objectives.

There was more to Cooper's crudeness than mere mistake but much less than a revolution in ideas. He was always disturbed by the convention that a virtuous woman must be passive in love until spoken for. In his next novel, *The Spy*, a girl who has loved "unsought" is killed for her sin, by a stray bullet. Her deathbed explanation of the system shows that while Cooper accepted its morality he was troubled by it intellectually: "Woman must be sought to be prized; her life is one of concealed emotions; blessed are they whose early impressions make the task free from hypocrisy, for such only can be happy with men like [the hero]." The conflict between his respect for the moral doctrine and his uncomfortable awareness that women do in fact have feelings accounts for one of the serious technical defects of much of his work, the celebrated woodenness of his heroines. They have enough emotion for us to expect them to do something with it; we are impatient with their acceptance of silence as the price of virtue. His two most successful women, the sisters in *The Deerslayer*, break the rule and tell their love —the one sister because she is a half-wit, the other because she is wickedly intelligent.

Cooper started on *The Spy* immediately after finishing *Precaution*, dashing off sixty pages in a few days. He was so confident of his talent that he had his new publisher print the story as it was being written. It was the great age of careless writers for whom a false start was impossible, and like his contemporaries Scott and Dickens, Cooper was never to think of a manuscript as a mere draft serving as a basis for thorough rewriting. But after the first volume was printed he feared he would not cover his expenses and he stopped writing for several months while trying to decide whether to abandon the work entirely. He was persuaded to go on by the argument that the favorable English reviews of the pirated edition of *Precaution* were a sufficient assurance against loss. As the second volume was being slowly printed, the publisher in his turn worried about profits; the story was getting too long. "To set his mind at rest, the last chapter was actually written, printed, and paged several weeks before the chapters which precede it were even thought of." Although Cooper was never to be solemn about the problem of composition, he admitted later that he had made a mistake in obliging the publisher: "This circumstance, while it cannot excuse, may serve to explain the manner in which the actors are hurried off the scene."

Despite the enthusiasm with which he had begun *The Spy*, Cooper had doubted from the first whether Americans would really be interested in a novel about America. Success seemed so little likely that, in order to explain away failure in advance, he wrote a preface to the first edition showing that the reasons against choosing his own country for the scene of a story far outweighed those in its favor; above all, it was too familiar and had no moats, castles, lords, or any of the other artificial distinctions of life which made English novels so attractive to American readers, particularly women. His hedging was unnecessary. *The Spy* had an immediate popular success when it came out at the end of December 1821; Cooper had guarded skilfully against the supposed barrenness of the American scene.

This story about Westchester during the Revolution was unmistakably American and at the same time straight out of Scott. Cooper had taken as his setting the neutral ground between the two armies in which the struggle had the intense and pervasive character of border warfare. The Westchester of *The Spy*, constantly invaded by the regular armies who fight according to the rules of elegance and chivalry, raided for plunder by the local partisans, the American Skinners and the British Cow-boys, is in the main part a land of Waverley romance and glamorous ambiguity. Harvey Birch, the peddler who brings goods from the enemy-held city, New York, is in reality Washington's favorite spy, and the stranger who seeks shelter from the rain is Washington himself, in disguise. By the historically implausible but aesthetically perfect opening in which Washington rides through the countryside alone, much more in the style of the Bonnie Prince than of the commander of the American armies, the exact tone of the adventures that follow is firmly set.

In *The Spy*, as in most of Cooper's other novels and in Scott's, the characters of high social station are less interesting than the low ones. This cannot be attributed to conscious democratic prejudice—Scott was thoroughly undemocratic in his political principles, and Cooper recognized the value of rank—but stems rather from the recognition of the restrictions rank places on conduct and of the formality of rhetoric it demands. Washington cannot act openly to save Henry Wharton, the young loyalist officer who has imprudently crossed the American lines out of uniform to visit his family; he can only order Harvey Birch to effect his rescue from the American army. The plight of young Wharton does not move us deeply, because he is so fettered by the code which forbids his showing fear; the Wharton slave, Caesar, one of the first of a long line of faithful comic Negroes in American literature, is a freer man, for he is allowed to tremble at danger and act sensibly about it. Major Dunwoodie, the technical hero (that is, the man who marries the heroine, Henry's sister Frances), is priggish about the unfortunate necessity of having to arrest his fiancée's brother. He is alive merely for the few moments in which he is so much of a prig that he is funny. When Henry escapes from his custody, he asks Frances, "What will Washington think of me, should he learn that I ever became your husband?" On deciding to marry her anyway, he boasts, "I will show the world a bridegroom who is equal to the duty of arresting the brother of his bride." "And will the world," asks Frances, for she has a real, if slight, touch of life, "comprehend this refinement?"

The most significant example of the freedom of conduct of the low character is the central figure, Harvey Birch. He had to be of humble origin for the practical reason that he was to be an efficient peddler, and for the theoretic reason that no gentleman could be a spy—he could at most hire one. Harvey performs his working role admirably—drives a good bargain, is greedy for the profits of his apparently immoral trade in British goods, conveys military intelligence to Washington while chatting with his customers. But he is compelled to be much more than amusing; his life is intended to illustrate the disinterested love of country. He refuses money for his services even after he is robbed by the Skinners, and must endure disgrace, for his neighbors believe he is a British agent. Cooper never explains satisfactorily—perhaps in consequence of his writing the postwar last chapter before the story had been thought out—why Harvey's reputation was not rehabilitated after the war was over; it strikes us now that fame would then come to him naturally.*

However, our chief objection to the patriotic Harvey is

---

* One Enoch Crosby was in fact to attain a modest celebrity by claiming, after *The Spy* came out, to be the original of Harvey Birch, the man who insisted on lifelong obscurity. Crosby may or may not have been the anonymous spy of whom John Jay had told Cooper years before and who had been the inspiration of the story; but the success of Crosby's claim at least denies the inevitability of Harvey's cruel fate. Nor is that fate made more likely by the fact that some years later the name "Harvey Birch" was assumed by a French secret agent who refused a reasonable reward for his work; Cooper's authority as a world-famous artist explains this imitation of Harvey but will not do as an explanation of Harvey himself.

literary. Under the burden of patriotism he abandons his racy speech and adopts the dull rhetoric of the upper classes, indulging in high-flown self-pity of his lot as a supposed traitor. That he chooses the moment of greatest danger for his longest outburst is merely an instance of the old dramatic convention, which survives now solely in opera, that the characters are to comment at length on their predicament and the action must pause to let them. What we regret is that Harvey's comment has lost its earlier flexibility and homeliness; as a patriot he is made to forfeit his literary life.

Having been noble to excess about Harvey, Cooper maintains a sensible balance about patriotism in general. The sincerity of a loyalist like Henry Wharton is taken for granted. While an English officer, Colonel Wellmere, is the nominal villain, he is villainous obviously for the sake of the plot and not of any truth about Englishmen. The Skinners, described by an American officer as "Fellows whose mouths are filled with liberty and equality, and whose hearts are overflowing with cupidity and gall," are much worse than the British partisans, the Cow-boys, and are the true villains of the piece. Respectable historians assert that Cooper has exaggerated the Skinners' activities; he may have been trying to justify the anti-American position of the De Lanceys, one of whom had been the leader of the Cow-boys. His prejudice saves the story; it relieves the American cause of the tedium of unmitigated nobility and makes the great patriotic effort more interesting and credible for having been supported in part by wicked men.

Similarly the contrast between the rules of honor of the regulars and the cruelty of the partisans gives *The Spy* its finest drama. The court martial by which Henry Wharton is condemned to death is conducted with the nicest punctilio and the most scrupulous regard for the forms of law, but its verdict is unjust. The Skinner chief when he attempts to desert to the Cow-boys is hanged by them so casually and callously that they do not even wait to see him die in screaming agony but ride away smug in the success of their joke; yet their deed, the reader feels, has its own rightness. Cooper does not explicitly connect the two cases or comment on the relative virtues of wild and formal justice. He was a loose, slovenly writer throughout his entire career, but on great occasions, especially in his early work, he kept quiet so well that we can only wonder idly how he learned such restraint, or whether—and this is perhaps the highest form of critical praise—he really knew what he was doing.

Readers knew at once that they enjoyed *The Spy* immensely, but it was more difficult for American critics to make up their minds. With a few exceptions, they were, considering the book's true importance, mild in their praise or noncommittal. They could not of their own initiative assert that it was the answer to Sydney Smith's recent question—"In the four quarters of the globe, who reads an American book?"—; for they accepted the question's infuriating assumption that the answer "Americans" was totally irrelevant. Their dilemma, for which we have too little sympathy today, was genuine; the self-conscious clamor for a national literature arose as much from a desire to impress England as to escape her influence, so that until the English reviewers had spoken one had no way of knowing how well a native writer had done his work. Fortunately, although there was some objection to Colonel Wellmere, the English magazines reviewed the pirated edition of *The Spy* favorably, and it was translated into French, German, Spanish, Italian, Russian, Swedish, Danish, Low Dutch, and several other languages. American opinion became unanimous, but on the whole the process had to be repeated with each of Cooper's early novels: foreign praise was a prerequisite to American critical esteem and assured it.

Cooper's third novel, *The Pioneers*, appeared after some delay in publication, in February 1823, and by noon of the first day sold 3500 copies, an amazing figure. In accordance with publishing devices of the time, it had been preceded by an extract in the newspapers. The incident chosen, the shooting of a panther who is about to attack the heroine, may have indicated to readers more melodrama by the author of *The Spy*, and it may be because this promise was not fulfilled that on the total count *The Pioneers* was only moderately popular. The first of the five novels in which Natty Bumppo appears, it has generally been considered the least good of the great Leather-Stocking series. But it has always had loyal admirers; critics as different as William Cullen Bryant and D. H. Lawrence have found it peculiarly moving. I believe that for the modern reader it is one of the most profitable and interesting of Cooper's novels.

The Pioneers is a varied and unhurried unfolding of all the aspects of life through the four seasons of the year in a raw frontier settlement like Cooperstown in 1793. Templeton and its leading citizen, Judge Temple, are not to be taken literally for Cooperstown and Judge Cooper. The author is not writing autobiographically of the world he saw at the age of four but of the world he missed and of which he must have heard in childhood. Like Henry James's *Washington*

Square, *The Pioneers* has the haunting quality of something just around the corner from memory. The reader responds with an embarrassed enthusiasm to the simplest materials: the cold of winter, the warmth of household fires, Christmas cheer in the tavern, the congregation in the unfinished Academy that serves as a church, night-fishing on the lake, the morning spent shooting the endless flock of pigeons returning northward in the spring. "Perhaps my taste is childish," writes D. H. Lawrence, ordinarily the least bashful of critics, "but these scenes in 'Pioneers' seem to me marvelously beautiful."

The mood of the book is that of the sophisticated pastoral that mocks, as tenderly as it loves, the wholesome life it portrays, and is as skeptical as it is sentimental about its pictures of sweet rural cooperation and communal labors affectionately shared. In Cooper the doubt is not whether this simple world ever existed but whether men ever liked it. The reader is always made aware that social necessity, and not men's own wishes, created this interlude, set apart from the ordinary course of life, in which men must live close to one another and to Nature until they can afford once again to be selfish uncooperative individuals. We see them during this interlude playing awkwardly the pretty roles which are so ill-suited to their original training. The elegant judge must drink in the tavern with his meanest settler because it is his only club. The settlers worship together because they are few in number rather than one in spirit; one of the finest touches of comedy is the struggle to maintain the decencies of Episcopal form in a village that mainly favors the "standing orders" and thinks it idolatry to kneel at prayer. Gratitude for the bounty of Nature, the formal theme of the pastoral, is shown by man's enjoyment of its destruction: the wood-chopper cuts down trees in a frenzy of delight; when millions of pigeons darken the sky a small cannon is brought out for their slaughter.

The story has to do with two moral problems of Judge Temple, one always present to his mind and one unsuspected by him. The Judge has profited by an act of apparent treachery. His business partner, Edward Effingham, was a loyalist in the Revolution and Temple bought up his land on the confiscation sale. At the end of the story he learns that the mysterious young stranger who loves his daughter Elizabeth is Effingham's son; without real cost to himself the Judge is able to restore the Effinghams to their rights as he has always wanted to. He explains that he has held the land on a secret trust for them which he has never declared openly because his declaration might prevent their obtaining compensation from the British Crown for their loss; in short, he has been trying to cheat the Crown and not them. This is the one point in *The Pioneers* in which Cooper is a little dull; more like a good son than a good novelist, he has taken the Judge's professions of honesty solemnly.

The story of the Judge and Natty Bumppo has all the hard clarity of perception missing in the Effingham-Temple relation. The old hunter who has lived for years on the shores of the lake welcomed Temple on his first trip there alone, but now resents the new settlement whose very existence makes game scarce. The Judge, however, is determined to be kind to Leather-Stocking, as the villagers call him, and to tolerate him and his drunken Indian friend, John Mohegan, even though they are something of a nuisance. When Leather-Stocking kills a deer out of season in violation of the new game laws, the Judge is certain he can manage the necessary prosecution with propriety: Elizabeth is to pay his fine, so that the old man who has saved his daughter from the panther will not be inconvenienced and the law will be satisfied. The worldly arrangement is spoiled by Natty, who resists the search of his cabin for the deerskin. The matter is now beyond the Judge's control, for his own feelings about the dignity of the law are involved; he sentences Natty to an hour in the stocks and to a month's imprisonment. After the public humiliation of the stocks, Natty escapes from the jail and again saves Elizabeth, this time from a forest fire. The Temples are all kindness once more; he is pardoned and is to live with them as a favored retainer. He refuses. Indian John has died by his own choice in the fire, and Natty knows there is no place for him in this new world; he leaves alone for the West.

Leather-Stocking and his Indian friend are so successful as characters that Cooper had to write of them again; three other novels tell of their earlier friendship, and one tells of Natty alone and of his death. It is usual, in publishing these five novels as a series, to list them in the order of the events of Natty's life, beginning with his youth in *The Deerslayer* and ending with his death in *The Prairie*. Under this arrangement *The Pioneers* is the fourth of the series. Although formal logic and Cooper's own sanction justify this practice, I believe that the adult reader should try them in the order in which they were written. The true fate of these two characters is their development in Cooper's hands; it is not an accident that they grow younger, starting in old age and ending in timeless youth.

One of the great charms of *The Pioneers* for the adult today is that he is always aware (whether from his own vague memory or from literary hearsay of *The Last of the Mohicans* and *The Deerslayer*) of the use Cooper is to make of Leather-Stocking and John Mohegan. This surly quarrelsome garrulous coarse old man who boasts tiresomely of past deeds on every occasion and even in the midst of danger, who wipes his nose with his hand and gets into childish disputes about the rules of a shooting-match, will be the mature dreaded warrior, Hawk-eye, and the romantically chivalrous youth, Deerslayer. John Mohegan, the childless old man who has abandoned the warrior's profession for basket-making, who piously thanks the clergyman in church for his sermon and passes out in a drunken stupor in the tavern, will be the noble Great Serpent, Chingachgook, and the father of the doomed Uncas; John is in literal and sordid fact "the last of the Mohicans," as in the novel of that name, Uncas is the poetic and beautiful symbol of the doom of his race.

The modern reader feels the need of some explanation for Cooper's ultimately idealizing his two main characters; however, from the viewpoint of Cooper's own world what is surprising about Leather-Stocking and the Indian is not that they ended so far away from but that they began so close to reality. Eastern America, secure from the Indian and rid of the squatter, was ready to be sentimental about them and weep for their wrongs. These two annoying old men who had been pushed aside by progress were for the later beneficiaries of that progress the embodiment of what little authentic romance the country had and were to be cherished in memory if not in fact. Cooper in *The Pioneers* has caught Natty and the Indian at the very moment when for his Eastern contemporaries and himself they are about to drift away from the scene and from reality, the moment at which the past is about to cease being a presently oppressive fact. Disgraced and degraded by the way of life imposed on them by the little community, their characters take on dignity and form by their death and departure. It was inevitable that having once freed them from a harsh cramping world, Cooper, if he was to write of them again, had to continue the liberating process until they were beyond the corruption of any world we know, so that the series is, in D. H. Lawrence's phrase, a *decrescendo* of reality, and a *crescendo* of beauty. Because Natty is less wise and spiritual in *The Pioneers* than in the other novels, some critics have said that the first is inferior to the other versions; but this is only another way of saying how faithful Cooper has been in the first instance to the hard reality from which the dream has sprung.

In 1823 Charles Wiley, Cooper's publisher, was in financial difficulties. To help him Cooper wrote two short stories for young girls which he gave to Wiley and which the latter published as *Tales for Fifteen* by Jane Morgan. The two stories, "Imagination" and "Heart," are interesting in revealing, respectively, potentialities for sprightly gaiety and morbid sentiment that Cooper never fully developed in his fiction.

"Imagination" is a pleasant set piece about the dangers of forced sentimental friendships between girls. A calculating girl, Anna, is hard put to it to appease the romantic demands of her sentimental friend, Julia, a typical young victim of novel-reading, and writes her that she has an unknown lover who will visit her in disguise. Julia first thinks he will come as a wandering harper, then remembers that as there are none in America, this would only make him the more conspicuous; she rejects the idea of an organ grinder whose stooping over the unwieldy box would be ugly and unattractive. When the coachman in answer to her question as to the distance to Schenectady says "Four miles, ma'am" and points to the milestone, she is certain it is he, and that the stone is intended to mark the spot where they first spoke and which they will visit in annual commemoration in after years. In the end Anna confesses to her invention; Julia gives her up in disgust and marries her sensible and helpful cousin. A warning against the evils of novel-reading was part of the standard morality of the domestic fiction of the time. Cooper, in this sustained bit of farce, while apparently repeating the old lesson has changed it slightly but significantly: the danger isn't in fiction itself but in mistaking it for life. Along with this good sense, the story throws out an odd xenophobic hint that girls will do better to have friendships in their own family rather than with outsiders.

George, the hero of "Heart," catches cold when he gives his coat to a poor man who has fainted on the sidewalk; that evening at a party George plays the flute because he has been inconsiderately requested to do so; his cold gets worse and he dies; the heroine, although wooed by a wealthy man, never marries. This sickly little tale, which is palpably intended as a moral warning against the heartlessness of "society" and not against the evils of generosity, is the first glimpse in Cooper of vulgar overindulged pity for virtue unrewarded by a wicked world. He will not show it again in his fiction as a mere matter of heart; his sentiment can be florid and high-flown for a modern taste but except in this one instance not downright unhealthy. However in his polemical writing and in his comments about himself he will on occasion betray a similar lachrymose strain; and because in his comments about his wrongs at the hands of his country it will be himself that he is pitying, this pity, although never so wallowing as in "Heart," will be almost as harrowing for the reader.

One day at a dinner-party in New York City the talk turned on the authorship of the Waverley Novels. There was no real mystery but readers liked to create one as a way of showing admiration: How could a man of Scott's background know so much about so many things? Where, for example, could the lawyer and Scottish antiquary have acquired the familiarity with the sea displayed in *The Pirate*? Cooper argued that the detailed expert knowledge was simply not there; the author, as always, had created an illusion of reality (*vraisemblance* is Cooper's own term). Lack of true seamanship was not a fault of *The Pirate*, but the claim made for it aroused in Cooper an immediate determination to show what a sailor could do with the sea as a subject. His friends discouraged him—it could never be made interesting, and women, an important part of the novel-reading public, would not like it. Cooper persisted, and *The Pilot*, his fourth novel and the first of his sea tales, was published in January 1824.

He had invented a new kind of fiction. Its most obvious characteristic, the deliberate and uncompromising unintelligibility of its details for the average reader, may perhaps be accounted for by the circumstances of the book's origin; certainly it gave Cooper an advantage over his critics which he exploited shamelessly. He called them lubbers in his original preface and warned: "If they have common discretion, they will beware of exposing their ignorance." Criticism has submitted meekly ever since to this bullying, assuring readers of the excellence of Cooper's technical knowledge and at the same time disclaiming the ability to judge it. Sensible people who like to understand what they are reading have never enjoyed the sea tale, but its unintelligibility is one of its charms. Lost somewhere between the knightheads and the taffrail, the unaided reader somehow makes out, as in a masterpiece in a foreign language dimly understood, the beautiful broad outlines of naval warfare or the ship's struggle with the storm. The daily life of the ship has its own touch of mystery; with a seaman's arrogance and insistence on his separateness from the rest of the world, Cooper uses nautical terms to describe those simple objects a landsman would recognize at once if only they were rightly named. Cooper delighted in confounding the ignorant with the mystification of jargon. In *Red Rover*, his next sea novel, there is an admiral's widow whose husband for amusement had mistaught her the technical talk of ships, so that whenever she speaks she says the opposite of what she means; the reader, following the joke at a respectful distance with his dictionary, makes an uncomfortable identification with the victim, for the author could at will play just such tricks on him.

Cooper had come on something so new that he did not realize at once the full use of his invention. He came around slowly to the discovery that the true subject of a sea story is not the sea or even a ship but a ship's company, and that its finest value for the novelist is in being regarded as the concentrated essence of society and not as something apart from it. In *The Pilot* Cooper has been impressed by the obvious newness of his material and has stressed the difference. Tom Coffin and Boltrope, the perfect seamen, have lost the faculty of living on land. Tom particularly, who has sometimes been admired by the critics as an original character study, strikes me as being too much the product of mechanical extravagance presented more as a marine animal exotic in its simplicity than as a man.

Like Tom, the story itself, which is about a fictitious raid by John Paul Jones on the English coast, becomes awkward and confused when on shore. The object of the raid, as in Jones' actual attempt to seize the Earl of Selkirk, is to kidnap hostages of high rank to assure the better treatment of American prisoners whom the British hold. Conveniently for the love interest the intended victims cannot be found, and most of the time on land is spent in the successful effort of the heroes, two naval officers, to carry off the heroines, two American girls who have been taken to England by their loyalist guardian. The splendor of the sea fighting is sadly diminished by these land adventures. Waging aggressive war for women—for this by actual result is what the fighting in *The Pilot* comes to—is too strong for the modern taste; the humanitarian reader is shocked to see the American Revolution turned into the Siege of Troy.

It was not until *The Last of the Mohicans* that Cooper was to hit on the formula by which war can be successfully perverted from its historical ends to those of a love story: any amount of fighting for a woman can be justified so long as its aim is to protect her from danger or rescue her from a savage enemy. He was not to repeat the mistake of *The*

Pilot and use war as an instrumentality for furthering the hero's love for an unthreatened woman. The formula was more easily applied to land than to sea warfare. In a few stories he had considerable difficulty contriving a plausible means of getting his heroine on board a fighting vessel. He solved the problem best by abandoning it: in some of his finest sea tales, such as *The Two Admirals, Wing-and-Wing,* and *Miles Wallingford,* the sea fighting is carried on without the heroine's presence on the ship. About the same time that Cooper was thus physically separating love and war, in the Leather-Stocking tales he was tying them together more closely; in *The Pathfinder* and *The Deerslayer* Natty Bumppo himself is fighting either for a woman he loves or for one who loves him. While in their broadest aspect, the Leather-Stocking tales were moving from the real to the romantic, in the sea stories Cooper's progress was in general from the romantic to the real.

Cooper had moved to New York City after the publication of *The Spy* to find a school for his daughters and to be near his publisher. He enjoyed being one of the leaders of the town's small intellectual society and founded a club of writers, artists and professional men that was known as "The Lunch" or "The Bread and Cheese." Among the members who attended its weekly meetings were William Cullen Bryant the poet and newspaper editor, Chancellor Kent the great conservative judge, Wiley the publisher, S. F. B. Morse the painter and later inventor of the telegraph, Gulian Verplanck the literate politician who was to edit Shakespeare, Fitz-Greene Halleck the poet who was to become John Jacob Astor's clerk. Washington Irving, still in Europe, was made an honorary member of the club.

The accounts we have of Cooper at the time suggest enor-
mous energy and high spirits that could not find an adequate
outlet even in his voluminous writing, and overflowed in
endless talk. "I have seen him," a friend said admiringly at
the memorial meeting a few months after his death, "in the
highest flights of his genius, at the table where numerous
friends were convened together; I have heard him converse
on national affairs . . . the literature of his country . . .
that monster of the ocean, the Kraken . . . on trout-fishing,
and the Otsego bass." Bryant, who delivered the formal eulogy on this occasion, remembered "being struck with the
inexhaustible vivacity of his conversation," and also "being
somewhat startled, coming as I did from the seclusion of a
country life, with a certain emphatic frankness in his manner, which, however, I came at last to like and to admire."
On first meeting Cooper at a literary dinner in April 1824,
Bryant wrote to his wife: "Mr. Cooper engrossed the whole
conversation, and seemed a little giddy with the great success his works have met with."

Cooper was by now an established writer and planned a
group of American historical novels to be called "Legends
of the Thirteen Republics." He brought out only one of
them, *Lionel Lincoln* (1825). It was his first setback. This
story about Boston at the time of Lexington and Bunker Hill
is remarkably successful in the handling of the purely historical material but a dismal failure as a whole. George Ban-
croft thought the account of Bunker Hill the best ever written. It has the very merit a historian would appreciate, for
the battle is presented in the most part as a spectacle watched
by intelligent military observers. The description of Lexington and Concord seems to me better as novel-writing. Here

profitable use is made of a technique of the novelist that is denied to the formal historian: an intelligent observer is placed in the midst of a confusing action in which known history does not unfold to its appointed end but things simply happen because they have got out of hand. The first killings in the early morning at the Lexington church by the tired troops who have marched all night is just such a bit of brutal casualness in the display of force as happens every day, and is regarded by the good-natured young British officers with the same ineffectual transient horror with which we read our daily newspaper. With the retreat of the British from Concord, hemmed in and fired on from behind trees, fences, barns, unable to strike back at the invisible enemy, all question of guilt disappears in the resentment aroused by the nagging unorthodox deadly attack on the weary plodding men.

Much of the apparatus of the story—the proud Boston family in which some great wrong has been secretly done; the wise old patriot who glides mysteriously through the dim streets and is so strangely attached to the half-witted boy; the spectral shadow on the church wall at the midnight wedding—inevitably reminds the modern reader of Hawthorne. It strikes us as so much like a bad jumbling of the Grey Champion and of the curse of the Maules that it is difficult for us to realize that Cooper is the forerunner and not the imitator. He has transplanted the old Gothic tale to New England but cannot make it grow on what seems to us now, after Hawthorne, its native soil.

The story itself arouses an expectation in the reader which it is its function to disappoint. The hero, Lionel Lincoln, an American-born officer in the English army, has come under the influence of Ralph, the wise old patriot, and has been oddly attracted to Ralph's equally patriotic protégé, a half-witted boy. We are certain that under Ralph's guidance Lionel will be converted to the American cause. In point of fact, he stays loyal to the king; when he does cross over to the American lines we learn later that it is the result of a moment of aberration, and his return to the English army is the sign of his return to his senses. At the dénouement Cooper by a stroke of melodrama reverses the entire meaning of the story. Ralph is revealed as the father of Lionel and of the illegitimate half-wit. Also, and more amazingly, Ralph, who at the beginning seemed to be the personification of mellow rational wisdom so tolerant that he can find kinship even with the poor half-wit, turns out to be a violent maniac whose love of freedom is embarrassingly literal; he has escaped from an English madhouse and regards the keeper who would recapture him as the deadliest foe of liberty.

It is one of the novelist's best tricks, when it is well done, to stand his story on its head and make good evil. We are taken by surprise by the change in Ralph, but become aware, after it has been established, that it has been led up to with some skill; what seemed an intolerable increase in the windiness of his patriotic rhetoric, toward the end, was actually the resurgence of his madness. Yet, for all of the effort that went into its preparation, the reversal, too tremendous and too unexpected, doesn't come off, and the story is a failure.

The parallel between madness and revolution had been a conventional one for Federalists to find when the revolution was French, but not when it was the American one. His American contemporaries and Cooper himself apparently

never suspected the presence of any such unpatriotic parallel in *Lionel Lincoln;* his formal ideas seem at this period
to have been entirely correct, whatever heresies his fantasy
entertained. But some of the English reviewers saw what
was wrong with the book. As one of them sneeringly put
it: ". . . we . . . are . . . instructed that the separation of
the colonies from the mother country was effected principally through the agency of a mad old gentleman, called
Ralph . . . and an idiot lad."

The Last of the Mohicans (1826), Cooper's most famous
and most widely read work, is his first great adventure story
of Indian fighting and perhaps his best. In contrast with
the ambitious *Lionel Lincoln,* and indeed with all of his
previous books, it is relatively free of social complication. It
is almost but not quite (for Cooper was incapable of holding his interest in human society in abeyance) the "pure"
adventure story in which in an arbitrarily simplified world
everything happens for the sake of the excitement of the
action.

Two young women, Cora and Alice, attempt to join their
father, Colonel Munro, the commander of Fort William
Henry which is besieged by Montcalm. Good Indians, aided
by Hawk-eye, protect them from bad Indians; the girls'
alternate rescue and recapture are the main incidents of the
tale. Virtue is the exclusive possession of one side, vice of
the other. Uncas can be only good and noble in his love
for Cora, Magua base and wicked. Moral choice is never
necessary, although its forms are presented to give variety
to the incidents; we know Cora will refuse to be Magua's
squaw even to save Alice's life. The possible problems that

might be raised by Uncas' love for Cora and by Cora's love for the man in love with Alice are conveniently avoided by the deaths at the end of the tale of both Cora and Uncas.

The "pure" adventure story is deliberately superficial. It has no serious concern with the outside world which it uses as a decoration and an aid to the action. It owes no duty to truth, and we recognize this by judging it not for its general truth to life but for the accuracy of its details; we object violently to such minor impossibilities as bullets fired from empty weapons, and accept without question such major impossibilities as its simplified morality.

The Last of the Mohicans exploits with particular ability the broad setting for its narrow adventures. The lonely fights of a handful of characters are made to seem a part of the French and Indian War and of the whole struggle for the Continent by the shifting of the scene, in the middle of the tale, to the armies at Fort William Henry, and in the latter part to the village of the ancient Delaware chief Tamenund. In terms of the action the function of these scenes is merely to furnish an opportunity for the resumption of the chase; in the confusion of the horrible massacre at William Henry, Magua again seizes the girls and must be pursued again; and out of the profound deliberations of Tamenund emerges the necessity of the Delawares' surrendering Cora to Magua and the Mingoes, so that there can be one last chase and fight.

As setting, these magnificent scenes intensify our personal interest in the characters. The women butchered at William Henry excite our pity and terror not so much for themselves but—by that peculiar egoism of identification which fiction sometimes encourages in us—for the two girls seized in the midst of the horror. The final struggle of Uncas and Magua for Cora gains dignity from Tamenund's great prophecies of the extinction of his race. The doom of the Indians, which was later to become a true theme with Cooper, is his most beautiful social decoration in the setting of this socially insignificant tale. Uncas' death in his effort to save Cora would be absurd if the theme were the extinction of the Indians, for this is not the way the Indians met their end. But no absurdity is felt here, as in *Lionel Lincoln*, because here no meaning has been implied.

Uncas and Cora are contrasts in color. *The Last of the Mohicans* uses race as a painter might use coloring arbitrarily for effect. The scale from the higher to the lower—represented by Hawk-eye, the white man without a cross in his blood, Uncas, the noble red man, and with Cora at mid-point—has no more moral significance than the values in a painter's chart. Cora is at mid-point because she has a slight touch of Negro blood. Although the Indians do not know of it, this accounts for their being attracted to her. It is intended to give propriety, instead of significance, to Uncas' attachment to her. The device succeeded so well that a contemporary reviewer was disappointed that a marriage was not arranged between them ("Uncas would have made a good match for Cora, particularly as she had a little of the blood of a darker race in her veins") and found the unhappy ending unnecessary. Cooper more cannily knew that the death of the last Mohican was worth more than a happy marriage, and contented himself with the funeral lament of the Indian maidens celebrating the union of the pair beyond the grave.

Cooper's noble Indians have imposed themselves so completely on the world as actual history that one of our first acts of intellectual emancipation is to turn against them, and, in the process, against Cooper as well. We accuse him of idealizing his subject, as if this were a fault, when in fact it is the accomplishment of the very business he has undertaken. As he sensibly said in answer to his critics in the 1850 preface to the collected Leather-Stocking Tales:

"It is the privilege of all writers of fiction, more particularly when their works aspire to the elevation of romances, to present the *beau-idéal* of their characters to the reader. This it is which constitutes poetry, and to suppose that the red-man is to be represented only in the squalid misery or in the degraded moral state that certainly more or less belongs to his condition, is, we apprehend, taking a very narrow view of an author's privileges. Such criticism would have deprived the world of even Homer."

The reference to the Indians' degraded moral state should indicate to us that Cooper's sober views as a social historian are not those of a literal believer in the Noble Savage. Yet, as W. C. Brownell pointed out, discussion has been carried on in terms of the good Indians, Chingachgook and Uncas, and not of the wicked Magua. Brownell's claim that Magua is Cooper's typical Indian is extravagantly stated but fundamentally true. Cooper regarded Indian civilization as vastly inferior to Christianity, and when he undertook in his later novels a realistic rendering of Indian character his subjects were "bad" Indians—Saucy Nick in *Wyandotté* (1843), and Scalping Peter in *Oak Openings* (1848)—who could become noble only by becoming Christians.

Although Cooper claimed a romancer's privilege for *The*

Last of the Mohicans and the later Leather-Stocking tales,
he had not ignored historical accounts of the Indians but had
merely chosen among them. For his virtuous Delawares
and treacherous Iroquois of the eighteenth century he had
drawn heavily on John Gottlieb Ernestus Heckewelder, a
Moravian missionary among the Delawares, whose works
had been published in 1819 and 1820. His usefulness to a
novelist was quickly recognized; W. H. Gardiner in writing on *The Spy* in the *North American Review* in 1822
had recommended the Indians as a subject for fiction and
mentioned Heckewelder as their best historian. His generous account of the Delawares fitted in with a view of
American history that was becoming fashionable in the
East. Now that settlement of their own land had been long
since completed, Easterners were beginning to realize that
the accounts of the practical settlers were suspect. Their
vilification of the Indian was part of the necessary process
of settlement, because it made his extermination easier.

In the West the Indian was still a practical problem to
which religious idealism seemed to offer no solution, and
the first serious criticism of Cooper's Indians came from
a distinguished Westerner, Lewis Cass, the governor of
Michigan Territory. In the *North American Review*, which
seemed to delight in blowing hot and cold on Cooper, Cass
in January 1826 said that " 'the last of the Mohegans' is an
Indian of the school of Mr. Heckewelder, and not of the
school of nature." We can appreciate the severity of the
Western standard of Indian naturalism when we consider
that this is apparently a reference to poor drunken John
Mohegan of *The Pioneers*, whose only romantic qualities
were his flowery rhetoric and his death in the fire, and not

to the characters of *The Last of the Mohicans* which had been published only in February of that year. In 1828 Cass again attacked Heckewelder and incidentally Cooper, saying that "His Uncas and his Pawnee Hard-Heart, for they are both of the same family, have no living prototype in our forests." Cooper had made himself superficially vulnerable to this attack by mechanically repeating Uncas and Magua in his Hard-Heart and Mahtoree of *The Prairie* (1827) and making them Plains Indians, a group that the great Indian agent knew. But this unimportant bit of laziness is not decisive of the true question: Who knew the "real" Indian? the "ardent, benevolent missionary" of the eighteenth century; or the nineteenth-century government agent who dealt with them on the treaty-ground, poor and almost naked, exchanging their ancestral lands for food, brandy, firearms, trinkets? The opportunity for knowledge did not necessarily lie with the man of affairs. "As just would it be," Cooper somewhat cynically said in his 1850 preface, "to draw conclusions of the general state of American society from the scenes of the capital, as to suppose that the negotiating of one of these treaties is a fair picture of Indian life."

Chapter III

FOR SEVERAL YEARS Cooper had been planning a long trip to Europe with his family. There were good reasons for going abroad—the education of his children, the hope of improving his health, which had been poor, and the opportunity of making better arrangements for European publication. Since *The Pioneers* he had been paid something, not very much, for his English editions. If he could have his London publisher bring his books out simultaneously with, or before, the American edition, his British rights would be worth more; and by furnishing advance copies to Continental publishers it might even be possible to obtain some payment for the European versions of his works. Europe would be expensive but held out the chance of profit as well as pleasure.

By 1826 Cooper had made enough money from his books to undertake the adventure. His preparations were elaborate. The entire family studied French for more than a year. He obtained the usual letters of introduction, and through the solicitation of De Witt Clinton, Governor of New York, was appointed United States Consul for Lyons. This unim-

portant post without salary or duties was an absurd honor
for a grateful country to confer on a world-famous writer,
yet it might have its uses if conditions in Europe should become troubled. Cooper also hoped that by his official connection with his government he would avoid the appearance
of expatriating himself. The danger he feared was real
enough, but the precaution he had taken was inadequate. His
success was bound to create enemies; by going abroad he
gave them an easy point of attack, which in good time they
were to use against him.

At the moment of departure he was near the peak of his
fame. The Bread and Cheese gave him a splendid dinner just
before he sailed. The governor, an Episcopal bishop, and
General Winfield Scott were among the guests. Chancellor
Kent offered a charming toast to "The genius which has
rendered our native soil classic ground, and given to our
early history the enchantments of fiction." Charles King, the
editor of the *New York American* who was later president
of Columbia College, was even more laudatory and linked
Cooper's name with Scott's in the highest terms permitted
by the standards of the day: "Praise indeed can hardly go
higher than by merely alluding to the fact, that the works
of our associate & guest . . . are . . . almost instinctively
compared with those of the Great Enchanter of the North.
. . . To . . . have taken a place at once, if not beside, at
least in close approach to, the Great Master of the art,
proximus a proximo, is glory enough. . . ."

Cooper had planned a grand tour that was to take five
years and to include Scandinavia, Russia, Greece, Palestine,
and Egypt. Although he was in fact abroad for more than
seven years he carried out only a small part of his plan.

More than half of his time was spent, at different intervals, in Paris or near it—he had the inevitable American passion for "the queen of modern cities"—and in Italy, whose people he loved most, he lingered for a year and a half. There were also visits to England and the Low Countries, summers in Switzerland, and trips on the Rhine.

Cooper was an excellent tourist. He never lost his frank rapture at every ancient ruin and scenic beauty—a state of feeling that the family, after Byron, called "touzy-mouzy." While he had only contempt for such "cockney sights" as Napoleon's cradle, he was willing to look with an easy credulity at such pleasant impostures as Juliet's tomb and the house of the Montagues. ("These people must have had houses, and they must have had tombs, and it is as well for us travellers to believe we see them here at Verona, as to believe any thing else.") Shrewd enough to recognize that in Switzerland tourism was a business (". . . the Corydons and Floras of the vale were speculating on the picturesque, and . . . the whole district was in the market of admiration.") he did not let his awareness spoil his pleasure.

His greatest virtue, and the five travel books he published after his return to America are filled with it, is the exactness of his observation of manners and customs. No scene is too grand or too trivial for his use as an illustration of national institutions. In Naples, when the King's son tries to sit in the front of the royal coach, he notes the respectful violence with which the servants force the child into his proper seat while the crowd stands uncovered and the soldiers at present arms. At a poor man's funeral in England he comments on "the niggardly administration of the sacred offices, and the business-like manner of the whole *transaction*." The great scale of the theater, forum, temples, and baths at Pompeii, and the small private apartments in the dwellings there, cause him to doubt the "individuality" of the Romans who were willing to live voluntarily so much in public. A grand diplomatic dinner in Paris for George Canning, the English Foreign Secretary, brings forth two dozen pages of minute detail: the arrangement of the rooms, the function of the porter at the gate, how long it takes the guests to assemble, how far their footmen accompany them to receive their wraps, the refreshments served to the footmen in the room set apart for them, the manner in which the guests are announced and the titles that are used, the conflicting international and national rules that determine rank in pairing for dinner and seating at table (Canning, because he is a commoner, actually gives way on this occasion to his young son-in-law, a Marquis), the comparative food-consumption of the French, English, and Americans during the hour and a half of dinner.

The smallest problem fascinates him. At the diplomatic dinner, to find out how strictly the Papal Nuncio complies with the requirements of a fast-day, Cooper is careful "to taste every dish that had been partaken of by the Nuncio." On being told of "real *bonâ fide* ladies, women of sentiment, delicacy, taste, and condition, frequenting public eating houses" (here surely is the passionate desire of Proust and James, if not their skill, for precise definition of a social class) he pursues a ruthless statistical method to get at the truth: "I have put the question to nearly every French woman of rank, as it has since been my good fortune to become sufficiently acquainted with, to take the liberty."

Cooper enjoyed hugely the social success which made

possible his limitless observation, but never deceived himself about his position in European society: "To be shown about as a lion, when circumstances offer the means; to be stuck up at a dinner table as a piece of luxury, like strawberries in February, . . . can hardly be called association. . . ." His success came to him suddenly after a few initial lonely months in Paris. The loneliness was caused by his own mistake. On arriving he had delivered a letter of introduction to a cousin of his good friend William Jay. He had been coldly received and used none of his other letters, waiting for the world to come to him. He was to learn later that the stranger had to take the initiative; as a free man it was his social right in Europe, if not in America, to be left alone. In his elaborate discussion of French etiquette Cooper insists so repeatedly on the fundamental and inviolable nature of this rule, and warns so feelingly against the stubbornness of morbid provincial pride as the propensity most likely to make the American visitor uncomfortable in Europe, that we are certain he is speaking from his own experience and his own proud hurt in the months of waiting.

Lafayette, who had met Cooper during his visit to America in 1824, did take the initiative and soon became his friend. But the hero of two revolutions, although he was subsequently to present Cooper to a king of his own making, Louis Philippe, could not do much in the world of Charles X for an American protégé. Cooper apparently owed his introduction into Bourbon society to the wife of the American minister, Jacob Brown. At about the same time, by his own act of disinterested kindness he met Sir Walter Scott who was then in Paris working on his life of Napoleon.

Scott was in the midst of his financial troubles and heavily in debt; Ballantyne & Co., his own printing firm, and Constable, his publisher, who had made themselves liable for each other's debts, had failed. Cooper wrote to Scott, suggesting that by an assignment of his work to an American citizen he might be able to get American copyright protection. He was probably wrong; the principle of injustice to foreigners was too clearly intended by the Federal statute to be so easily evaded. Scott called and offered a scheme of his own which was carried out. The author of Waverley addressed a letter to Cooper that was an appeal to the "liberality, perhaps in some sort to the justice, of a great people" to buy future works of Scott only in an authorized American edition; if Americans refused to buy from pirates, an American publisher could afford to pay the usual royalties. Cooper forwarded this letter with his own to Carey & Lea, his new publishers, urging them to undertake the edition as an act of tardy justice to Sir Walter in his present difficult circumstances. He added an interesting political argument: by denying copyright to foreigners the American government had made it possible for England to continue, through literature, her moral dominion over America, after her political sovereignty had ceased; "the law throws the resistless power of money into the foreign side of the scale." Nothing came of the plea. Sentimental interest in Scott's gallant effort to pay his debts was high, but perhaps in Carey & Lea's opinion—the younger Carey was an economist and the elder a pirate—sentiment could not be expected to compete with "the resistless power of money" over book-buyers and publishers.

Cooper may have been too logical, but Scott was grateful.

They chatted pleasantly in Paris about books and writing. The older author was flattering and particularly praised the "liberal hostility" of Cooper's treatment of England and America at war; the ascendancy of his own country was maintained without descending to vulgar abuse. The younger author made no return in kind. "As Johnson said of his interview with George the Third, it was not for me," he wrote in defense of his manners, a dozen years later, "to bandy compliments with my sovereign."

Cooper wondered whether so great and practised an author as Scott always felt despondent, as he himself did, about the quality of the work he had produced, and, to draw Scott out, described his own feelings in the course of writing. "The mere composition of a tale," by which he meant the buzzing in his own head, was a pleasure; so much so, that he invented twice as much, on his walks or in bed, as he put on paper; "much the best parts of the composition never saw the light; for, what was written was usually written at set hours, and was a good deal a matter of chance." But by the time he had finally gone over the proofs, he was so thoroughly disgusted with his book that he supposed everyone would feel the same way about it. Scott admitted to the surfeit, but apparently said nothing about the despair.

Cooper was surprised by the difference between Scott's "natural manner" when the two were alone together, and "the mask of society" he put on at a large party given in his honor. It also struck the American that tactful, self-possessed, quiet, dignified, and absolutely unpretentious though Scott was, he was nevertheless not a true man of the world: "he wanted the ease and *aplomb* of one accustomed to live with his equals." Mrs. Cooper thought him countrified.

This odd family judgment indicates a dangerous standard for a gentleman's behavior in public. It seems to imply that his manner should indicate a sense of his own importance— the last thing in the world, one would guess, that would help a man through the embarrassment of being lionized by a group of Russian princesses arrayed in tartan as a compliment to him, Scott's actual problem that evening. There were special reasons why Cooper should find such a manner desirable. Europeans looked down on Americans. They were often kind and welcomed visitors handsomely (more so on the Continent than in England), but they had a tendency, as Cooper knew, to do as much for fourth-rate Indian chiefs. As an American gentleman and an American writer he felt bound to assert his own position on all proper occasions; he could defer to Scott as his true superior, but to the world at large he could not, as a patriot, give in an inch. He would not be bumptious or provincial, he would respect all foreign forms and ranks; but his own rank would have to be respected too.

We have at least one malicious bit of outside evidence that he was too zealous in his effort. A paragraph of Hazlitt's admiringly describes Scott reading in an outer room of Galignani's bookshop unrecognized by the clerks. To round out his praise by a pretty contrast, Hazlitt adds:

"Cooper, the American, was in Paris at the same time: his looks and manners seemed to announce a much greater man. He strutted through the streets with a very consequential air; and in company held up his head, screwed up his features, and placed himself on a sort of pedestal to be observed and admired, as if he never relaxed in the assumption nor wished it to be forgotten by others, that he was the American Walter Scott."

This is obviously irresponsible caricature whose aim is to make a high virtue of Scott's pleasant but morally irrelevant conduct, by showing its grotesque opposite. But it is also so obviously the caricature of a man who thought Scott's quiet manner the wrong one that we suspect Hazlitt (who did not know Cooper's opinion of Scott) may have had some of the truth of malice in his wicked description.

In America Cooper had begun a book about Leather-Stocking's last days in the West. It had been interrupted by the preparations for his trip, and was perhaps further delayed by the excitement of his early months in strange lands. Cooper finished *The Prairie* in Paris and it was published in England in April 1827.*

Natty Bumppo in 1805, the time of *The Prairie*, is a very old man living alone on the Great Plains, surrounded by fierce mounted Indian tribes. His long absence from civilization has refined his speech: as Louise Pound has pointed out, he is here less given to dialect than in any of the other Leather-Stocking tales, and at times talks pure Ossian in his moralizing about Nature. In fact Natty has become almost a formal philosopher of the "natural" life and of the true equality of all men. He can tolerate the thieving of the Sioux, and the Pawnee chief's bright scarlet leggings fringed

* From this time on, practically all of Cooper's novels and many of his other works were published first in England, to assure his British rights, and came out in America after an interval ranging from a few months to a few days. Dates of publication used hereafter will refer to the English edition unless otherwise noted.

with human scalps; his sympathy stops short at towns, about whose unnatural laws and wicked civilized ways he is rigidly doctrinaire.

Natty's philosophical distaste for civilization has its sinister counterpart in the hatred of the squatter Ishmael Bush for its restraints. The rude sluggish patriarch who with his family is fleeing from the world of title deeds and sheriffs is the true "natural" man in action. He must himself seize the land that he needs, and defend it with his own rifle, for his need is his right, and some deep propriety would be violated if he were to receive from others what is not theirs to give. But this outcast from the law (he has murdered a sheriff and is engaged in a kidnaping venture into which he has been lured by his evil brother-in-law) is also its creator. Impatient of rules, he must impose them on his sons, lest they abandon him as he once abandoned his own father; and at the climax of the story it is his function to be the judge of all of the white characters, who in the course of the complicated fighting with the Indians have become his prisoners. Having declared his intention to punish Natty for the murder of his oldest son, he cannot, on learning that his wife's brother is the murderer, pardon the guilty man. "O! Ishmael, we pushed the matter far!" his wife wails, but she too feels that because her husband has announced his rule of retaliation, her brother must die.

Natty is charming not as a philosopher but as a touchingly weak old man, and there is a lovely serenity, despite its outmoded trappings, to his death which closes the story. But Cooper's great achievement in *The Prairie* is Ishmael Bush and his family. In their slow violence and unlovely ways they are at one with the unlovely ominous country of which they are the ultimate conquerors.

The Red Rover (1827) was written entirely in France. This exciting sea tale was enormously popular, but seems to me to be one of Cooper's few novels in which the excitement is purchased by means that are essentially cheap. The Rover is a mid-eighteenth-century American pirate, ferocious by reputation but in actuality an accomplished gallant gentleman. He is joined by a charming young man, Harry Wilder, who is as fascinated as we are by a career of piracy. The ability of decent attractive people to engage in an evil life, the apparent subject with which we are presented, is never honestly developed. It is merely explained away at a critical point. Wilder is an officer in the British Navy who has been assigned the task of hunting the Rover. The Rover himself was once a loyal colonial subject of the King, serving in the navy. When his commander insulted America, the Rover fought and killed him, and turned pirate, wasting his talent for loyalty on his vicious crew.

We are assured in the end that the Rover redeems himself by dying on the American side in the Revolution. It is of course the reader's and not the pirate's morality that is being redeemed. We need some excuse for liking a gentlemanly villain, and none is so convenient—it has been used frequently since—as his noble death in a just cause. But the excuse has the effect of destroying one of the serious and ironic themes of the novel, our own delight in the spectacle of polite wickedness.

Early in their European friendship Lafayette had asked Cooper to write an account of his triumphal American tour of 1824-25. Cooper could not refuse "the good old man," but he knew that a narration of official celebrations and speeches would be dull. He hit on the idea of a book about America itself, written by a European traveler arriving in the United States at the same time as Lafayette and meeting him often in the course of his own journey. As a further elaboration Cooper made his traveler a member of a club of bachelors who wander around the world and write long informative letters to each other about the strange countries they visit (much as Cooper himself was setting down in letter-form, interspersed with his own adventures, his current impressions of Europe, which he was to revise and publish on his return to America).

Notions of the Americans: Picked up by a Travelling Bachelor (1828) handles the incidents of Lafayette's visit so cleverly that one would never suspect that the long book was undertaken for their sake; they seem to be used solely to enliven a long descriptive work and to illustrate the excellence of American manners on public occasions. Of course Cooper had enlarged on Lafayette's suggestion because he wanted to write a book about America, and his elaborate apparatus was adopted for his own purposes as well as Lafayette's. He was shocked by the extent of European ignorance of America and insolence toward her, and was certain that travel books by Europeans contributed to the international misunderstanding. English travelers were the worst, the most prejudiced, and the most hostile. Radicals often harmed the truth as much as Tories, for as Cooper observed: "Finding that things fall short of the political Elysium of their imaginations, they fly into the opposite extreme, as a sort of *amende honorable* to their own folly and ignorance."

Notions had a double purpose: to explain America to

Europe, and to show what a sane, balanced book about America by an intelligent, open-minded foreigner would be like. Apparently Cooper could not conceive of a completely reasonable Englishman, and therefore made his foreigner a Belgian; but the lesson was aimed at England, so much so that the traveler refers to English instead of Belgian customs for comparison with American.

Unwilling to trust any European to discover America unaided, Cooper furnishes his traveler with a native guide, an educated New Yorker named Cadwallader. The entire traveler and guide device is an unhappy one. *Notions* is not a dishonest book because of it, but the use of a fictitious foreign observer as a medium of praise creates an unpleasant air of disingenuousness, as if Cooper were unwilling to assume responsibility for the defense of his own country. The traveler is too quickly converted by Cadwallader; an explanation by the latter always wins him over, so that Cooper has placed himself in the embarrassing position of seeming to boast of his own skill in persuasion. (In his European travel books, when he repeats conversations he has had, he never pretends to have made a thorough convert, although his arguments often seem to us unanswerable.) Cadwallader, because he is a fictitious character talking, and not the author writing carefully in his own person, at times speaks loosely and irresponsibly. He is accurate as the portrait of a patriot, but inadequate as the mouthpiece of Cooper's serious views.

Notions is a eulogy. It selects the facts one-sidedly: while it tells us of the Federal government's effort to aid the Indians, it hardly mentions the brutal treatment of the Indians by settlers and local governments. It draws only favorable inferences, ignores more probable unfavorable ones: the infrequency of libel suits is cited to prove that the press does not abuse its freedom, rather than that its abuse is without practical redress. Cornered with an inescapably ugly situation, slavery, it descends to vulgar retort: Europeans instituted the slave trade. It tries to offset faults of manners by irrelevant references to physical greatness: "How pitiful do the paltry criticisms on an inn, or the idle . . . comments on the vulgarity of a *parvenu*, become, when objects and facts like these [the vastness of the country's resources] are pressing themselves on the mind!" The frontier, which European travelers, like the later historians, considered the most significant and most American phenomenon, is hurried over in a few pages (Cooper had not been west of Buffalo and Niagara Falls); the Bachelor condescendingly explains that his predecessors have made the mistake of writing so much about the West and so little about the East from their understandable desire to find novelty in the New World. At every turn he minimizes the wild and eccentric elements in American life. The excesses of Methodist camp meetings, like the accounts of Thumpers and Dunkers and other enthusiasts, are enormously exaggerated. Violence is treated in a discussion of a European institution, dueling; its deadliness in America is ingeniously attributed to an unfortunate triumph of common sense in sneering at unhurt duelists: "This system of stripping a thing, that is foolish in itself, of all its inconsistent folly, has brought the custom under a certain set of rules."

Yet with all its faults *Notions* is a brilliant description of America in the third decade of the nineteenth century. It has something more valuable than accuracy and impartiality—the sense of a living civilization and the interplay of its institutions, manners, customs, politics, literature, ideals, and underlying physical conditions. The process of selection, omission, and accent that seems at each step so unfair, the individual judgments that seem so extravagant, together make a total that is remarkably sober both as present fact and prophecy.* America's greatest institution is its future. Its actual achievements in art, literature, science, and learning are as yet unimportant. Democracy is creating a uniform American character which Cooper views hopefully but in which he recognizes the same limitations that Tocqueville will note a few years later. Americans of all classes are decent, respectable, competent, and intelligent, but rarely distinguished. The aim of the system seems to be a high level of mediocrity rather than individual excellence. "What the peasant gains, the gentleman must in some measure lose." But while not afraid to admit that equality equalizes, Cooper is certain that in the long run the process must elevate the great mass of men. The justification of political democracy is not the infallibility or superior wisdom of the many, but the simple moral notion that the bare fact of life itself gives

* Some of Cooper's statistical guesses turned out amazingly well. The following table shows how closely his estimates of the future population of the United States correspond to the actual census figures (taken to the nearest million):

Year	Cooper's Estimate	Census
1850	24,000,000	23,000,000
1880	48,000,000	50,000,000
1920	100,000,000	106,000,000

In making this prediction, Cooper fixes the Rocky Mountains as the boundary of the habitable territory of the United States. On the basis of these boundaries Cooper's estimates, as a whole, come closer to the actual figures.

every man a stake in society: "A man may be a voluntary associate in a joint-stock company, and justly have a right to a participation in its management, in proportion to his pecuniary interest; but life is not a chartered institution. Men are born with all their wants and passions, their means of enjoyment, and their sources of misery, without any agency of their own, and frequently to their great discomfort."

To the modern reader Cooper's analysis of the present and future of American literature is perhaps too modest. He is so good on the reasons why it is not better that one wonders how it existed at all. In the peculiar circumstances of American settlement, a brand-new world that had immediately at hand all of the intellectual resources of the old, the printer preceded the author. English literature was part of the common heritage and first supplied American needs, and still continues (at the time of the *Notions*) to be preferred by publishers and readers. An American publisher not only avoids payment of royalties on an English book but can cut down all risks by waiting to see how a book sells abroad and how well it is reviewed, or, if he will not wait, by dealing in the great popular names that are sure to sell. Under these circumstances there are not a dozen American writers whose books can pay their way with an American publisher.

Unlike Tocqueville, Cooper is not afraid of the trading spirit that democracy introduces into literature; "a good, wholesome, profitable and continued pecuniary support, is the applause that talent most craves." He fears democrats not as readers but as subjects for the writer. In a passage similar to Henry James's famous enumeration in his *Hawthorne* of "the negative side of the American social situation," Cooper lists "the poverty of materials" in his native land:

"There are no annals for the historian; no follies (beyond the most vulgar and commonplace) for the satirist; no manners for the dramatist; no obscure fictions for the writer of romance; no gross and hardy offences against decorum for the moralist; nor any of the rich artificial auxiliaries of poetry. . . . I have never seen a nation so much alike in my life, as the people of the United States, and what is more, they are not only like each other, but they are remarkably like that which common sense tells them they ought to resemble. No doubt, traits of character that are a little peculiar, without, however, being either very poetical, or very rich, are to be found in remote districts; but they are rare, and not always happy exceptions. . . . There is no costume for the peasant, (there is scarcely a peasant at all,) no wig for the judge, no baton for the general, no diadem for the chief magistrate."

The notion that American life was too simple and American character too undifferentiated to be satisfactory literary material was one of the most persistent in the long course of the self-conscious development of American literature. It antedates Cooper and was to be expressed after his time by writers as distinguished as Hawthorne and Henry James. It is hard for us to be sympathetic with these views. So many of the elaborate European institutions which American novelists thought would be useful to their trade have lost their meaning, even for their supporters, that we cannot understand the old envious feeling that they order these matters more complicatedly abroad. Our sense, moreover, of the difference between actuality and imagination, fact and fiction, is much more blurred than Cooper's. We are disturbed by his casual assumption that democracy can be useful in actual life and useless as a subject for art. Art and life, we are sure, have more to do with each other, and a good life cannot be bad art. We insist that it is the duty of the artist, if he believes in democracy, to find in its way of life his richest materials.

Notions did not do well. Possibly readers were bound to be disappointed in any work of nonfiction by Cooper, but there were good reasons why it did not achieve even a success of esteem. Educated Americans were embarrassed by high praise. It might well have been "Bonton," as Lafayette wrote Cooper, rather than true modesty, that caused them to find *Notions* an exaggerated account of American virtues. Good tone, of course, was set by Europe. The concern with foreign opinion—whether manifested in the refined self-depreciation of the upper classes or in the defiant noisy boasting of the professionals whose business was self-gratulation—was universal. Whatever its general validity, the question of foreign approval was relevant to *Notions*, a work obviously intended to persuade England of America's superiority. In this one instance at least, an American's pleasure in a native book could be legitimately spoiled by the thought of what England would make of it. Cooper had undertaken an impossible task and had to fail, not because his prophecies seemed absurd but because it was secretly feared that they were true. Well-informed Britons believed in America's future greatness but could afford to admit it only privately; in public they asserted all of the overwhelming arguments

that men can always marshal so plausibly against an unpleasant truth.*

Cooper did nothing to make his theme acceptable to a
prejudiced audience. In fact his treatment of his secondary
subject—English attitudes toward Americans—ruined what
little chance he may have had of partial success. He discovered prejudice everywhere, even in professions of good will
purporting to disclaim any share of Tory bigotry. Compliments were exercises in condescension. The English praised
an American by saying that he "could not have been a finer
gentleman . . . had he been educated in London or Paris!"
"An American lady was dancing in the midst of fifty Eng-
lishwomen" and a bystander stated "that he saw no difference in her grace and that of the belles of his own island!"
But when American innkeepers tell an English traveler that
they "are surprised to find Englishmen behave so well" this
is merely evidence of how badly earlier travelers from England have behaved.

The two groups of incidents I have cited are only superficially alike. Englishmen did patronize Americans; the latter
could not as yet retaliate in kind. As Cooper knew (but was
not willing to state in *Notions* as he had in his letter to Carey
& Lea about Scott), the new nation had not completely won
its independence. Culturally it was still dependent on the

* "I am afraid," Scott said to Cooper at their first meeting, "the
mother has not always treated the daughter well, feeling a little
jealous of her growth perhaps; for, though we hope England has
not yet begun to descend on the evil side, we have a presentiment
that she has got to the top of the ladder." But the Tory *Quarterly
Review*, which Scott had promoted, was so committed to the
proposition of the inherent inferiority of Americans that the only
serious question for discussion was the cause: was it the climate or
the food?

old country. The relation is usually referred to as a continuation of colonialism, but in today's terms Americans of Cooper's day might be described as a minority group surrounded by a dominant culture. They claimed the right to be free of it and to be themselves, a difficult aim, for they did not quite know what they meant and resented any discovery of a difference. They yearned for acceptance as equals but were offended on being assured of it in words; only in actions, never verbally, were they to be told by the English, "Why, you might be one of us."

Cooper was to write frankly and with great brilliance on the peculiar English domination of America. In *Notions* he denied its existence; Americans, he gravely said, were indifferent to foreign opinion. But the writing itself, the quivering indignation, the delight in small thrusts at England, betray his claim. The pettiness of his points often weakens the brute force of his physical facts and may well have lost possible support among well-intentioned Englishmen. Cooper was to trace the decline of his literary fortunes to the publication of this book: he had alienated England by it, and, through her, his own countrymen, who could not think for themselves. It is difficult to corroborate this contention; it can be true only in a loose and not a literal sense. His next novel was understandably a failure in its own right, but he was soon to have one of his greatest successes, *The Bravo*, for which he received the largest sum (£1300) he was ever paid in England.

The Wept of Wish-ton-Wish (1829) is a story of King Philip's War, attempting to combine the excitement of Indian fighting with a careful study of seventeenth-century Puritan theocracy in a small Connecticut settlement. The villain is the Reverend Meek Wolfe who as spiritual leader pries into the private lives of his congregation and urges the murder of Indian women and children as a religious duty; the hero is the noble, chivalrous Indian, Conanchet, who, after befriending the Puritans, is the victim of their treachery. His white captors, with a priggishness that makes their conduct the uglier, will not kill him themselves but give him up to his Indian enemies to deal with. The sheer good conscience of these people, their certainty that their own self-interest is the divine will, are terrifying. Cooper tries to indicate that there are milder members of the community and even a softer side to Meek Wolfe, but these are mere self-conscious efforts to be "fair" and are much less effective than his cold hatred of Puritanism. The triumph of hate has not so much distorted the truth (to the biased reader, at least, *The Wept* seems sound enough historically) as limited its value. We learn only what we already knew, and the pleasure of taking sides in a partisan attack against dead enemies soon grows stale.

Conanchet has a little too obviously the virtues that the Puritans lack and that are his undoing: delicacy, good breeding, honor, generosity, and a tolerance of the ways of others. He and the Puritan share, more interestingly, a certain austerity of manner and gravity in their view of life. In the Indian it is a means for the fit and decorous enjoyment of life and at the same time a sign of true submission to a higher law; in the Puritan it is a sign of the denial of life's worth, in worldly terms, and yet a means of making law correspond exactly to one's worldly interests. Unfortunately the two derive their speech, if in different degrees and with different authenticity, from the same model, the King James Bible.

Cooper shared the current view that the two races had to remain apart. With this premise, the theme of the marriage of Conanchet and the white captive is fundamentally unprofitable. The author can achieve only the negative success of good taste. The Indian has believed the girl's family dead, and on learning that they are still alive generously surrenders her to them. Cooper struggles honestly to dramatize the family's conflict between love and social embarrassment on getting back their heathenized daughter with her half-breed child, but he cannot under the conventions of his time develop this material fully. The solemnity of the taboo that separates the two races is saved from absurdity by a comic device: another captive, a half-wit boy, has become a stubborn renegade, more Indian than the bravest brave, boasting futilely that next snow he will be a warrior and childishly denying his white past; this parody of the desire to cross the forbidden line gives to the convention against it an appearance of health and good sense, and prepares us for its ultimate maintenance. The death of Conanchet, a stiffly beautiful and sentimental scene, is only in part the unjust historical dooming of the Indian by the white man; he has been doomed as well by the author for violating one of his taboos. His death loses some of the beauty of pure injustice by its obvious necessity as a novelistic means of dissolving a mixed marriage, a process that is completed by the simultaneous death of his wife from grief and from the shock of recovering her white identity.

It may be an accident that the stark, somber *Wept* was planned in Switzerland, a country unequaled, in Cooper's opinion, "in the sublimity of desolation." But there can be no doubt of the influence of place on *The Water-Witch* (1830), written chiefly at Sorrento on the Bay of Naples and having as its subject smuggling in New York harbor in the early eighteenth century. The two bodies of water were intimately connected by the fond American belief that they were equally lovely. On sailing into the glorious Italian bay, the Coopers, overcome by its beauty and by their growing independence of opinion back home, exclaimed, "What dunce first thought of instituting a comparison between the bay of New York and this?" Naples was not New York—*The Water-Witch* contains the longest and pleasantest of Cooper's many disclaimers of resemblance, which were to become cranky with the years—but her drowsy loveliness that made life so dreamily unreal and unserious might somehow be captured for a tale about his own bustling city.

The plot of *The Water-Witch* is absurd. The fantastic brigantine for which the book is named is too obviously intended as a symbol of unreality and is unsuccessful as one. She eludes her pursuers prettily and disappears amazingly off prosaic Staten Island, but Cooper has not the full courage of his fantasy and explains her disappearance as mere skilful navigation in unsuspected inlets and the trickery of false lights. The strange ship gives out oracles through its figurehead, a green lady; but too much of the mystery of the ship has been naturalistically explained for the reader to accept as magic rather than as carelessness those parts of the story which remain unexplained.

But if Cooper could not mechanically capture the magic of the Mediterranean, he has caught something better, a part of himself which had come to life in Italy. Italy relaxed temporarily the severity of his moral judgment. The energetic American loved the Italians for their indolence, their seeming "too gentlemanlike to work, or to be fussy"; he delighted in seeing the beggars at his door increase from one to ninety-six as the days passed. Nations in their decline, living off the accumulations of past energies, were happier, he learned, than nations busily accumulating in the present. American activity, viewed by an American who had learned such dangerous truths, was surely not what it seemed, and Cooper's finest effects of illusion in *The Water-Witch* are achieved not with physical but with social phenomena. It is not the ship but commerce itself that is so strange. The true romantic figure in the tale is not the conventionally daring smuggler who risks his life casually and gracefully, but his customer, the timid respectable merchant, Alderman Van Beverout.

The alderman is the poet of profit. His elaborate rhetoric, rich with the imagery of trade and ledgers turns the entire world into gold, much as some excessively romantic lover might find his beloved's face everywhere in Nature. When he speaks of beads made in England, traded with the Indians on the Mohawk for their furs, which are sold to an empress in Germany, the excitement lies not in the journey across the ocean and forests but in the mounting figures in his ledgers which reflect each step of the transaction. He is above the vulgar moral pretension, so fashionable in Cooper's age, that trade is the exchange of equivalents. The beauty of life is in its unearned increments of value, its terror in the unpredictable risks of the market. When his niece has apparently eloped with the handsome smuggler, Master Seadrift, he can express the seriousness of her position only by likening her to falling stock; he argues with her respectable lovers that a bargain is not to be interrupted by a little cheapening of one of the parties.

The alderman dares not search too hard for his niece lest his own connection with the smuggler be betrayed. Her reputation is saved by a turn in the plot that is allegorically justifiable but unfair to us as novel readers: Master Seadrift turns out to be a charming young woman, in fact, the alderman's legitimate daughter, so close in their relationship are lawful and illicit trade; and the high-spirited heroine has merely been on a visit with her newly discovered cousin. The stroke is a daring one in the completion of Cooper's private task of treating commerce, a respected institution, with amusement and contempt, but is at the same time his timid surrender to another solemn institution, female respectability, which he had seemed for a time to be treating with equal lightness.

Chapter IV

THE IMMEDIATE suggestion for Cooper's first novel with a European setting, *The Bravo* (1831), came from a brief stay in Venice in the spring of 1830 and a reading of Venetian history; but its scope and avowed message must have been influenced by immediate European events of the last half of 1830—the July Revolution in France that overthrew Charles X and made Louis Philippe king, the Belgian revolution against the Dutch, and the Polish insurrection against the Czar. Cooper was connected by sympathy and personal interest with this sudden turn of history. His friend Lafayette was again the great man of the moment. Lafayette had assured the French people that they might have liberty through a citizen-king, "a throne surrounded by republican institutions." He had secretly encouraged the Poles and after the revolt broke out urged intervention on their behalf. Cooper was further linked with Poland by his friendship with Adam Mickiewicz, the Polish patriot and poet, whom he had met the year before in Rome.

In the long and dreary course of the Polish revolt Cooper

was one of its active foreign supporters. He served on a committee in Paris to raise funds, presided at dinners, drafted appeals to the American people for aid, first for the support of the war and ultimately for the relief of the refugees. The French revolution was on the other hand not a call for action but a call for thought. Nominally successful, it had failed in actuality, as Cooper early saw, not because the throne had been preserved, but because the republican institutions that the throne was to support had not been immediately established. Such a step would have been opposed by the bankers, manufacturers, and great landed proprietors, and might have caused foreign intervention; but the strength of the opposition was the very reason why the new institutions had to be set up during the period of revolutionary ardor, or not at all.

The monarchical principle, Cooper was convinced, was virtually extinct. Monarchy versus republic, which popular opinion took to be the great question of the day, was purely a matter of form obscuring the true conflict, that between the interests of the few and the many. A monarchy, the Russian as well as the English, was now actually an aristocracy in disguise, but it could be made the basis of responsible popular government. A republic—and this was the point of *The Bravo*—might conceal even more effectually than a throne the rule of an irresponsible and ruthless minority.

Cooper furnished *The Bravo* with the conventional characters of historical romance: an heiress destined for a loveless marriage, a gay young nobleman who succeeds in eloping with her, a jailer's tender-hearted daughter, and an assassin—all using unfortunately an even more stilted language than the author normally employs. But in the course of developing his subject, as Cooper said, ". . . the government of Venice, strictly speaking, became the hero of the tale."

The human agencies are dwarfed by the impersonal working of a system of exploitation that publicly observing all of the forms of justice operates tyrannically in the interests of the small senatorial class. Even a senator who profits from it does not understand its true nature ("To him Venice seemed a free state, because he partook so largely of the benefits of her social system."). He is free to act selfishly because he sees himself acting always in the public and not in his private interest.* The system can make use of individual virtue as well as vice, can pervert good impulses to its own ends. When the Council has secretly murdered an old fisherman for protesting too vehemently against the impressment of his grandson into the state galleys, a virtuous senator sug-

---

* "A senator, he stood in relation to the state as a director of a moneyed institution is proverbially placed in respect to his corporation; an agent of its collective measures, removed from the responsibilities of the man. He could reason warmly, if not acutely, concerning the principles of government, and it would be difficult, even in this money-getting age, to find a more zealous convert to the opinion that property was not a subordinate, but the absorbing interest of civilized life."

In this and his two succeeding novels Cooper's aim was "a series of tales, in which American opinion should be brought to bear on European facts." But occasionally, as in the sentences just quoted, he glanced at American facts to note that they were startlingly like the European. The reference to a bank is particularly significant since political radicals back home had already begun their attack on the Bank of the United States. And the observation that the corporate form permitted individuals to escape moral responsibility for their acts was typical of liberal opinion in the Jacksonian era. Compare W. M. Gouge, *A Short History of Paper Money and Banking in the United States* (1833): "As directors of a company, men will sanction actions of which they would scorn to be guilty in their private capacity."

gests that the bravo, whom he abhors, is the real criminal, and diverts the mob from its incipient wrath against the government.

The impersonal machine that is beyond the understanding of its beneficiaries and its victims, and greater than either, is a dramatic character which has no fit antagonist in the story. Cooper has made up for this deficiency by himself taking a personal part as a zealous advocate of freedom. He intrudes his own views throughout the book and sometimes lectures for several pages on the nature of true republican institutions. It is not the happiest device, but, although Cooper was to abuse it later, in *The Bravo* it works, so great is the reader's need for some opposition to successful evil.

Cooper's usual faults as a novelist strengthen the point of the book. The faintness of our interest in his upper-class characters allows us no feeling of victory when the young Neapolitan nobleman wins his heiress against the Senate's wish. Our indifference is politically astute. The state has suffered a money loss (the girl was its ward and a fine prize) but not a real defeat in principle, for its fundamental activity is the exploitation of the poor at home and the rich in the colonies, and an occasional brush with a wealthy outlander raises no serious issue.

Jacopo, the bravo for whom the book is named, is by reputation the government's favorite assassin. The quiet dignity with which he bears his ostracism, his cynical understanding of his honorable employers, the fact that he has been forced into his profession to protect his father—a prisoner in the terrible jails of Venice—, make him a strangely attractive figure. As we know that he has been the poor old fisherman's friend, we are as indignant at his being falsely accused of that particular murder as if he were a completely innocent man. But when we learn that he is innocent, has never killed anyone, we feel that Cooper has once more (just as with Wilder in *The Red Rover* and the heroine in *The Water-Witch*) had a failure of nerve. He has given to an attractive character a mere appearance of wicked conduct to heighten our interest, but has not dared to carry through and make the conduct real.

The good priest and Gelsomina, the bravo's fiancée, rush off to the doge with the news of Jacopo's complete innocence. We are certain he will be pardoned, but Cooper with a seemingly cheap theatricality insists on an execution scene with the elaborate preparations going on inexorably while the pardon is awaited. It is only when Jacopo is actually on the block that the signal at last comes from the palace. "The clarions sounded, and another wave stirred the multitude. Gelsomina uttered a cry of delight, and turned to throw herself upon the bosom of the reprieved. The axe glittered before her eyes, and the head of Jacopo rolled upon the stones, as if to meet her. A general movement in the living mass denoted the end."

This brilliant reversal stuns us into enlightenment. As our feelings have not been given time to change, the cynicism with which as readers we have followed what seemed to be a mock drama becomes dramatically the cynicism of Venice itself, and our sense of mock drama persists through the horrible reality of the execution. The mere appearance of evil in Jacopo has not been another betrayal by Cooper but the essence of the bravo's role as a tool of the state. The state has supported its own reputation for virtue by creating a false reputation for him, so that its unofficial murders can be performed without detection by its real assassins or if discovered be suitably punished, for the business of the hero-state is not only crime but punishment. Jacopo's execution is the logical final discharge of his strange employment, to seem wicked that his employer may seem just.

For Cooper the highest praise for his book was an English reviewer's complaint that while Byron had seen in Venice her palaces and renown, the American "had seen only her populace and her prisons." Actually he had not gone so far in realism but had made liberal use of the glamorous Venetian past as an aid to his story.

In *The Heidenmauer* (1832) he went the whole way and undertook the bold experiment of handling realistically materials that were the traditional delight of the romantic writer—a drinking bout between a worldly abbot and a haughty baron to settle a dispute over feudal rights, a pilgrimage to a shrine, the midnight destruction of a monastery.

In this "legend of the Rhine" we see the Reformation being effected in Germany not as an exciting adventure in new ideas but through the operation of greed and worldly interest on a dull and still superstitious people. The townsfolk of Duerckheim, encouraged by their good neighbor, the baron, sack the monastery to which they have paid feudal dues and seize its land. They insist on holding on to their booty, but as a hedge against risk baron and burgomaster go on a penitential journey to a Catholic shrine. In the end the burgomaster discovers that his town has only made a change of landlords; it pays tribute now to the baron instead of to the abbot of the monastery.

The story is intended as an illustration of a theory of history: progress is slow and doubtful; the leaders of thought can never be too far ahead of their fellow-men if they are to influence them at all, for the old is abandoned reluctantly; the sudden revolutions of popular thought in which "we frequently see whole communities making a moral pirouette in a breath" occur when the practical needs of men coincide with ideas that have been long abroad and that are accepted at last only partially and without full comprehension.

To emphasize his theory Cooper has played down the dramatic possibilities of his tale. His new quietness of manner is not becoming to him. He is one of those writers who to be at their best must also give themselves room to err on the side of extravagance and melodrama. Long passages of *The Heidenmauer* have that particular respectable dullness that we feel we ought to like because it is "honest" writing. Perhaps the best parts are the few paragraphs of direct historical theory. And yet, although we read the book as a whole without much lively enjoyment, its intellectual keenness commands our respect.

The Headsman (1833), the last of the European problem novels, promises in its first half to be the best. It pursues with irony and subtlety (I mean of fictional device, for Cooper rarely found in his novels a felicity of expression worthy of the brilliance of his ideas) his study of aristocratic society, this time in terms of hereditary liabilities instead of hereditary rights. Adelheid, the daughter of a minor Swiss nobleman, loves a Swiss commoner. The difference in rank can be overlooked, for Sigismund is a mercenary soldier with a good future and his foreign master can confer some title on him. Adelheid proposes marriage to him—in a strict caste system the duty of passivity is stronger for the inferior class than for the inferior sex. He refuses. His social position, he tells her, is worse than she thinks; his father is the headsman of Berne, a hereditary office that the son cannot legally decline. His family is ancient and wealthy and in the dark ages was deemed honorable, but the world has by now (around 1700) become squeamish in its enlightenment; although it claims law as its highest achievement it regards with illogical but passionate loathing the man who is "the last avenger of the law." Pressed by Adelheid, Sigismund admits that his parents are happily married, but points out that his mother is herself the daughter of the headsman of another canton; marriage within the group seems to work out best.

Adelheid decides to reconsider her proposal. To marry the son of an executioner, a possible future executioner himself, to become voluntarily the member of an accursed class and race, is a greater misalliance than the sensible young woman had bargained for. The novel exploits the gross and the subtle aspects of her problem. The prejudice against her lover's family takes on external reality as we are confronted with crude, even violent, manifestations of public feeling. Superstitious travelers on Lake Leman try to throw the headsman Balthazar overboard to appease the wrath of a storm. His daughter is publicly jilted when Balthazar is identified as her father; the marriage contract had stipulated that the family connection should not become known, for even a handsome dowry cannot compensate her mercenary lover for such a disgrace. The people side with the man; once they know who the girl is they can see the family "taint" in her face.

These vulgar feelings have their refined complement in Adelheid. Immediately aware of the injustice that threatens her lover, she still views his father with distaste, although he is in actuality a man so humane and mild that he had great difficulty in learning his trade. She is pleasantly surprised that Sigismund's mother and sister are women of education and culture, as if money could not do as much for them as it does for others. When she first hears his mother speak intimately of her son, there is "a chill, resembling that of death, at her heart . . . owing to the shock inseparable from being presented with this vivid, palpable picture of Sigismund's close affinity with the family of an executioner. She could have better borne it, had Marguerite spoken of her son less familiarly."

Not only Adelheid, who struggles through to enlightenment, but Sigismund also, shares the general prejudice, and in him it has a corrupting ambiguity. Out of love his parents have had him brought up as another's son, but the same love has made them reveal themselves to him. Grateful to them for his chance to escape, but at the same time bitter that they have not disowned him entirely, the brave young soldier lives in dread of public disclosure of his parentage and in shame and self-hate for not daring to claim it. It is only the novelist's arbitrary control of our emotions that makes the brother who sits inactive through his sister's humiliation an object of sympathy and the fiancé who rejects her an object of disgust, for both have been gambling on secrecy and cannot face exposure.

There is absurdity as well as pathos in Sigismund's horror of becoming the executioner of his country's laws and in his naive pride in the career of his choice, killing for the highest bidder in foreign wars to whose merits he is indifferent. As a mercenary he is following the highest calling of his time and one that still pleases us as novel readers if not as serious citizens. We like him for his trade, which must have reminded readers of Cooper's day even more sentimentally than it does us now of the Swiss Guard at the Tuileries. Although the father has as much chance as the son of dying bravely at the hands of a mob, we cannot like him for it; the overwhelming violence of persecution, unlike overwhelming violence directed at armed men, never makes its victims glamorous. The constant interplay of the reader's attitudes and those of the characters of the story to the different kinds of mercenary in it (in addition to the soldier, the executioner, and the lover, there is even a pilgrim—a paid penitent) extends its scope beyond an ancient prejudice against hereditary headsmen, of which we are happily and smugly free. The ancient prejudice suggests throughout the deep unreason at the bottom of the "natural" feelings which are so often the source of our own prejudices and persecutions.

Having built up his problem so well, Cooper unforgivably ruins his story by its solution. In the end Sigismund turns out to be not the son of the Headsman of Berne but of the Doge of Genoa. Adelheid is marrying (she had decided, to be fair to her, to take the risk before she knew her reward) above and not below her station. There is an old fairy tale in which a princess loves a swineherd and finds him to be a prince; it has its own moral truth, but it is not a truth that is useful to the solution of a problem of prejudice.

While working on *The Headsman* Cooper decided that it would probably be his last novel and that he would give up writing entirely. The immediate occasion of this strange

decision was the reverberations in a few American newspapers of a minor controversy he had engaged in at Lafayette's request.

In September 1831 Lafayette called Cooper's attention to
an article in the *Révue Britannique* discussing the proposed
French budget. The author, a government writer, compared
the costs of the French and American governments and
naturally found that the monarchy was cheaper than the
republic. Lafayette wanted Cooper to reply. It was an easy
task for him as he had just written an article refuting Basil
Hall's misstatements about American expenditures, but
Cooper was reluctant to get into a foreign political dispute
and refused. Someone explained to him that as Lafayette
was always asserting that the government of the United
States was the least expensive of any, the article had in
reality attacked him. Cooper now, both as an American and
as a friend, had to help, and he wrote his *Letter to Gen.
Lafayette*, which the General presented to the Chamber of
Deputies early in 1832 when the budget came up for con-
sideration.

The *Letter* is an able pamphlet, carefully restricting itself
to the facts of the American situation and never commenting on the French. Cooper points out that America has two
peculiar features distinguishing it from Europe, its geo-
graphical position and its political institutions, and that foreign writers attribute all favorable American phenomena to
the former and all unfavorable to the latter. He manages
to reverse the process: to blame expenditures on geography
(a widely scattered population requires a greater number of
courts and post roads per capita, and considerable protection
from Indians on the frontier); and to make the institutions

responsible for all of the savings (the popular character of the government makes a large peacetime army unnecessary). His thrusts in favor of republican institutions are quiet, and the tone of the piece is pleasantly mild and inoffensively "American."

The French writer answered and Cooper replied. The "Finance Controversy," as it is called, took a surprising turn when the Premier in the course of debate stated that William Cabell Rives, the American Minister to France, was on the government side. This declaration seems to have been unauthorized, but it was not publicly repudiated. Rives' position was difficult; he had negotiated a treaty for the satisfaction of claims arising out of Napoleon's raids on American shipping, but the payments called for by the treaty had still to be appropriated by the Chamber and he was unwilling to offend the party in power. Worse, however, an attaché of the legation, an American named Leavitt Harris, wrote a letter on the French side of the financial dispute. Cooper had always believed that Americans abroad, especially official representatives, compromised their country's interests and principles out of a desire for foreign social success, and now felt that by Rives' silence and Harris's action he himself was being compromised. He was supporting his country and his country should support him.

Instead, a sharp attack came from home at about this time. A remarkably unfriendly and stupid review of *The Bravo* appeared in June 1832 in the *New York American*, a Whig newspaper which had earlier commented favorably on the novel. Cooper had always had some bad reviews but he was convinced that ever since his defense of his country in *Notions* he had been shabbily treated in the American press

by its "deprecatory praise and pealing censure." He and
his good friend S.F.B. Morse found in the new attack in-
ternal evidence of its French origin: the review used the
French form "we" although signed by an individual—"Cassio"; it was based on the Paris and not the American edition;
it made a parade of academic rules such as French critics
loved. Another friend was certain that he had seen the article
in the *Journal des Débats*. Cooper was convinced that it was
actually a translation from a French original that had been
inspired by government hostility to him. America had always
been too dependent on foreign opinion—this was the country's greatest weakness, the source of a peculiar American
unmanliness and want of self-respect in the presence of the
outside world. Now the country was importing the foreign
poison unlabeled for use against a loyal citizen.

Cooper was to busy himself for several years with Cassio's
review. It is first mentioned in a piece he wrote in French
for a Parisian miscellany. "Point de Bateaux à Vapeur"
(1832), later translated as "No Steamboats—A Vision," is
a dialogue that Cooper has in a dream with three personifica-
tions of French political theory. He refutes their errors about
government and about America by showing that the American newspaper on which they rely for facts carries a review
of *The Bravo* obviously inspired in France.

In the summer of 1832 the Coopers were on another
excursion. Everything on this trip seemed calculated to show
the difference between European and American treatment
of a distinguished writer. A Belgian artist—famous it is true
for his painting of cattle—had the author detained by the
Governor of Liége and himself traveled sixty miles by post
to have the honor of doing his portrait. German postmasters

visited him "in compliment to the republic of letters." A Swiss gentleman "sent a handsome expression of regret" because his agent had failed to rent him his chateau. A French customs officer turned a rude search into a gracious recognition of rank by explaining that duchesses were the worst smugglers.

Cooper believed that if he remained abroad he could still write, but "the idea of becoming a hack writer in a foreign land" was not to his humor. As an American gentleman, and a father who did not want his daughters to marry foreigners, he had to go home. He had been putting off his return and now it seems to have posed itself to him as an unpleasant alternative—abandoning his country or his career. He chose America and in November 1832 wrote to William Dunlap of his decision. He could not continue to court a public that repudiated him, or fight a press controlled by men without taste and without sympathy for "the real opinion of the country" (that is, its fundamental principles). His publisher was treating him badly, the final proof that his position with the public was being undermined. He would be home next year, looking for a new way to earn his living, or, as a gentleman expressed it, "I shall certainly be forced (even were I disposed to idleness) to do something to eke out an income. . . ."

Morse had returned to America and considered that he had a roving commission to investigate the Cassio review. Cassio was in fact a young American writer named Edward Sherman Gould; he had written his review in Paris and had therefore used the French edition. This was too simple an explanation for Morse who had a taste for conspiracy. (A few years later he was to find an Austrian-Catholic plot against the United States, and after that was to believe Maria Monk's "awful disclosures.") The obscure review would have been forgotten if Morse had not kept it alive by inquiries, conjectures, and letters to the press. Whig papers became sharp in their criticism of Cooper's "meddling" in foreign politics. At the same time the Democratic administration in Washington seemed to rebuke Cooper by making Leavitt Harris, of all people, chargé d'affaires in Paris.

This must have been especially irritating because in September 1832 the Administration had indirectly vindicated Cooper's stand in the Finance Controversy. At Lafayette's request, Edward Livingston, the Secretary of State, circularized the American governors for information about local expenditures to refute (as Cooper put it) "the extravagant pretension . . . that freedom is more costly than despotism." Cooper on learning of the circular addressed a "Letter to the American Public" (published in a Philadelphia journal in December 1832) commenting on the irrelevance of local figures as a basis of comparison, because the French budget made no provision for many local costs. He used the opportunity to justify his participation on Lafayette's side of the controversy and to warn the nation that some Americans in Paris sided with the French government. Despite the warning, the Administration, presumably with full knowledge (Rives had been elected to the Senate and might conceivably have blocked Harris's appointment), was now rewarding the man whose position it had officially undertaken to refute.

Under the double blow Cooper was induced by Morse in April 1833 to write to an American newspaper his opinion that the Cassio review was a translation of a venal attack on him by a French government hack. Privately he was even more extravagant; he connected Rives with the newspaper abuse, and wrote Dunlap, "Rives is at the bottom of all this, and he may ride to the presidency on this and a few other expedients of this quality."

His friends warned him that he would find that America had deteriorated. Some were Whigs, frightened by Jackson's war on the Bank; some, like Morse, were struggling artists disgusted with the universal drive for money and the pigs literally at large in New York's streets. Undismayed, Cooper went ahead with his preparations. He started negotiations to buy back Otsego Hall, which was unoccupied and in a sadly dilapidated state, and in November 1833 arrived in America.

The Europeanized family that set up house in New York, with its French furniture and Swiss servants, its younger children more French than American ("Even the family cat was French"), must have had a hard time in a community at once so fond and so suspicious of foreign manners. Cooper had become accustomed to a society in which the highest tone was "the graceful semblance of living less for one's self than for others, and to express, as it were, their feelings and wishes rather than to permit one's own to escape him," and in which deference to rank had its complement in deference to age. A few days after his return he was a guest at a public dinner given for a distinguished naval officer. He knew half of the people present. Most of them, with the remarkable American coldness of manner that Cooper had once defended as a reasonable reserve, did not speak to him; those who did were as casual as if they had seen him a week ago. He knew that no rudeness was intended, but the chill was so thorough that he left before the dinner was over.

Shortly afterward at a social gathering he was "attacked by a man young enough to be my son and who was never out of sight of the smoke of his father's chimney, for thinking like an American." The note was struck that was to echo through the rest of his life: to the wealthy mercantile community he was the aristocrat with foreign airs; to himself and a few friends, he was the true democratic American, free from the influence of foreign political ideas.

His admirers cordially offered to give a public dinner for him. He thanked them graciously but declined. Perhaps he felt that the inevitable predictions of further achievements customary on such an occasion could only embarrass him and his friends, for he was persisting in his determination to give up writing.

He prepared a formal farewell to the American people that was to be his vindication and a disinterested warning against America's greatest danger, deference to foreign opinion. *A Letter to His Countrymen* appeared in June 1834. It is a mixture of personal nonsense and profound analysis of political institutions. The first fifty pages, about half of the *Letter*, are a detailed and at times dreary account of his ill-treatment in the American press for his participation in the Finance Controversy. The Cassio review, the unfriendly newspaper comments, Hazlitt's paragraph about the American Scott, which had been reprinted in America, are dissected minutely. The finicky overrefined argument betrays (to apply his own phrase to himself) "that most pernicious gift of providence, a whittling intellect." On the other hand, the rest of the *Letter*, chiefly a demonstration of the folly of reasoning in American political situations from English analogies, is a work of intellectual freshness and power.

One cannot separate the two parts—dismiss the first as mere apologia, or the second as irrelevant to the personal story—for underlying each is the country's bad practice of quoting foreign opinion to help make up its own mind about its public men. Fenimore Cooper in the Finance Controversy, as well as Andrew Jackson in the war on the Bank, is one of the public men whose conduct has been judged by alien standards. It is unfortunate that he used himself as an instance, especially since a leading point in his own case—the French origin of the Cassio review—is so shaky; one is not sure whether he is still insisting on it or only explaining the grounds of his earlier belief. But the first part of the *Letter*, personal as it is, is intensely relevant to the abstract question, and his few pages defending *The Bravo* are a masterly bit of objective criticism. Nor is the second part always severely impersonal. In the midst of a warning against exceeding constitutional limitations on appointments to office, Leavitt Harris pops up as an illustration of the evil to be avoided.

President Jackson had removed the government deposits from the Bank of the United States, and to do this had first had to remove an unwilling Secretary of the Treasury. The Senate in March 1834 passed a resolution censuring the President for acting unconstitutionally. The party in opposition to "King Andrew" was beginning to use the label "Whig," a good name in American history for it had been one that the colonists had taken in the early stages of their struggle with George III, while in English history it signified opposition to the royal prerogative. To Cooper, the new-Whig talk of "withholding the supplies," the modern imitation of the libertarian oratory of Burke and Chatham, all for the benefit of the Bank, involved no mere question of taste in rhetoric but the very nature of English and American institutions. The English Whigs had not fought for England's freedom but for themselves, and had perverted the monarchy into an oligarchy. "The ascendancy of the thousand families who control the British empire has been obtained under the cry of liberty." Withholding supplies had been the means by which an aristocratic Parliament had destroyed the King's power and increased its own. Applied in this country it would destroy a balance of power that had been deliberately created in the interests of freedom. Englishmen, accustomed to Parliamentary supremacy, liked to call the complicated American balance "only a compromise," but to Cooper "Every government is a compromise, or something worse." The danger of usurpation, he warned his countrymen, came not from the Executive but from Congress—an idea still fresh, at least in popular thought, because we still refuse to examine American experience but persist in thinking, as Cooper would say, in European terms.

The farewell to writing, at the end of the *Letter*, is a gentle and dignified reproof to his public for supporting him magnificently while he wrote of American "things" and failing him when he wrote on the one true subject for a national literature, American principles. Before the year was out he had finished a new book, on the very theme for which, so he had told his countrymen, they were not yet ready, and on the aspect of it that they would like least—the failure of America, as well as Europe, to understand the principles underlying American freedom.

The Monikins (1835) is, as Carl Van Doren has said, "an unbelievably dull satire." The elaborate apparatus—a visit to two nations of monkeys near the South Pole, Leaphigh (England) and Leaplow (the United States)—often obscures Cooper's meaning instead of clarifying it. The animal fable is usually a method of simplifying our views of human nature and institutions. Cooper, against the best practice, attempts to preserve the complexity of his political ideas in all of their vast detail and to translate them into the arbitrary allegorical terms that his form demands. The allegory, chiefly about the processes of mystification at the bottom of law and government, is brilliant but fatiguing in its tightly reasoned ingenuity. The disconnected episodes demand so much diligent application on our part that the author's marked but incomprehensible gaiety, like a scholar's chuckling over some bit of pornography safely hidden from us in a learned language, adds to our irritation.

Only the simpler instances of monkey allegory are easy to follow. In aristocratic Leaphigh, monkeys are ranked by the length of their tails, the seat of simian reason. In republican Leaplow, by its own boast the most enlightened nation on earth, the tail is docked, for natural inequalities are deemed antirepublican and must be removed to prevent an aristocracy of the intellect. But Leaplowers when they visit Leaphigh in a diplomatic capacity put on extra long false tails. The human visitors to the court of Leaphigh adopt the practice so that the king will not be shocked. On seeing them the king praises his savant for "bringing us these specimens of the human family. But for his cleverness, I might have died without ever dreaming that men were gifted with tails."

A wealthy Leaplow merchant, Gilded Wriggle, is ashamed of his country's democratic institutions and of his fellow-citizens as a foolish jacobinical rabble. Only the physical—the size of the largest city, Bivouac, and of its main street, Wide-path—need be praised. He fawns on the travelers from Leaphigh, seeking to extort eulogy by disparagement ("A poor place, no doubt, after your own ancient capitals") and is deeply hurt when they hint that it is not the finest town in the world. His patriotism is but a part of his love of property; his houses, cats and dogs, the very stones in the street, are sacred. Leaplow, like America in the 1830's, is in the midst of an orgy of speculation and is undergoing a moral eclipse. Under the pervasive influence of dollars a Leaplower must give a selfish reason for his conduct, for if he claims to have acted disinterestedly in anything the basest motives will be attributed to him. (Whig papers had asserted that Cooper wrote the *Letter to His Countrymen* in the hope of a political appointment.)

While most of the American satire is against the commercial class and its Whig politics, some is directed against Democratic candidates and practices. Foreigners are naturalized even before they land in Bivouac and are run for Congress because of their special appeal "to our adopted fellow citizens." They are elected despite opposition slanders—Cooper cannot let the Whigs alone even when making fun of his fellow-Democrats—that in their own country they have three wives and seven illegitimate children, have gone bankrupt, and have been obliged to emigrate on account of sheep-stealing. Rotation in office—the philosophical abstraction which in practice became Jackson's spoils system—is in Leaplow as blindly mechanical and oblivious to merit in order to assure "pure" democracy, as it was to become later in the imaginary England of Chesterton's *Napoleon of Notting Hill.*

The voyage to the monkey countries is prefaced by an account of the life of the English narrator and his father. The father's is a sordid tale of amassing a stock-jobber's fortune at the cost of a progressive loss of human feeling: the poor foundling who began life in generous sympathy with his fellowmen, crying "Wilkes and Liberty," ends it in dread of them, with the cry of "Property is in danger," and talking all day of the need of force, "regiments and bayonets glittering in every sentence." The son, to avoid his father's narrowness, decides to broaden his interests. As wealth is his chief means of contact with the world, the kindly young man buys a rotten borough in England and slaves in America; the enlargement of his "social stake," he is certain, will automatically enlarge his sympathies. Even love must not be confined but must be made a part of his system of diversified investments; "the terrible thought of monogamy, and of its sympathy-withering consequences," keeps him from marrying the rector's daughter whom he has always loved. Unfortunately his failure to convince this proper young woman of the soundness of his views sends the narrator off on his travels and brings the much duller monkey world on us, just as we have begun to like the young man for his naive ability to combine Tory political theory with Shelleyan notions suggestive of *Nightmare Abbey*. The broken-off story, unlike the rest of the book, is written in a cocky, jaunty style, often vulgar and knowing but peculiarly suited to it. It has the promise of a gay and original social novel that the author could not apparently complete—it is patched up feebly at the end by the triumph of monogamy. Cooper, as Yvor Winters has pointed out, is at his best not in his books as a whole, but is above all a writer of great fragments.

A retired novelist could not have chosen a worse vehicle for returning to public favor than a book holding out the hope of a good story and sinking almost immediately into crabbed, difficult allegory. It was a complete failure. "The man who read *The Monikins*" was for some years a newspaper by-word for an odd, improbable character. Perhaps the satire's chief effect was to prejudice Cooper's audience against the clearer presentation of the same ideas in the excellent series of travel books that he next brought out.

Cooper seems to have thrown his travel notes together somewhat hastily, to have revised some carelessly so that speaking from a given moment of time they describe future events, to have left others uncorrected so that they are contradicted later in the text, and to have published the five books without logical sequence. But these are trifles. The carelessness gives them an air of spontaneity. They have preserved the contemporaneous freshness of impressions of a lively and curious mind, and yet are almost always mature and reflective in content.

The five books in order of publication are *Sketches of Switzerland* (1836) about the 1828 trip there; *Sketches of Switzerland. Part Second* (1836) about France in 1830 and 1832, and the Belgian, German, and Swiss travels of 1832; *Gleanings in Europe* (1837) chiefly about France in 1826-28; *Gleanings in Europe. England* (1837) about the visit to London early in 1828; *Gleanings in Europe. Italy* (1838) about the Italian travels from the fall of 1828 to the spring of 1830.

Italy is the most charming. It glows quietly with the joy

of happy surrender to the people who live so irresponsibly in the past. As the English, for all their admirable qualities, can never be quite right, the Italians can never do anything very wrong. In England in the midst of wealth Cooper is reminded of the hard, grinding lives of the poor; in Italy even poverty is enchanting. In other countries he is intensely practical in his suggestions of what America can learn from them, in Italy merely wistful: if there could be a cultural exchange of the populations of Rome and New York for a year, "while the one party might partially awake from its dream of centuries, the other might discover that there is something valuable besides money." At moments *Italy* has a sophisticated poignancy, a mocking self-indulgence in its longing for the past, not unlike Washington Irving at his best. Attractive though it makes the book, it is also its weakness that Cooper's love for the Italian way of life has at bottom the comfortable safeness of a hopeless passion such as minor poets live on forever; for Cooper was too committed to adventure, whether physical or intellectual, to be entirely at home with minor poetry or with safety in any form.

Cooper knew that *Italy* was much less significant than *England* and despised the reviewers for preferring the pleasanter book. The most important of the series, *England* suffers from the author's refusal to be at ease with his subject. It is in part a chronicle of comic misadventure, honestly recorded but stubbornly unaware of the fun. Well received by the highest Whig society and meeting on cordial terms even a few Tories like Coleridge, Scott, and his son-in-law Lockhart, Cooper feels bound, nevertheless, for his country's good, to play the role of the hostile, suspicious guest and to recommend it to others. A good American must contradict his host's political platitudes lest polite acquiescence compromise fundamental principle. An invitation to an exclusive party given by the Duke of Devonshire brings forth not only a discussion of the factitiousness of social exclusiveness in England but also a display of patriotic rage at the offhand informality of the invitation.

He is constantly on the alert for things to dislike and occasionally descends to obtuse cant. In a lovely cathedral close he is piously astonished—surely, as Trollope has since taught us, not the most profitable emotion for a novelist to enjoy at such a spectacle—"that a man of liberal attainments should possess one of these clerical sinecures, grow sleek and greasy on its products, eat, drink, and be merry, and fancy all the while, that he was serving God!" Still, his unremitting search for social evil is rewarded, and the book's great virtue is that he finds it almost everywhere, and above all in the most unlikely places. Lady Holland's herring, which he is urged to eat because it is contraband brought in by an ambassador, makes him aware how much the English arbitrarily prize privilege for its own sake and determine value by rarity and price; he finds the corrupting influence of this false standard on English comon sense in such a simple phrase as "ridiculously cheap."

The days of repression and violence were ending and those of emancipation and reform at hand, but Cooper will not be taken in by the fine talk. England is and will remain in all its institutions a complex system for the maintenance of the aristocracy, which is supported now at home and abroad not by force or obvious wrong but by such diverse and apparently innocent means as loyalty to the king, the "enlightened" doctrines of free trade, the newspaper society columns that delight the lower middle classes. The aristocracy, he predicts during his 1828 visit, will use even reform for its own preservation, will abolish rotten boroughs and admit the commercial class into alliance with itself to strengthen its position against the poor.

Cooper so dislikes the social machine which the aristocracy has created that at times he speaks of it as if it were some conscious hypocritical monster; but the machine's product, the individual aristocrat, he likes or at least reluctantly admires. Perhaps the sense of strain that one feels in *England* is the result not only of his personal discomfort but also of the intellectual discomfort caused by his honesty of vision, which has denied him the cheap consolation so dear to us, the notion that wicked systems are invariably run by wicked men.

The book about France (confusingly called *Gleanings in Europe* without any subtitle) is midway between the happy surrender of *Italy* and the unhappy aloofness of *England*. It accepts the Bourbon world on its own terms, for France, unlike England, is so obviously different from America that Americans need no warning against it. Cooper relishes the minutiae of social life and the abundant good talk with an easy conscience, indeed with a sense of virtue, for he is certain that his countrymen can learn much from the graciousness of manner and the free play of the mind that he has found in the French upper classes.

The worldliness of tone that is on the whole pleasantly maintained in the entire series is especially noticeable in *France* and is at times touching in its frank enjoyment of the immemorial license of the American in Paris. Women's bodies really appear for the first time in Cooper's pages:

French women's "good busts, inclining to be full"; a grisette's "sauciness of expression, . . . mincing walk, coquettish eye"; a girl on a donkey with her gown pinned up about her waist, "the well-turned legs, and the ankles, with such a *chaussure* as at once marks a *Parisienne*. . . . Truly, it is no wonder that sculptors abound in this country. . . ." But even in England, where opportunities are more limited and a self-imposed propriety must be observed, his new daring does not desert him. On seeing a statue of Queen Anne in a regular set of petticoats, he reflects, "Ladies who are not disposed to go all lengths, had better not be ambitious of figuring in marble."

The secondary subject of the European travel books is America. Cooper is concerned only with the defense of American principles, and—contrary to his practice in *Notions*—sacrifices American "things" ruthlessly, often gaily. The lovely American girl, whose voice had been praised in *Notions* as "particularly soft and silvery," too frequently reminds him of "a nightingale roaring." He likes pointing out how much smaller the Catskills are than the Alps, or Trinity Church in New York than St. Paul's in London. (His sense of heroism in reporting the obvious may seem out of place, but his daughter has assured us that on his return home friends begged him to avoid all such dangerous remarks, or, if something like that had to be said, "Let him, at least, attest the fact in a corner, and lower his voice to a whisper!") Where he has had direct experience of his countrymen's inferiority to Europe their failing is stated with extravagant boldness. In praising German love of art he must add, ". . . blocks are not colder, or can have less real reverence for letters, arts, or indeed cultivation of any kind, than the great bulk of the American people."

This judgment may be based even more on his experience as a patron of the arts than on that as a writer. In Europe he had commissioned the young sculptor Horatio Greenough to make a statuary group after two chanting cherubs in a Raphael and had sent the sculpture home for exhibition to arouse interest in the arts. The Chanting Cherubs failed in New York because the literal public was disappointed when they did not actually sing; in Boston the newspapers suggested that they should be draped in muslin.

The random observations about government, scattered throughout the five books but more concentrated in the two Switzerlands, constitute an informal statement of a liberal political faith, both optimistic and shrewd in the extent of its reliance on the sense of right and wrong in the great mass of men. The optimism is directed at the past, to explain —possibly too glibly, we are inclined to feel today—its failures: the worst excesses of the French Revolution were due not to the inherent evil of the masses but to the instigation of English agents. The shrewdness is reserved for the present: "free trade" (which in Cooper's broad use of the term is much like today's "free enterprise") is a pretentious humbug that hides the unrestrained operation of greed—the cheating of a poor Indian by an unscrupulous trader or of a helpless traveler in a foreign land by a cab driver; a government that wants men to be truly free will regulate conduct that needs regulation.

Cooper must have seemed deliberately perverse in some of his ideas of liberty. Americans, he thought, could learn from the French aristocracy to tolerate the expression of individual opinion and individual conduct that did not conform to the conventional notions of the community. On the other hand, America's favorite libertarian institution, freedom of the press, which was of English origin, was a source of danger. A free press, an excellent instrument for opposing tyrannical government, was itself, once a free government had been established, an instrument of tyranny. It reflected the vices, the capricious interests, the pecuniary cupidity of the commercial class whose members controlled it, and by the blackguardism of its attacks put down all opposition. Soon after the publication of the books on France and England in which these two unpopular theories appeared, Cooper was to experience what he regarded as the tyranny of an American community and the tyranny of the press. He had been right about life in America, but perhaps in part because he had foreseen its dangers, which were of the kind more likely to befall the man who is aware of them than the one who does not know that they exist.

Chapter V

THE COOPERS on coming back to America had planned to live in Cooperstown for only part of the year and to spend their winters in the city. But the reception of *The Monikins* and the *Gleanings* made it clear that the author's great commercial success was over. Although Cooper himself often had to go to New York or Philadelphia on business and might occasionally afford the luxury of taking his wife with him for a few months, Otsego Hall was to be the family's only home. Elaborately remodeled in the new Gothic style with Morse's help, it looks unpretentious and sweet in the old pictures, but some of the villagers disapproved of it as foreign. Current popular taste dictated that a gentleman's country house should be a copy of a Greek temple, which in fact might have been a more practical model, for the castellated Gothic roof held back the snow and leaked.

Cooper's fellow-villagers, or rather some of them, had two other grievances against him. During the many years that the Hall had been empty they had fallen into the habit of crossing its large grounds which cut one of the village streets into two parts. They resented having to give this up and to walk around the block merely because the new owner wanted to enjoy the privacy of his own home. And they disliked even more his attitude toward their use of Three Mile Point.

This small, pleasantly wooded point of land on the west shore of Otsego Lake, about three miles from town, was one of the few pieces of property that Judge Cooper had not sold. It was useful only for pleasure, a perfect place for a picnic after rowing on the lake. Since 1801 it had been used for this purpose by the Judge and his family and of course by the rest of the village, for the Coopers went there only a few times in a summer and the Judge was a good neighbor both by disposition and by profession. In his will Judge Cooper left Three Mile Point to all of his descendants in common until 1850, to be inherited then by the youngest William Cooper. It was certainly Judge William Cooper's purpose to keep the property in the family, but his devise most likely had the effect of continuing its general use, since every Cooper was legally entitled as one of the tenants in common to visit it and invite friends.

Some memory of its theoretic private ownership lingered for a while. When the small house the Judge had built on the Point burned down through the carelessness of the "public," it was suggested to George Pomeroy, the village druggist who had married Judge Cooper's daughter and was in effect therefore a co-tenant, that he replace it. He did not want to do this but consented, as far as he was concerned, to building a house by public subscription, and at the same time warned that the "real owners" might later object. A shanty was put up, costing about $20. Picnics flourished. Each Sunday school—there were about half a dozen churches in the village—must have had its own, for it was unthinkable that a Presbyterian boy, for example, should go on a Universalist outing ("No, sir-ee! I believe in a hell!" one said in refusing an invitation). The bit of land that had so much sentimental association for the absent Fenimore Cooper must have had equally sentimental associations for many of the villagers. When Hannah Pomeroy, George's daughter, and five other girls founded "The Society of Fine Arts, of Elegant and Precious Literature" and dedicated themselves to the annual task of drinking Madeira, eating hickory nuts, and writing to each other in verse on Hannah's birthday, the members as a matter of course ceremonially carved their initials on a tree at the Point. Newcomers to Cooperstown could not remember a time when the public had not used the Point freely as its own; literally they were enjoying a right which, as they claimed later, they had exercised "from time immemorial." It has been said that Americans do not have the love of place that comes from long association, but perhaps it grows, as well as dies, more quickly here.

After Cooper returned from Europe he qualified as executor of his father's will. By then, a comfortable legend had been established that Three Mile Point was public property. Some thought that the Judge had abandoned the land, others that he had expressly willed it to his beloved townsmen. Cooper "took pains to correct this error" but without success. A few years after he came back a tree was cut down "that had a peculiar association connected with my father"; also, the shanty needing repairs, workmen were sent to the Point without permission from anyone.

Cooper felt that he had to do something. Like a Venetian

senator or a bank director, he was acting not in his personal interest but for the collective good of a mythical entity, in his case an estate and a perhaps as yet unborn William Cooper whose rights had to be protected. The conventions of Cooper's position both as executor and as head of the family prescribed a pettiness of conduct on behalf of others that he probably would not have stooped to for himself. In July 1837, he sent a card to the *Freeman's Journal*, the local Democratic weekly, stating that the Point was private property and cautioning the public against injuring the trees. Word of it got out before it was published and produced that exacerbated political feeling then known as "excitement." "Menaces and messages" induced Cooper to withdraw his first notice and substitute a stronger one, an advertisement that warned against trespassing, announced his intention "rigidly" to enforce the estate's title to the Point, and declared that the public had no right to it "beyond what has been conceded by the liberality of the owners."

On only a few hours' notice about sixty villagers met publicly at an inn to protest. They went through the parliamentary forms of indignation—appointed a chairman and secretary, made speeches, adopted resolutions, ordered their proceedings published in the village papers. It was resolved to "disregard the notice given by James F. Cooper," to "hold his threat to enforce title . . . as we do his whole conduct in . . . the matter, in perfect contempt," to "request . . . Franklin Library, in this village, to remove all books, of which Cooper is the author," to "denounce any man as sycophant, who has, or shall, ask permission of James F. Cooper to visit the Point. . . ." According to report, a more extreme suggestion, that his books should be burned, and a more reasonable one, that his title to the Point should be investigated, were turned down.

Wild though these resolutions are, they nevertheless show some grasp of the issue presented by Cooper's unhappily worded advertisement, which was not the practical question of whether the villagers were to use the Point at all, but the metaphysical one of whether they were to use it only with Cooper's consent. He had acted from his understanding of the metaphysics of property, they from theirs of the metaphysics of freedom. But as news rather than as a subject for speculation, the controversy had to be presented in a more simplified form. The first report, in the *Chenango Telegraph*, a paper in an adjoining county, by stripping the affair of its details put Cooper hopelessly in the wrong. A churlish landowner, to show his authority, had forbidden anyone to set foot on a worthless bit of land. "This gentleman," so the editor began, stating his conclusion in the first sentence, "not satisfied with having drawn down upon his head universal contempt from abroad, has done the same thing for himself at Cooperstown, where he resides." The brief account was reprinted in the *Albany Evening Journal*, run by the great Whig, Thurlow Weed, and became the authoritative version that was spread throughout the country.

The *Otsego Republican*, Cooperstown's Whig paper, also reprinted the article and added a nondefamatory if inaccurate statement of the citizens' supposed rights, for the Chenango editor had called on it to give all of the facts to the public. Cooper immediately bought space in the *Freeman's Journal* for two letters of rebuttal. Apparently his side of the matter was so unpopular that his friend and fellow-Democrat, Colonel Prentiss, would not give him free use of his columns. The first letter set forth the facts of the Point's history at length and argued the question of title cogently; the second mockingly published the resolutions, which the secretary of the meeting had failed to do, having given them to Cooper instead of to the papers as ordered. Cooper's letters had no effect on national opinion, for they were not copied by any other papers; nor is it clear that they had any local effect.*

At the same time (August 1837) Richard Cooper, Fenimore's nephew and lawyer, wrote to the *Otsego Republican* threatening to sue for libel unless there was a suitable retraction of the offending article. The inexperienced young editor, Andrew Barber, did not realize that he was legally responsible for the repetition of the Chenango piece. Unaware of any wrongdoing of his own he was certain of his duty to the press to resist "an attempt to compromise its high tone and independent bearing, . . . it is its legitimate privilege, and the right of the people, to promulgate their sovereign will and pleasure, and disseminate truth, justice and morality" *et cetera*. Such exalted notions required an editor to stand firm and refuse to correct his mere errors of fact. In September 1837 Cooper began suit against the brash young man and also against his brighter colleague, the editor

---

* It is true that the villagers did nothing further in the matter, but there is no indication that they ever intended to go beyond their original gesture of defiance. They seem to have continued using the Point which was in due time inherited by a William Cooper. In 1871 it was leased to the Village Improvement Society of Cooperstown, and in 1899 was bought for a moderate sum for the townspeople. It is still one of the few places for public swimming and picnicking on Otsego Lake.

of the *Chenango Telegraph*, but not against the powerful Thurlow Weed. He went no further than the initial step of serving the writs. He had a more urgent task than teaching these two small fry a lesson about Three Mile Point; his countrymen needed instruction in "the principles involved in that controversy."

Cooper's next two works, *The Chronicles of Cooperstown* and *The American Democrat* (both published in 1838 and only in America), may have been undertaken before the controversy, but there can be no doubt that they were influenced by it. The *Chronicles* is a dry, dull narrative. The author professes belief in the value of "the love of particular places," but in his desire to avoid the exaggerated "land and water" patriotism that he had so often ridiculed, he has left no room for love. One gets little sense of the antiquarian delight in local history and none of the charm of the village and surrounding country. As an impartial and anonymous historian, he gravely accords himself the respect to which his social position entitles him: except when he is "that gentleman," he is "James Fenimore Cooper, Esquire," even in the same sentence in which older settlers are "James White, a carpenter," and "Joseph Baldwin, cooper"; in describing his "improvements" at Otsego Hall he notes, ". . . this dwelling . . . promises to be one of the best country houses in the state, again." The Three Mile Point affair figures without name or facts in a generalized reference to the rudeness and troublesome interference of the floating population and to its defeat, which he celebrates smugly: "One or two instances of audacious assumptions of a knowledge of facts, and of a right to dictate, on the part of strangers, have recently met with rebukes that will probably teach others caution, if they do not teach them modesty."

The American Democrat, a formal exposition of his views on government and society brought up to date, suffers a little from its orderliness and unrelieved abstractness. One misses the trifles that in *Gleanings* were so frankly revealed as the sources of his thought. "The work is written," as he disarmingly says in his Introduction, "more in the spirit of censure than of praise, for its aim is correction. . . ." He believes as firmly as ever in the superiority of democracy. Every system, however, has its inherent defects, depending on where power resides. It is more useful for democracy's supporters "to guard against the evils peculiar to that particular system, than to declaim against the abuses of others . . . [and] to be glorifying ourselves. . . ." Because in a democracy the people really rule, they are most to be distrusted. "The publick, then, is to be watched, in this country, as in other countries kings and aristocrats are to be watched."

Democratic tyranny takes the form not of evil laws but of substituting public opinion for law. The public as such has no legal rights except by acting through the instrumentalities of government and law, but it does have the power to act extralegally and is often tempted to do so. As a king has his courtiers, it has its own special flatterer, the demagogue. Few dare attack the errors of public opinion, but in the case of individuals "there is a singular boldness in the use of personalities, as if men avenged themselves for the restraints of the one case by a licentiousness that is without hazard." Americans have reversed the standard of most civilized countries, "where personalities excite disgust, and society is deemed fair game."

Flattery of the people has resulted in false notions of the meaning of the democratic doctrine of equality, which is limited strictly to equal political and civil rights for all (with the exception, as Cooper likes to point out, of women, children, criminals, aliens, slaves). It does not mean equality of property or that men are in fact equal in talents. No one really believes the cant saying, "One man is as good as another," for no one suggests that all offices should be filled by lot. "Choice supposes a preference, and preference inequality of merit, or of fitness." Nor does the democratic ideal seek to make all men alike. "Individuality is the aim of political liberty." But the tradition of religious fanaticism handed down from colonial days, the mistaken tendency to increase the extralegal authority of the public and set up "They Say" as an absolute monarch, the general indifference to the invasion of private rights by an intolerant press, make this country, whose political liberty is greater than that of nearly every other civilized nation, the one in which men have the least individuality and personal liberty.

To Cooper, whose observation of American life is in so many ways like Tocqueville's, social classes were as inevitable in America as in Europe, "but the classes run into each other more easily, the lines of separation are less strongly drawn, and their shadows are more intimately blended." To his contemporaries the class structure of society was an inadmissible fact, and they denounced all signs of it as "aristocratic." In his private correspondence at this time Cooper was referring to "the present political struggle . . . between men and dollars," but in *The American Democrat* the dangers of a class society appear much less immediate and are outweighed by its advantages. Cooper never quite brings together the two parts of the dilemma: politically, a class society threatens majority rule, because a minority of wealth and talent can always subvert democratic institutions if it ever conspires seriously against them; socially, it assures "the utmost practicable personal liberty" by recognizing the right of association of men of like interests and tastes. Cooper disagrees with what he understands to be a typical European theory, that the people should always elect the "noble." "Power cannot be extended to a *caste*, without *caste's* reaping its principal benefit. . . ." Yet, to win its support for democracy the gentlemanly class should be admitted to a fair share of the government. And, since "no rights can be dearer to a man of cultivation," a gentleman must be allowed in his private life the full exercise of his democratic right of social exclusiveness. It is as unjust to the refined minority to deny it the enjoyment of its own tastes by forcing it to associate indiscriminately with the majority ". . . as it would be to insist on the less fortunate's passing the time they would rather devote to athletic amusements, in listening to operas for which they have no relish, sung in a language they do not understand."

The American Democrat is the intellectual scenario for Cooper's contemporary novel that was to dramatize the principles of Three Mile Point. His plan for the new work was simple: the rediscovery of America by a family of educated Americans who after many years abroad return to their own village. With brilliant novelistic economy Cooper made his family the descendants of Judge Temple of *The Pioneers*, and their village, Templeton. The Effinghams—Judge Temple's only child, Elizabeth, had married Oliver Effingham—would have the advantage of a documented past that could be contrasted with the present without wasting a word. But the head of the family, Edward Effingham, would also have the disadvantage, of which the novelist seems to have been naively unaware, of being taken for a self-portrait of Fenimore Cooper.

Originally the story was to open at Sandy Hook with the returning travelers about to land. But the cry for "more ship" persuaded him to push back the beginning to the embarkation at Portsmouth and to expand the adventures. Ultimately a whole book, *Homeward Bound* (May 1838), was given over to the Atlantic crossing; and, as if reluctant to come to grips with his unpleasant subject, the American scene, he put it off to a sequel, *Home as Found* (November 1838).

The evasion of a stern duty had its happy reward. By keeping his characters at sea Cooper invented a new setting for the comedy of manners, the ocean liner. After a century of hard use it may seem almost too pat a symbol of a stratified society, too convenient a stage for the meeting of the ill-assorted world that was never meant to meet. But it is still the right instrument for a master who is not afraid of the obvious, and Cooper in the early pages of *Homeward Bound* uses the American packet *Montauk* with unashamed boldness, working his material for its full worth. The great problem for cabin passengers—the question of each other's social position at home—is studied with equal care by the genteel Effinghams, anticipating the horrors and pleasures of enforced intimacy on a long voyage, and by the colored stewards whose answers to casual inquiries about the weather are measured out according to rank. To get the maximum return from his garish assembly of passengers—the Effinghams who are trained mechanisms of recoil from the vulgar; the vulgar Steadfast Dodge; an embezzling clerk disguised as a baronet; the baronet himself, masquerading under his valet's name; a young man so reasonable on touchy national questions that no one can tell whether he is English or American—Cooper has placed at its head a ship's master who is a genius of social intercourse. The homely Yankee Captain Truck, Cooper's most delightful sailor, has a passion for marine protocol that ranges from the great question of international law, the right of search on the high seas, to the smallest amenities of the ship's daily life. He has a mania for introductions among his passengers, and when one doesn't take he does it over.

The novel's subtitle, "The Chase," refers to a double movement: the external pursuit of the *Montauk* by an English corvette seeking to capture the embezzler, a long chase that might have been avoided if Captain Truck hadn't been too punctilious to ask questions; and the pursuit of the cabin passengers by each other. In the end flight is ineffective against brute force. The man-of-war overtakes the packet. Steadfast Dodge, the pushing, ferociously egalitarian newspaper editor, establishes a lasting acquaintance with the Effinghams, who have no defense against his aggression except a snub so dignified that he cannot recognize it.

The obnoxious ignorant envious boastful cringing little country editor from whom the Effinghams cannot escape is one of the makers of America. Cooper is too honest to pretend that his refined protagonists can handle such an adversary, but hates him too much to allow him his formal dramatic triumph. At the very heart of the gay *Homeward Bound* is an unwritten tragedy of conquest (which has been written in part in D. H. Lawrence's imaginatively inaccurate description of the book); instead we have a static character study of the contemptible conqueror and his consistent discomfiture in scenes that are irrelevant to his victory in history.

This "stubborn friend of liberty" (as Captain Truck agrees, "That is he. . . . He has no notion of letting a man do as he has a mind to") is the perfect false democrat: "I think you will agree with me, sir, in believing it excessively presuming in an American to pretend to be different from his fellow-citizens. . . . I do not know that any man has a right to be peculiar in a free country. It is aristocratic, and has an air of thinking one man is better than another." He cannot stand the necessary despotism of a ship ("majorities were his hobbies") and suggests to the captain that a committee of passengers be appointed to help run it. He works up an "excitement" and is amazed when Truck is indifferent to his report of it; for Dodge's awe of public opinion is so great that he lives in trembling respect even of the "public" opinion he has himself manufactured, just as his faith in the truth of newspapers is too firm to be shaken by the lies he publishes in his own.

It is easy to defeat a demagogue by pitting him, as Cooper has done (and Conrad was to do later), against an autocrat of the sea—in fact, so easy that in the process landsmen's democracy itself suffers from an unintended comparison with shipshape autocracy. Not content with this, Cooper must take Dodge further afield, force the ship to land on the African coast and fight Arabs, for no other reason—if we except the readers' pleasure in adventure—than to show Dodge up as a physical coward. This is mere dream revenge on a man who lives comfortably off his moral cowardice.

The fighting makes a break with the book's theme but never quite suppresses its mood of civilized gaiety. A pure adventure story like *The Last of the Mohicans* does not strike us as quite "real" because violence has exempted life from its ordinary embarrassments with which we are so familiar. In *Homeward Bound* Cooper has discovered that the fear of being ridiculous and the pompous freedom from that fear, two prime conditions for the comedy of manners, can flourish amidst physical dangers. Captain Truck tries humanely by means of pantomime to tell a captured Arab that Americans are *not* cannibals and will *not* eat him, and is humiliated when all that the prisoner apparently gathers from the vigorous gestures and disgusted negative shakings of the head is that the Americans will eat him but will consider him loathsome food. Steadfast Dodge insists at a tense moment that a secret ballot rather than a rousing cheer is the legal way of getting the crew to undertake the fight for the recapture of the ship from the Arabs.

The comic spirit, having managed to live through high adventure, accompanies Captain Truck tenderly to a scene at which Cooper has heretofore been uniformly solemn, a deathbed. Truck's nice sense of the problems of social intercourse makes him worry fussily over what part of the Bible to read to a dying man (". . . a chapter is the very least we can give a cabin-passenger . . ."). When he wistfully realizes that he has a further inescapable duty, and he and the mate go down on their knees in prayer, it is such honestly hard work on their part, so much worse than fighting wild

Arabs, that the reader, like the dying man, is for the moment piously touched.

Homeward Bound is really complete in itself; in fact, an incidental virtue is its formally unfinished state that leaves the polite lovers, the hero Paul Blunt and the heroine Eve Effingham, dangling in mid-courtship. It is one of Cooper's freshest books and, for a landsman, one of his finest sea tales. The story, it is true, has interfered with the theme, but we do not mind because the story is a good one.

In the sequel, *Home as Found* (November 1838), the author took such care to avoid this error that he eliminated the story almost entirely. He had deliberately chosen a subject which he was certain a novelist could not treat successfully, the flat ugliness of ordinary American life. Today we expect a dull world to furnish at least an interesting tale of revolt. But this solution was not available to Cooper, who had no taste for the attitudes of rebellion and arrived at his most original and unpopular views by believing that they were the true orthodoxy. It was impossible for him to make Eve Effingham a rebel like Carol Kennicott against the Main Streets of New York and Templeton. She can only watch the disappointing spectacle and listen to her elders' endless talk about it. Because she has grimly made up her mind to love her native land, she tries conscientiously to side with her mild father, Edward Effingham, who likes to think that his country is not so ugly as it looks, rather than with his cynical cousin Jack, who is happy in the certainty that it is much uglier. Jack is not Cooper's licensed mouthpiece, and neither Eve nor the reader ever fully believes him, but he manages always to be authoritative in his gloomiest forebodings. "Whited sepulchres!" he mutters, when the others admire the neat houses of the Hudson Valley. "Wait until you get a view of the deformity within."

Home as Found is a huge loose catalogue of the infinite varieties of provincial deformity observed by the Effinghams on a round of visits in New York and on their return to Templeton. It is a narrow, mean, intolerant world, deprived of the graces of civilization, so shifting and unstable on account of its "go ahead" spirit that, as Jack Effingham puts it, ". . . an American 'always' means eighteen months, and . . . 'time immemorial' is only since the last general crisis in the money market." No one, except the Effinghams and a few intelligent friends, dares avail himself of a free man's first privilege, to think for himself. Everyone has opinions on everything, derived ready-made from authority and accepted without examination.

New York's social life is an imitation of Europe's, misapplied with childish zeal but without the charm of a child's corruption of adult forms. Cooper has the clearest cruel vision of the sadness of living at second-hand and of the pathetic dreariness of his city. Literary New Yorkers are so starved for culture that on Jack Effingham's statement they accept Captain Truck as a great English writer, "much the most interesting man we have had out here since the last bust of Scott." The noisy belle who must "entertain" five gentlemen simultaneously is in reality a poor overworked drudge; if her bright chatter stops for a moment her young men will gape and talk to each other about the price of lots. By a typical American combination of mechanized standards and mystic faith, everyone who has been to Paris is, because of this sacred pilgrimage, a "Hajji." No grades are recognized in this high social distinction, except that there is a risk in having stayed away too long. "Are you reconciled to your country?" is the tell-tale question every New Yorker asks Eve.

In Templeton the Effinghams are among a people "so saturated with liberty, that they become insensible to the nicer feelings." These are the "I'm as good as you" Americans of Mrs. Trollope's phrase, but Cooper finds their social claims even more exorbitant: equality with God; superiority to everyone else. A church is to be altered, for, as Steadfast Dodge says, "To my notion, gentlemen and ladies, God never intended an American to kneel." Old neighborly forms of cooperation from the pastoral age of *The Pioneers* persist in the new age of individual struggle, but with a new purpose—to prevent the assertion of individual differences. The community that loves the unlimited right to acquire property despises its proprieties. Mutual helpfulness has degenerated into a one-sided duty to submit to trespassing. Borrowing has expanded to the extent that a neighbor can be asked for the use of her better-sounding name on a trip to Utica, the borrower assuring the lender that any incidental damages will be paid.

Cooper's inability to create rounded and functioning upper-class characters had not heretofore been a serious fault, because he had usually entrusted the business of adventure to competent lower-class people like Harvey Birch and Natty Bumppo, who act with cool efficiency while the fine sensibilities of their betters paralyze them into inaction. The novelist had probably arrived at his lopsided pattern of the world, strong at the bottom and weak at the top, rather from the deliberate imitation of Scott that had begun with *The Spy* than from conscious theory about the relation of social classes in America. (In the field of his own invention, the sea tale, professional skill goes hand in hand with rank.) In *Home as Found* the disproportion becomes serious when, for the first time, the upper-class characters are challenged by their environment to demonstrate the right to live on their own terms. The Effinghams can face the issue intellectually. They have just the right thin vitality to carry on a philosophic dialogue, where the doses of life must be small enough for reason to swallow them comfortably. But dramatically the Effinghams are so feeble that they cannot directly confront the forces to which they are opposed. At the great crisis over the "Fishing Point" (as Three Mile Point is called) Edward Effingham, like a too rational William Tell, can only give his land agent, Aristabulus Bragg, messages and advertisements for the attention of the turbulent villagers who, according to Jack Effingham, are playing the part of Gessler. Liberty—or at least this is what a romantic tradition teaches us—cannot be won by so easy a defiance of a tyrant.

In the sketch of the stock-jobber's rise in *The Monikins* Cooper had given a new and sophisticated rendering of the time-worn tale of the virtuous apprentice. With Aristabulus Bragg, in *Home as Found*, he arrives at an American version of this theme, the making of a self-made man. Like his great contemporary, Julien Sorel (of whom Cooper had probably not heard), Bragg has the sense of life as conscious choice and of the moral right to aspire to the highest social position. If we arbitrarily ignore the difference in Stendhal's and Cooper's talents, what in large part makes Julien still so "modern" for us is his desperately anxious awareness of how limited his opportunities are, and the terrible need, imposed on him by his own nature as well as by external circumstance, to seize them ruthlessly. The aristocratic society that shut him out has disappeared, but the emotions of exclusion, from self-pity to terror, are with us yet. Bragg's world, nominally continuous with our own, is in reality unrecognizable; it offers so many chances that an ambitious man can afford to be careless about them and let go of some easily. Where the Frenchman must treacherously calculate the seduction of his employer's daughter as the only possible means of marrying her, the American can feel entitled to casually propose marriage to his, while whittling.

Bragg is a pleasant scamp who, like some impudent but always fundamentally cautious servant in an old comedy, does not know his place. The question of place, however, had become an extremely complicated one in democratic America. Bragg is willing to undertake any menial errand for his employer, even the hopeless one of trying to fetch the village barber to Mr. Effingham's house to cut his hair; at the same time he is a lawyer—that is, if we are to believe Tocqueville, a true American aristocrat. He is delightfully indifferent about the precise ends and means of his ambition, but will some day undoubtedly be a great man in American politics. After Eve Effingham refuses him, he makes an excellent marriage with her French maid. When Edward Effingham instructs him to drive away some apprentices who are playing ball on the lawn, he coaxes these future voters off by telling them that it is aristocratic to play among roses and dahlias and much more libertarian to play in the street where games are forbidden by law.

We would say today that Aristabulus Bragg had a flair for "public relations," a gift that Edward Effingham, like

Fenimore Cooper, lacked. It is not entirely our fault—for after all Cooper must have liked him too—if our fondness for Bragg lessens the force of Cooper's point in *Home as Found* that a civilized country would be one without any need for "public relations" other than justice and truth. As so often happens in the novel with a purpose, the dramatic means are in the wrong hands and undermine the author's avowed moral ends. Bragg's flexibility, his willingness to accept America's raw vulgarity, give him an attitude of open welcome to life, while the high-minded uncompromising Effinghams seem in their stiff uprightness to turn their backs on it; so that in the end the unforgivable aesthetic sin, denial, seems to be theirs, and the highest virtue, affirmation, his.

Since *Home as Found* had its immediate source in a personal controversy it was easy for Cooper's contemporaries to belittle its serious criticism of America by treating its author as a personally embittered controversialist. Cooper was in fact developing a liking for bitter controversy, or finding a great social need for it. A month before the exhaustive attack on his country in *Home as Found* he had attempted to overturn one of its great idols, Sir Walter Scott, who just because he had been so shabbily treated by America in his lifetime was to be spoken of only with reverence now that he was dead. Behind Cooper's review of Lockhart's *Life of Scott* (in the *Knickerbocker*, October 1838), as behind *Home as Found*, there was enough of a personal situation—which Cooper of course with his gratuitous honesty had to make public—to give color to the claim that he was making his attack for personal reasons and not for the sake of the truth that he professed to maintain disinterestedly.

The *Quarterly Review* which was edited by John Gibson Lockhart, "the Scorpion," published in its October 1837 issue an anonymous review of Cooper's *England* so abusive that it was generally assumed in America, where it was gleefully copied, to be the Scorpion's own work. It seems in fact to have been written by Lockhart's friend, John Wilson Croker (and is listed as his work in Myron F. Brightfield's biography of Croker). Cooper's mistakes about English life are attributed to the fact that he spent the most important years of his life as a common seaman and evidently had "a late and scanty acquaintance with polished society." Cooper, who had learned to tell a lord from a commoner by his knock, had been minutely observant in a field in which the spirit of scientific inquiry is most easily identifiable with snobbish curiosity, and the reviewer made the author sound like a fool who "cannot . . . mention a lord . . . without getting into a flutter between awe and envy, that confuses his very senses." The American who boasted about invitations to breakfast at Rogers' was unaware that they were given "when the guest is one about whose manners, character, or social position, there is *some uncertainty*." He had been in "a state of probation," and the inference was that he had not made good, for he had not met the best people, not even the reviewer.

Cooper had written at some length both in the *England* and in the *France* about his pleasant meetings with Scott. To his chagrin the diaries quoted so copiously by Lockhart in the monumental *Life* compressed the entire relationship into two brief entries, a half-dozen sentences in all, of which the one given solely to Cooper read: "This man, who has shown so much genius, has a good deal of the manners, or want of manners, peculiar to his countrymen." *

Cooper wrote a long letter to the *Knickerbocker* (April 1838), incidentally to defend his manners, which he did gracefully, and primarily to prove that he knew Sir Walter better than the latter realized. We are indebted to it for the fullest account of Cooper's generous efforts on Scott's behalf and for a copy of their appeals to Carey & Lea. Along with these letters, Cooper published in the *Knickerbocker* formal proof of their authenticity, as if now that he was back home he doubted—and expected others to doubt—whether he had ever been one of the great men of the world in a position to offer aid to another. He protests with pathetic crankiness against the older author's diminution of his junior's stature by the careless disproportion of the diary entries: Scott might well have omitted the Frenchmen bouncing in and exploding their compliments, to make room for a few words about his serious business with Cooper. The diarist's opinions were reprehensibly superficial: at Princess Galitzin's evening party where, as the diary put it, "the Scotch and American lions took the field together," the Scotch lion found an eighty-year-old lady the most interesting person present; but all that he knew of her personally, Cooper points out, "was obtained in an interview of a very few minutes, in a crowded room, and through the medium of a language that he scarcely spoke at all, or understood when spoken!"

* Scott had actually written "manner, or want of manner," and the additional *s*, which gave the passage so much crueler a meaning, had somehow crept into the published text. The error was not corrected until almost forty years after Cooper's death.

Cooper mentions, only to deny, his friends' suggestion that Lockhart had mutilated the diary in the same spirit in which he had reviewed the *England*. He argues with considerable detail that Lockhart could not have been the reviewer, for if he was he had lied in asserting that he had not met Cooper—*England* described two dinners at which they were both guests—and could never have spoken of breakfast as an "equivocal compliment" when his own father-in-law, Scott, as the diaries showed, had breakfasted out so frequently in London.

The *England*, however, contained the answer to the riddle of the diary. Cooper had explained painstakingly to his countrymen that they did not count with Britons as the latter did with them, and that it was a provincial failing for Americans to believe that they did. His own experience illustrates this general law, which inevitably he always observed more accurately in others than in himself. Sir Walter was a real force in Cooper's career, a part of his life; he could never hope to rid himself of the annoying tag, "the American Scott." But Cooper was not part of Sir Walter's and could be dismissed with a few words in the fullest record of it, an awkward figure glimpsed for a moment among a throng of extravagant admirers.

Reading Lockhart's *Life* as a whole convinced Cooper that the subject far from being a model of virtue, as the biographer piously claimed, was a selfish unprincipled worldling. Scott's faults were of the sort least appealing to an incorruptible man. Hiding under his anonymity as the "Author of Waverley," he had reviewed his own work with amused, discriminating admiration. As an orthodox literary politician he had publicly praised Southey's poetry, and privately admitted that he would have had more fun tearing it to pieces. He fawned on the ducal head of his clan for loans, and on his worthless king, George IV, for promotion for his son. As the secret partner of Ballantyne & Co. he had recklessly borrowed huge sums for the purchase of Abbotsford, and when heavily in debt bestowed it on his son as his marriage settlement.

If we cannot take Scott's faults seriously, it is not merely because of his heroic struggle in his last years to pay his debts, but also because in his fortunate years the gift of enjoying life lends a charm to his meanest and most devious acts. But to Cooper the pleasant qualities were an aggravation of Scott's faults, a mask of hypocrisy that made them more effective. In his elaborate review of Lockhart's *Life* Cooper took on himself the duty which the biographer had failed to perform of unmasking the monster and showing the hideous ugliness beneath the lovely surface.

Scott's peculiar talent was "the art of seemliness." In his novels it hid his inability to create noble characters; in his conduct it hid his "innate want of principle." To sustain this broad proposition Cooper had to find everything about Scott bad, and the signs of his evil nature everywhere in his life, in his most trivial acts and most understandable reticences. He is denounced as a base flatterer, for speaking of George IV as king *de jure* in disregard of the claims of the Jacobite Pretender; as a scoundrel, for indicating to his brother Tom a convenient device by which he would know when Tom's letters of introduction were not to be taken literally; as either having kept a false diary or as a heartless unfeeling man, because his diary records no great grief at his wife's death (for, Cooper argues with a pettifogger's love of an artificial dilemma, "If he did feel it, what are we to think of the Diary?").

The biography was Scott's final effort "to maintain his assumed character with posterity." For this purpose he had deliberately picked a biographer whose training had been the editorship of the *Quarterly Review,* a periodical conceived in fraud—as Scott knew, for he had been one of its founders—and "reckless alike of truth and decency." He had been even more culpable in authorizing the use of his diaries. A diary read after death, Cooper argued, is at best a kind of misrepresentation, because we read it as "the parting sentiments of a dying man," when in fact it has been written under the passions and impulses of the living moment. In Scott's case, where posthumous publication had always been intended, the air of confidential communication with the reader was "a sheer deception."

Cooper had arrived at a literary truth which we accept today but usually value differently. A great "Life" is in part something manipulated and contrived, an act of creation. Lockhart, like Boswell, had a subject who was himself a writer, among other things, of lives, and who lent himself with a sympathetic skill, not unlike that of a professional model's, to making a work of art out of his own. Depending on our point of view, we can label the portrait of such an accommodating sitter "the real thing" or—if we have Cooper's horror of manipulation and contrivance—"a fraud."

Cooper recognized that under his theory there was no room for any working cooperation between artist and subject. "None but a strictly conscientious man . . . should ever leave a diary for publication." When his own turn at dying came he requested that there be no authorized biog-

raphy of him; and it may be no accident that of the few
fragments of diary that have come down to us, those which
are subsequent to the review of Lockhart are almost all as
barrenly factual and stripped of life as any writing is likely
to be.

Chapter VI

ON NOVEMBER 15, 1838 Cooper in a typical letter
to his wife gossips about a marriage, her brother's
election to a bishopric, a pamphlet by the Ballantyne family against Lockhart and Scott, arrangements for
lodgings in town for the winter. At the end he mentions,
"*Home as Found* is published, and will not take, of course.
. . . " He was prepared for another failure, but not, despite
his knowledge of Steadfast Dodge, for the new intensity of
insult in his reviews.

James Watson Webb of the *Morning Courier and New
York Enquirer* made the leading attack. With that shrillness
of vituperation of which only sincere outraged feelings are
capable, he called Cooper "a base minded catiff who has
traduced his country for filthy lucre and from low born
spleen; . . . the *slanderer* who is in fact a traitor to national
pride and national character." If all Americans do their duty
and read Cooper's works, ". . . then there will ascend to
Heaven one universal prayer, that the *viper* so long nour-
ished in our bosom, may shortly leave our shores never again
to disgrace with his presence a land to which he has proved

an ingrate and . . . been anything but a reputable, useful, or even harmless citizen." This is political rhetoric, and Webb proceeded to accuse Cooper of a political crime more serious, in the code of the day, than treason: he was an aristocrat.

Since Judge Temple of *The Pioneers* was clearly Judge Cooper, and Templeton was Cooperstown, and Edward Effingham's Fishing Point Fenimore Cooper's Three Mile Point, obviously the mild handsome thoughtful philosophical Mr. Effingham, so superior to all of his countrymen, was Fenimore Cooper's notion of himself. Eve had argued with a provincial cousin that an American gentleman of good family, like her father, was better than a mere baronet and the equal of dukes and princes. To Cooper this idea of equality with the highest European social rank was indispensable for American independence; stated with his normal prolixity and passion for explicitness in matters of social theory, it sounds a little ridiculous. By slight omissions Webb took away its general applicability and made it apply only to the Effinghams, that is, to Cooper. One of the novel's fundamental purposes, the reviewer claimed, was to create the impression abroad that the novelist came from a long line of noble ancestors. To contrast with this pretension Webb invented a family background for Cooper: his father had been a wheelwright, proud of his trade, regretting only that his wagons weren't as good as his competitors. In a later article Webb said that the father of the aristocrat who now lived in English baronial style had started even lower in the social scale, "an humble hawker of fish," and that the aristocrat's maternal grandmother, "old Mother Fenimore," had kept a vegetable stall for twenty years in Philadelphia.

Webb's review was widely reprinted and commented on. Thurlow Weed delightedly called it "a skinning alive." Park Benjamin, according to Poe the most influential literary editor of the day, playfully disputed Webb's claim that Cooper had been motivated by the mercenary desire to make his works sell in England. Blackguarding was his nature, and he was literally going mad; he was already "the craziest loon that ever was suffered to roam at large without whip and keeper."

Cooper and his enemies were at an impasse that could not be solved by any rational use of words. *Home as Found* was an infuriating book; even so good and rash a friend as Morse wrote to the author, ". . . I wish you had not written it." Its most infuriating aspect was that as a novel "by the author of Homeward Bound, The Pioneers, etc., etc.," it was certain to reach an important European audience. Translated into other languages—many more, Cooper gloatingly noted, than his detractors admitted—it would go, unrefuted and undenied, where their shouts and clamor could never follow; even if badly received abroad as a book, it would still as the work of one of America's chief writers testify against American civilization. Editors only screamed the louder from sheer ineffectuality, not quite sure whether they were encompassing the author's ruin at home or merely recording the fact that he was bringing it on himself.

Most of what Webb and the others wrote was an unanswerable mixture of misstatements and sneers, as Cooper knew, yet never able to lay logic completely aside he was, at his leisure, to undertake painfully detailed replies. But a logical answer besides being tedious was useless. After all,

Home as Found, the source of his present trouble, had been just such an answer to the Three Mile Point affair. ". . . I have learned to know," Cooper wrote a few years later, in explaining his course of action, "that the refutation of a lie, in this country, is of little importance. It must be *punished,* to do any good." He immediately took the necessary legal steps to get his pending libel actions in shape for trial. Against Webb he proceeded more drastically than by civil suit. He had him indicted by the grand jury of Otsego County for the crime of libel.

According to the editors, Cooper admitted weakness by transferring the controversy from the press to the law; he was acknowledging "either his own incompetency to wield his proper implement or the superiority of the courts of judicature to the high court of Public Opinion in which he is by right a practitioner." In his polemical writing Cooper had been incompetent, if we assume rather narrowly that his purpose was to defend himself or to persuade his country-men of the soundness of his views. In his new field he was an able practitioner, often arguing his own cases—doing rather better, however, in his legal arguments to a court than in his appeals to juries for their sympathy. But the law was not the perfect medium for his purposes; just as the traditions of the press were too loose, those of the law were too tight. Before he had finished with his libel suits he obtained judg-ments or forced retractions in more than a dozen cases; but since these victories sometimes involved the application of a technical rule of procedure which his opponents did not understand they were able to assert with some plausibility that he had won not because truth had triumphed but be-cause it had been suppressed.

In his first trial, that against Andrew Barber (May 1839), the editor had not attempted to justify the malicious remarks he had reprinted from the *Chenango Telegraph* but had given notice that he would prove the truth of what he had himself written about the title to Three Mile Point. Cooper accepted the challenge, and the plaintiff's opening statement went into the matter fully. But when the defendant's turn came, Judge Willard on his own initiative excluded all evidence offered about the Point. The judge was legally correct. Courts were fond of saying that truth, to be a defense, must be as broad as the charge. From this harmless general principle they established an absurd subsidiary one: partial truth was no defense, not even in mitigation of damages. A defamatory statement that might be true in part was to be considered as if it were entirely false. "Good morals, as well as the law," so the reviewing court in the Barber case glibly explained, "forbid that the addition of some truth should be deemed a palliation of the wrong of publishing a libel."

This reasoning was more than a young country editor could understand, and the result, a $400 verdict against him, was more than he could afford to pay. William L. Stone of the *New York Commercial Advertiser* suggested an Effingham Libel Fund for the relief of the novelist's victims. The proposal, which was regarded by Cooper as positive evidence of a conspiracy against him, seems to have been merely a bad newspaper joke, for as yet the editors were not afraid of the lawsuits. Barber proudly refused any help from his fellow-editors, and Stone himself was soon in trouble with Cooper on account of the review he published of Cooper's new book, *The History of the Navy of the United States of America* (1839).*

   As long ago as 1826, at the dinner given in his honor just before he sailed for Europe, Cooper had responded to the praise of his novels by the promise to write something more serious and lasting than his fiction. No American writer, he said in the correct style of so grand and happy an occasion, had invaded the sacred precincts of the Muse of History with greater license and frequency than he. As an expiatory offering before the altar of the offended Goddess, he would record the deeds and sufferings of a class of men to whom the nation owed a debt of lasting gratitude and among whom he had passed many of the happiest days of his youth. Truth would be a pleasant duty, for the more nearly it was attained,

   * Cooper did not press Barber for payment, but the young man's creditors sold him out, either because of the judgment or their own desire to put the *Otsego Republican* into other hands. When the Whig candidate, William Henry Harrison, hero of Tippecanoe, defeated "the little aristocrat," Martin Van Buren, in the presidential election of 1840, Barber sought the Cooperstown postmastership on the ground that he had been ruined by Cooper's oppression. Cooper, annoyed, issued execution, and the sheriff legally seized the banknotes found in a box which he had to break open. Barber wrote an open letter to Cooper, via Webb's paper, complaining that all he had left in the world was a pair of pocket combs, hair and shoe brushes and box of blacking, *et cetera*, a likeness of "Old Tip," and a miniature log cabin, 1½ by 2 feet. The mention of these was of course to prove his deserving poverty and his loyalty to the Whig party and to appeal to the victor of the "Log Cabin Campaign" for a political job. Cooper told the whole story in a letter to his friend Bryant's paper, the *Evening Post*, and asked that a copy of his letter be sent to the Postmaster General. He was unable, however, to block Barber's appointment as local postmaster, and the Democratic weekly, the *Freeman's Journal*, was soon complaining that the papers it mailed its subscribers were not being delivered on time.

"the more certain I shall feel of contributing to the renown of many of my nearest and dearest friends."

During the thirteen years that passed before Cooper, at the age of fifty, published the *Naval History*, he wrote 10 novels, 7 books of nonfiction, 3 pamphlets, and a number of magazine articles and letters to the newspapers. Yet somehow he found the time for the research necessary for his long history, which began with a naval battle of colonists and Indians in 1636 and ended with the conclusion of the War of 1812. He used records and materials that had not been published in book form and obtained first-hand information about the sea fighting of 1812-15 from naval officers whom he knew.

Cooper's exalted notions of the dignity of history and of the historian forbade his making any use of the story-teller's art or even of the material of biography. The *Naval History* is a severely impersonal work. The reader rarely feels the urgency of battle or sees the heroes of whose deeds he is told. To maintain a highly professional point of view, the author plays up a quiet victory like Chauncey's on Lake Ontario, and is relatively cool about a showy incident like Oliver Hazard Perry's going in an open boat from his disabled flagship, the *Lawrence*, to the brig *Niagara* at the Battle of Lake Erie. "This was the least of Perry's merits," Cooper writes in a footnote intended to rebuke popular opinion; and he proceeds to explain that the American commander's determination to win and the manner in which he fought once he gained the *Niagara* were more important than the personal risk of the passage to it, for there was personal risk everywhere in a naval battle—in all of the boats that went from one ship to another during the action, and in the ships themselves. But this pedantic argument about the universality of danger conveys less sense of it than even the vulgar selection of one man's acts as a symbol of gallantry.

Against the background of much foolish writing by Englishmen and Americans on the merits of their respective navies, Cooper's air of exact impartiality was a happy effect to achieve. An American could be sure enough of his country, the book seemed to say, to record its victories and defeats quietly, and to a considerable extent Cooper was immune from silly national prejudices. He might attack the British press, or speak cheaply, when his narrative went ashore at New Orleans, of a "licentious soldiery," but he was too fond of navies and of naval officers as a class to speak ill of them merely because they were foreign. Yet patriotism seems to have had its effect, not on his tone, but on his facts. According to Theodore Roosevelt, who was certainly no Anglomaniac, they are slanted in favor of the Americans and against the English, a result in part of Cooper's failure to use English sources sufficiently as a corrective of American versions, and in part of his desire to be kind to American commanders and to praise them all.

Perhaps Cooper had never been so kind in print as in his treatment of the Battle of Lake Erie, and for this kindness he was to be involved in one of his bitterest controversies. Immediately after the battle rumors had got around that the second in command, Jesse D. Elliott, had failed, deliberately or through incompetence, to bring his brig, the *Niagara*, to the support of Perry on the *Lawrence*. Perry said that he was indignant at these rumors, and in his official account of the victory praised Elliott so highly that Congress voted gold medals for both men. But five years later the two heroes quarreled. Elliott challenged Perry to a duel, which the latter refused on the ground that he had new evidence about the battle and intended to prefer charges against Elliott for misconduct. Perry died soon afterwards, and no action was taken on his charges. The matter came to life again in 1834 as a political affair when Elliott placed a figurehead of Andrew Jackson on the frigate *Constitution;* Whig papers attacked him for his indecency and brought up his cowardice at Lake Erie. In the next year there appeared in reply a biography of Elliott presenting him as the chief hero of the battle. Months before the *Naval History* came out, Whig editors knew that Cooper would be on the wrong side of the Perry-Elliott feud and for the worst reasons. "This part of the work is, we understand," so James Watson Webb wrote, "to be dictated by Elliott. . . ." Matthew Calbraith Perry, the dead hero's brother, tried flattery: a friend of his, he said in a letter to Cooper, feared that "the machinations and falsehoods of others had diverted your mind . . ." but Matthew himself was certain "you are too intimately acquainted with naval matters to be deceived. . . ."

Cooper had studied critically all of the evidence of the battle and came, as he explained later, to "a firm conviction that the controversy that had grown up out of it, was not in a fit state to pass into history. This was all I had to decide, and having made up my mind to this one fact, all I had to do was to follow the official account. . . ." This he did, and no reader of the *Naval History* could possibly suspect that an unpleasant word had ever been spoken about Lake Erie. Cooper's decision was assuredly honest. It was also convenient for his purposes as the writer of dignified history. He avoided an ugly squabble that did the Navy no good;

suppressing it was the only way to be kind both to the living Elliott and to the memory of the popular hero after whom forty counties, towns, and villages had been named. Cooper could not have fairly attacked Elliott (at least to the extent that the Perry clan expected) without showing how Perry had contradicted himself shabbily, under disagreeable circumstances. It must have been a relief to Cooper to find that there was no necessity for an attack and that for once the truth was the easiest way.

The Perry clan disagreed. William A. Duer, a distinguished but remote member—he was president of Columbia College, and the uncle of Alexander Slidell Mackenzie, a naval officer who was Matthew Calbraith Perry's brother-in-law—wrote a purported review of the *Naval History*. In several issues of the *Commercial Advertiser* Duer devoted columns to Lake Erie as if the dozen pages about it were the sole subject of the book. His article is nasty, scurrilous, pompous. Cooper, disregarding justice and propriety, callous to the perceptions of good taste, insensible to his obligations as a historian, with the infatuation of vanity or the madness of passion, has made himself the apologist of an official sycophant, a man who owes his continuance in the Navy to his superior's forbearance and magnanimity, which he requited with ingratitude and perfidy; the power of sympathy, Duer consoles himself, is irresistible, the patron worthy of the client—the evidence that the one has falsified, the other has deliberately used in his history, "and hopes that his work may be appealed to as an authentic record, by future generations and to the latest age. It shall not be our fault," the reviewer writes, apparently bidding for an equal

immortality, "if the bane be not accompanied by the anti-
dote."

Even before the Duer review was published Cooper had
been planning legal action against Stone of the *Commercial
Advertiser* as well as several other Whig editors. It was
humanly possible to sue for only a small fraction of the libels,
and whatever principle of choice he hit on was subject to
the criticism that he let much worse go by. He had Webb
indicted again, this time for saying that the most wholesale
libeler of any man living had succeeded "in smuggling an
indictment against us through a Loco-Foco Grand Jury,"
but failed in an effort to obtain a third indictment. With
Stone he waited almost a year before suing on the Duer
review. This suit led to one against Park Benjamin. Webb
had asserted that Cooper was suing Stone to create a little
excitement for a second edition of the *Naval History;* Benjamin reprinted this with a hanging defense of Cooper: "Vain,
weak, self-inflated, silly and preposterous as his conduct has
been since his return to this country, we cannot believe him
capable of such baseness. Yet why defer this suit for so long
a period? . . . Why single out Mr. Stone from the number
of those critics who have fairly riddled his book with their
sharp shooting? . . ." Benjamin was infuriated by a $375
verdict. Any litigation—a breach of promise suit in which
the defendant pleaded in extenuation the plaintiff's bad
grammar—reminded him of how he had been punished unjustly for defending Cooper. Against Thurlow Weed, who
was currently libeling him, Cooper did nothing for almost
three years after the publication of Weed's articles on Three
Mile Point; then he demanded a retraction and failing to get
it, sued on these old libels.

Since his return to America the novelist had carried out his intention of giving up his career to the extent of abandoning the kind of writing that had made him famous. Only parts of *Homeward Bound* were the old Cooper, and everything he had written had been controversial or, as with the *Naval History*, considered so. He had been urged frequently to have done with controversy and write like himself again. His detractors when they made the plea indicated that they thought it hopeless: he was written out. *The Pathfinder* (1840), which appeared just as his war against the press was spreading, seemed deliberately contrived to answer his critics and restore his popularity: it combined his two best subjects, a ship and Indian fighting; it brought back his greatest character, Natty Bumppo, and gave him a new role, that of a lover. "The idea of associating seamen and savages" had in fact occurred to Cooper a decade ago as the basis of a novel, but he had hesitated for a long time about reviving Natty, whom he had buried at the end of *The Prairie*.

The Pathfinder has much the same opening as *The Last of the Mohicans*. Natty and his friends rescue a girl who is traveling through an Indian-infested forest on an inopportune visit to her soldier father. The similarity of the two openings smooths over the change that Cooper has made Natty undergo for the story's sake in the mere year or two that has elapsed in Natty's life since *The Last of the Mohicans*. The scout at the height of his fame has attained sufficient middle-aged respectability and regularity of employment at a British garrison on Lake Ontario for a prudent sergeant to consider him an excellent match for his daughter. It was he who sent Natty into the forest to meet Mabel, at the beginning of the tale; and near its end, dying in battle, he brings about their engagement. The girl has told Natty that she is not good enough for him and they ought not marry; the sergeant explains that this is the timidity of youth, the girl's mother had said the same to him. Natty, who sees clearly how other men are untrue to their "gifts"—it is his theme, as for years it had been the critics' whenever they spoke of Cooper—is about to betray his own, to give up the forest and Chingachgook for a home and wife. Desperately ill at ease in love, he talks of it with his young sailor friend Jasper, and learns that Jasper too loves Mabel and believes, although she has not said a word, that she loves him. Natty insists that all three talk the matter over sensibly, for he has the Noble Savage's faith, as naive and strong as a Shavian hero's, in reasonable discussion. Civilized sentimentality cannot hold out against him. Mabel protests that she will be true to her promise, but when she is certain of Jasper's love, goes off with him, guilty and happy. Natty is left with a keen sentimental grief, but we already know from *The Pioneers* that he has made the most of his gifts in staying in the forest with his Indian friend.

Mercedes of Castile (1840), a novel about Columbus's discovery of America, combines sound historical sources—Prescott's *Ferdinand and Isabella* and Washington Irving's *Life of Columbus*—with bad fiction to make one of Cooper's worst books. Don Luis, a Castilian nobleman, has traveled in other countries, "and as, like all observant travellers, he was made doubly sensible of the defects of his own state of society on his return, a species of estrangement had grown up between him and his natural associates. . . ." He is considered "unsafe," and to win back the pious heroine, Mercedes, goes with the Admiral on his crusade to Cathay A

Castilian Fenimore Cooper as a companion of Columbus, who has his own touches of Cooperism in his bitterness at the harsh treatment accorded him by his native Genoa, promises much. But Don Luis does no more than become mildly entangled with a Carib princess whom he finds in the New World. She has the false ingenuousness of savage innocence, and the reader knows from the moment he meets her that like her more famous successor, Melville's Fayaway, Ozema will at the first convenient opportunity take off her one garment.

Ozema is the sort of literary savage whose directness of desire results always in misunderstanding the forms of civilization. Bewildered and seasick in a storm on the voyage to Spain, she construes Luis's religious instruction and gift of a cross as a declaration of love, and on her arrival at the Spanish Court announces that they are married. Set right on this mistake, she consents to baptism only upon the marriage of Luis and Mercedes. When both ceremonies are completed, she asks to be made Luis's second wife. The archbishop scolds her so fiercely for this that the poor girl—Spain has made her physically ill as well as confused her morally—dies on the spot.

It was inevitable that Columbus should be treated with deep reverence and that this heavy mood should spread through the whole book. (Only one minor character, a sailor who goes on the great voyage for money, escapes it.) Irony would have been inappropriate for Columbus's story; its absence, however, is fatal to Ozema's. The solemn high-mindedness of tone officially invites only tears for her fate, and denies the reader's right to enjoy honestly the comic social and moral malapropisms that lead up to it. He is left with the unacknowledged half of a double meaning on his hands, that is the more indecent because the author seems so wilfully to ignore it. Cooper's blindness was purely occasional; the ironic possibilities of the Noble Savage, which he missed so completely in *Mercedes*, were developed in his next novel, *The Deerslayer* (1841).

The last of the five Leather-Stocking Tales is the simplest in plot and most equivocal in meaning. The unspoiled beauty of Otsego Lake, or Glimmerglass, as the lake is rather fancily called by the few hunters who visit it in the 1740's, dominates the story and gives it a tone of deep and lovely unreality. Time has mercifully run backward for Natty Bumppo and Chingachgook, and they are half a century younger than when we met them on this very spot in *The Pioneers*. Natty, the Deerslayer, is on his first war-path, and with charming reluctance and much tender soliloquizing kills his first Indian. This slow and long-drawn-out episode would be a little absurd and tedious if taken by itself. It is, however, not an isolated incident but the crucial point of a legend, the moment of choosing the inevitable, and the killing with its lingering detail is the first hesitant awkward affair in the career of some traditional great lover.

Intruding on Natty's idyl of violence is the nonidyllic violence of the two other white men of the tale, the ex-pirate, Tom Hutter, who lives on the lake, and the breezy young hunter, Hurry Harry. They kill brutally and wastefully for they are urged on not by inner necessity, which has its own restraints, but by the reasoning of civilized society. In attacking an Indian party they seek to scalp the women and children as well as the men, for the Colony pays a bounty for the scalps of all alike, much as it does for a wolf's ears, to encourage extermination of a pest without regard to its age or sex. Cooper refers only occasionally and obliquely to the contemporary world he has treated so fully in *Home as Found,* but we wonder uneasily in this simple tale of escape whether we are watching the working out of the commercial values we live by. Even the Indians who torture their white prisoners have more respect for the mere humanity of their enemies than the white men who engage in warfare as a profitable alternative to other forms of hunting wild life.

The two murderous white men and the beautiful Judith Hutter, who has been seduced by a British officer, are all that we see of civilization. The other white character, the half-witted Hetty Hutter, has fallen below it to a state of grace. "An idiot she could not properly be termed, her mind being just enough enfeebled to lose most of those traits that are connected with the more artful qualities, and to retain its ingenuousness and love of truth." A white Ozema, her innocence makes her betray her love for the worthless Hurry Harry whenever she speaks of him. But her most embarrassing faculty is her simple literal faith in the truths of Christianity and her certainty that they must prevail. After her father and Harry are captured by the Mingoes she goes to the Indian chiefs with her Bible to explain to them that they must not kill but should return good for evil. When they ask her why the white man has himself forgotten what his book says, the unfortunate girl bursts into tears.

Hetty is the ambiguous end of a great tradition. She is the Noble Savage, restored to the race that invented the myth, and being asked, instead of asking, the unanswerable stock question of moral literature. In opposition to the happy myth of a natural alliance between reason and virtue, Cooper seems to say, like the Russian novelists later, that the mind must be somehow mysteriously spoiled before it can be good. And Hetty's virtue is remarkably impractical. Her feeble-minded uncompromising love of truth becomes a nuisance as the story progresses, and hinders Natty's escape from the Indians who have captured him.

Beside Hetty, Leather-Stocking is a sophisticated being. "A magnificent moral hermaphrodite, born between the savage and the civilized states of man," as Balzac described him in a famous review of *The Pathfinder*, he has judiciously tempered the methods of warfare learned from the Delawares with Christian doctrine learned from the Moravian missionaries who dwell among them. He will not absolutely return good for evil, but he will kill only from necessity. The point of honor makes him admirable, chivalrous, and just a little smug. It is also useful. His respect for human life teaches him an efficiency in the art of taking it that makes him the dreaded enemy of the Mingoes in *The Last of the Mohicans* and *The Pathfinder*.

Between the nightmare of Tom's and Harry's sordid butchery and the nightmare of Hetty's virtue one has the sense of an orderly, stable society only among the Mingoes, who in *The Last of the Mohicans* were merely a group of convenient villains. The Mingoes are as treacherous under Rivenoak as they were under Magua, but we see now through the kindlier and younger eyes of Natty that treachery is part of their lawful gifts and becomes them. We are more sympathetic to these hostile Indians because we glimpse their homely needs. Rivenoak is willing to forgo the torture of Natty if he will marry the widow of the brave he has killed and take this middle-aged, ill-tempered squaw off the hands of the tribe. We are for the moment in the midst of a truly Homeric age, where grand heroic warfare goes hand in hand with opportune domestic arrangements between victor and vanquished.

In *The Deerslayer* Natty is given the refusal not only of the ugly squaw but also of Judith Hutter. He has moved slowly through the five books from a minor figure who took up more room in *The Pioneers* than seems to have been intended for him, to the very hero of the piece. But although he has achieved the hero's right to be the object of love, his character has been molded in the novels already written of his later life, and there is never any doubt about his choice. The drama turns rather on a question of manners. Positive and rude as he was with the Indian widow, he is so well-bred with Judith that she is not certain, until she asks him point-blank, whether he realizes that she is proposing marriage to him.

With his refusal of Judith *The Leather-Stocking Tales* come to a close. It is a negative note, but Natty Bumppo is one of the great negative characters of literature, the man who will not be encumbered with the ordinary obligations of life and for whom freedom is the absence of permanent involvement. In *The Deerslayer*, the true end of the series, Natty, free of all of life's hampering restrictions, has the gift of youth not as the young live it but as old men dream of it. There is a recurrent American legend of the man who suddenly drops the burdens of civilization, usually a wife, and goes off by himself. Release may be sought by brutal direct action, as it is by Hawthorne's Wakefield, or may come gracefully of itself, as it does to Rip Van Winkle. In

Natty Bumppo the grace is in never having become entangled. Cooper has invented, to use his own words in a context quite different from his own, "a being removed from the every day inducements to err, which abound in civilized life."

Natty in keeping clear of civilization's responsibilities and errors has held on to its higher and also to its pleasanter values. The primitive forest in which he lives in his youth and the naked plains on which he dies are scenes of horror and violence because of the deeds of the other white characters in the story, but for Natty they are always the great good place, an inviolable retreat from the pressure of reality. His life there is a kind of ideal bachelor existence, fastidious and untouched by the lives of others. He can afford to be helpful to every stranger, loyal for the duration of the adventure but without risk—except for his temporary infatuation with Mabel—of committing himself too far. His one permanent friend, Chingachgook, is a member of another race, and strong though their feeling for each other is, a correctness of tone pervades their relation and saves it from intimacy. Natty turns the wilderness into a salon and indulges with every newcomer the passion for endless talk that is characteristic of so many lovers of solitude.

It is of course Natty who holds the five novels together and makes them a related series. Cooper's great success is in large part because he has allowed Natty so much diversity in his unity. Between books he changes abruptly and without explanation; yet even when we suspect that he is responding primarily to the needs of the particular story (for whose sake the very details of his biography are often altered), he seems still to illustrate some law of development and growth. Created before the days of petty truth to local color, he absorbs the habits and traits of entirely different regions when they are convenient, as easily as a hero of ancient myth gathers inconsistent cults to himself. It is true, as Mark Twain complains in his witty but parochial essay, "Fenimore Cooper's Literary Offenses," that Natty at times "talks like an illustrated, gilt-edged, tree-calf, hand-tooled, seven-dollar Friendship's Offering in the beginning of a paragraph . . . [and] like a negro minstrel in the end of it." But this misses completely how much Natty's few and rather limited ideas are enriched by the careless profusion of his means of expression. It is in fact Natty's inconsistency—his facility in turning from flights of formal rhetoric to such incisive statements as "I peppered the blackguards intrinsically like," his mixture of superhuman skill in shooting and disregard of elementary precautions, his fluctuations between philosophic indifference and childish showing off— that makes him emerge from the series a magnificent whole, one of the great rounded characters of American literature.

Chapter VII

THE PATHFINDER and *The Deerslayer* had a mixed critical reception. Cooper had kept his unpopular views fairly well out of sight in these two books, but hostile papers were unwilling to forget them. The *Evening Signal*, whose editor, Park Benjamin, was soon to be sued, suggested that *The Pathfinder* was as unreadable as *The Monikins* and that Cooper had made its villain a Scotchman to get revenge on Sir Walter.* Even when he was sincerely praised, a note either of relief or of worry would

* This odd deduction from the nationality of a character may not be malignancy. Balzac in his laudatory account of *The Pathfinder* complained that its one Frenchman, Captain Sanglier, the commander of Indian warriors, held France and French officers up to ridicule. Balzac was the more astonished, he said, because the American writer owed his renown to the universality of the French language, which made his works known among nations unacquainted with English; and he added plaintively, "Is it for an American, whose position demands of him exalted ideas, to invest a French officer with a gratuitously odious character, when the only succor which America received during her struggle for independence came from France?" Provincial sensitiveness, according to Cooper, was peculiarly American, but perhaps national honor was making the whole civilized world provincial.

mar the occasion. He was hailed as if the resumption of an old uncontroversial way of writing were a return from madness to sanity, and the anxious hope was expressed "that hostilities between our novelist and the public may henceforth cease."

Cooper had no intention of giving up his fight, which he insisted was not against the public but against the press that influenced it unfairly and by illegal means. He was blocked in his efforts to have Webb tried in 1840, by the appearance on the eve of trial of a belated review of *Homeward Bound* and *Home as Found* in two issues of Park Benjamin's *New World* which were mailed to the prospective jurors. Fearing that his own neighbors were permanently prejudiced against him, Cooper had the venue changed from Otsego to Montgomery County. ("You will gain nothing by a change of *counties*," Stone, Webb, Weed, and Benjamin boasted in an open letter to Cooper, "a change of *countries* is what you want . . ."—a jury not of Americans but of Halls, Trollopes, and other prejudiced British travelers.) In November 1841 at Fonda, the Montgomery county seat, Webb was at last brought to trial for his libel. The jury disagreed; eleven were for acquittal, one—the only capable juror, so Cooper told his family—stubbornly held out for conviction. Cooper suspected that the jury had been corrupted by something more powerful than bad Whig logic, for after the trial some of the jurors drank champagne with Webb in his room. The editors claimed that Webb's lawyer had won by the honest tactic of reading aloud to the jury every word of *Home as Found*.

At the same court term in Fonda, Cooper's case against Thurlow Weed came up for trial. It had been adjourned once for six months because Weed had forgotten about it. Now, on the calendar call a lawyer not formally retained by Weed told the court that the editor was detained in Albany by the serious illness of his daughter. The case was put over for one day with the understanding that there was to be no further adjournment, but on the next day Weed still did not appear. Cooper and his counsel suspected a trick; they refused to consent to a further delay and standing on their rights proceeded to have an inquest taken on Weed's default. An unfriendly jury ignored Judge Willard's suggestion that damages should be assessed in a punitive amount and brought in a verdict of $400.

After the case was over, Weed arrived in Fonda and wrote an anonymous report of it as correspondent for Horace Greeley's *New York Tribune*. This account, in itself only mildly defamatory for an Effingham libel, was reprinted in many papers with horrified comment on Cooper's cruelty. Park Benjamin wrote that counsel had "appealed to Mr. Cooper's humanity, but he might as well have appealed to the reddest of the Great Novelist's Indians, when the war-paint was on him, and the scalps of the pale-faces hung reeking at his belt." Weed ran a special department in his paper in which he reprinted items about Cooper, and within a month Cooper had brought five new suits against him. Cooper also sued Greeley. The latter on learning of the threatened action very fairly published Cooper's letter to a Democratic paper giving the novelist's own version of the facts, but mischievously added, "Mr. Cooper will have to bring his action to trial *somewhere*. He will not like to bring it in New York, for we are known here, nor in Otsego, for *he* is known there."

The results of the two trials at Fonda were not satisfactory. The courts having let him down for the moment, Cooper switched back to the press and wrote a series of letters justifying his litigation, which appeared in *Brother Jonathan* between January and April 1842.

The popular defense of newspaper calumny, then as now, was that no one believes it. "This mode of talking," Cooper answers, "deadens the sensibilities of the public, and is one of the reasons why the American public shows so little of a generous sensibility in general. . . . Men cannot hear character coarsely assailed, from day to day, and maintain a just appreciation of its importance." Cooper proves at too great length that the Whig press and not the author of *Home as Found* is the real wholesale libeler of America and American womanhood. The respectable papers had recently waged a "moral war" against James Gordon Bennett's sensational penny journal, the *Herald*, and had tried, unsuccessfully, to frighten Bennett's readers off by assuring them of their moral degradation. Webb in a typical passage had asserted that "a virtuous and honorable young man would almost as soon go into a public brothel, to choose a partner for life as to take to his bosom one whose purity of feeling and thought has been contaminated by gloating over the lascivious and disgusting essays of The Herald." In a "Lost Chapter" of *Home as Found* (published with one of the *Brother Jonathan* letters) the English baronet hears all of this newspaper nonsense, and, believing what Americans say of themselves, breaks off his engagement with his American fiancée, who for all he can tell may be a *Herald* reader.

Cooper also wrote exhaustively in *Brother Jonathan* on his supposed identity with Edward Effingham. In any serious

sense the two were not alike, but the novelist was the victim
of an inevitable law of literature. While in a biography a
mass of facts is rarely sufficient to give its subject "reality,"
in a work of fiction a single recognizable "fact" about a character can color a whole mass of invention and give all of it
the appearance of literal representation. Readers of *Home
as Found* could hardly be blamed for confusing Edward
Effingham with Cooper, for they seemed to live in the same
house in the same village and to have the same fight with
their neighbors over the same point of land on the same lake.
Cooper had been "Mr. Effingham" ever since Webb's review, and now tried to rid himself of the odious name.

He did fairly well in a preliminary part of the task, a discussion of *The Pioneers*. Judge Temple was a type and not
an individual portrait; the novelist had borrowed from his
father, Judge Cooper, only what was "generally characteristic" of him and fifty other landed proprietors as well. But
when he came to his own generation it would have been
awkward to admit that for Edward Effingham he had borrowed from himself the general characteristics of a contemporary gentleman. He could only deny all likeness and point
out distinctions, some of which are so fine in their niggling
that they tend not to refute but to establish resemblance:
Edward had been abroad from 1823 to 1835, Cooper from
1826 to 1833; Edward was "tall," Cooper under 5 feet 10
inches, "a height that would never be described as *tall* in
this country"; Edward had French servants, "my domestics
were principally Swiss, who *spoke* French."

Above all, Edward was rich, and Cooper was not. And
in proof of this the man who hated intrusions on his privacy
breaks out suddenly with one of those personal revelations

that tell nothing yet leave us with the sense of having been spoken to much too intimately:

When I was traduced, *envied* and maligned by my countrymen, who fancied I kept aloof from them, in foreign countries, in order to live in the smiles of princes and nobles, I was toiling day and night, under a pressure of ill health that nearly brought me to the grave . . . to pay off debts that were not contracted in my own behalf, and which were not only paid by the efforts of my pen, but paid to the uttermost cent; and in many instances, with usury. . . . Talk of my being under obligations to the American people! . . . I lost thousands—ay, *tens of thousands,* by upholding the character of this country among those who delight in degrading it, and this without any return but abuse and calumny.

Earlier private statements of Cooper are quite different from this self-pitying publicity about his financial situation while in Europe. In December 1831, in urging his sister-in-law Caroline De Lancey to come abroad to be his copyist, he writes that his income for the year will be nearly $20,000 and that he expects to return to America in a few years with "a comfortable independence." But this calculation was too optimistic, for Cooper never achieved financial independence, and at the time that he was telling his readers about past difficulties his present ones must have been serious. The country was still suffering from the depression following the Panic of 1837. American writers suffered also from the insane frenzy of competition between old-line publishers and the new "mammoth" papers (of which *Brother Jonathan* was one) in pirating English authors. A new Dickens would be sold as an "extra" by newsboys at ten cents a copy; in the excitement of not paying an author anything, books were being sold below cost. Cooper himself, besides getting a bad press, was the victim of a shift in popular taste away from the adventure story. He made a living during these years, but it was always uncertain.

The new lawsuits against Weed were quickly brought to trial, and Cooper obtained four verdicts by September 1842. At the trial in May, Weed spent his spare time in the court room reading the new Cooper novel, *The Two Admirals* (1842). He liked it immensely, and, as Dorothy Waples has pointed out, he recorded the incident years later in his *Autobiography* but at the time said nothing of it in his newspaper. More remarkable than Weed's reading his favorite American author in the midst of litigation with him is the author's feat in having found the time and the temper in the midst of his suits to write a novel that was so free of their bitterness.

The Two Admirals realizes a project, formed as long ago as his 1828 visit to England, of "taking a subject from the teeming and glorious naval history of this country. . . ." The subject which he chose, the English victory over the French in the Channel during the Forty-five, gives him the opportunity of exploiting the large-scale maneuvering of a whole fleet and the ready-made romance of Jacobite intrigue. In outline the story is as romantic as *The Pilot* or *Red Rover:* a bastard is foiled in his plot to keep the true heir out of his inheritance; the junior admiral, a secret Jacobite, plans to keep his division of the fleet out of the battle, but at the last moment joins forces with his lifelong friend, the commanding admiral, and dies heroically in action. The details, however, are in large part solid and real, and events are so handled that they raise philosophical questions—the more interesting because Cooper keeps personally aloof and neither asks nor answers them directly—about the notion of legitimacy in government and the conventions of loyalty and obedience.

After the old squire has patriotically drunk himself to death in an orgy of toasts to the threatened House of Hanover, everyone feels that it is right that his hall should not go to his bastard nephew but to the stranger from America who is the true heir. Only Jacobites see any resemblance between the commonplace rogue whose very existence is a swindle and the illegitimate government that is keeping the other stranger from over the water out of the inheritance which is his by birth, the English throne. Yet the bastard's situation is a parody of the government's: filled with a greater shame because his misfortune is not attributable to his own conduct, he takes the lead in repeating the old lie of the Pretender's spurious birth, but knows each moment that he is really denouncing himself; fearing exposure, he brings it about by offering to show casual strangers his mother's supposed marriage certificate which he carries around in his pocket. The Jacobites have all of the formal logic on their side; they are maintaining the rights of property and succession against usurpers. They are answered in the story not by formal reasoning but by the logic of custom, the mere running of time that creates ties of loyalty and affection and in the end makes upstart wrongs ancient and beloved rights.

Without betraying his faith in the peculiar gloriousness of sea fighting Cooper writes of it in a new matter-of-fact way. In the amateur fighting of *Homeward Bound* he had allowed the comic awkwardness of life to survive amid adventure; now, more daringly, because he sees the fleet as a professionally run machine, men's ordinary habits and attitudes persist in all of their commonplaceness before and after the battle. The captains chat desultorily about the merits of the conflict ("I was a youngster under Queen Anne, and she was a Stuart, I believe; and I have served under the German family ever since; and to be frank . . . I see but little difference in the duty, the pay, or the rations"). An old captain who is a self-made man lives in dread of a reprimand from the commander in chief on inspection; battle with its risks merely of wounds and death would be a kindly release from the terrors of discipline. The commander in chief indulges his foible that he knows each common sailor, and the sailor, to hand the unbearably flattering pretense back undamaged, denies his own right to individual identity: "What's your name, my lad—Tom Davis, if I'm not mistaken?" "No, Sir Jarvey, it's Jack Brown; which is much the same, your honor. We's no way partic'lar about names."

In the *England* everything English had been part of an ingenious system for the support of aristocracy, making use of a native tendency to delight in the factitiousness of social arrangements and to avoid looking principles in the face. At the time of *The Two Admirals* Cooper's conscious opinion of the system had not changed.* But the novel presents this world, or rather, its more factitious predecessor, casually and without indignation. Absorbed in manipulating the com-

* In a magazine article called "Edinburgh Review on James's Naval Occurrences and Cooper's Naval History" (*Democratic Review*, May and June 1842) he had expressed his belief that the difference in tone of Tory and Whig attacks on his *Naval History* was the usual division of labor arranged between English political parties according to their talents, the one assuming the duty of scurrility, the other "the artful and more dignified office of mystifying."

plicated social and physical life of a whole fleet, Cooper feels
no need for either censure or praise. So much organized
vitality in a novel can never leave a moral vacuum; when it
does not urge us to surrender morally to the particular system that it skilfully portrays, it urges us more broadly—and
this is the effect of *The Two Admirals* as it is of no other
novel of Cooper's since *The Pioneers*—to the acceptance of
the world itself and of things as they are. Cooper had been
vigorously maintaining his right to think for himself and
scrutinize critically every institution in his own country;
but on looking at an alien scene of which he professes to dis-
approve, he has led his readers to the conclusion that taking
thought against one's own time may be—as it turns out with
the admiral who reasons himself almost into treachery—a
sorry business and that there may be a happier wisdom in not
struggling against our own unthinking ways.

In 1842 Cooper had his finest victory over a newspaper,
but it was not in court. Stone had complained that the Battle
of Lake Erie presented issues too complex to be decided in-
telligently by a jury, and Cooper had agreed to an arbitration. Three lawyers were to act as arbitrators and were to
make a detailed decision on Cooper's performance of his
duties as a historian and on Duer's of his as a reviewer. At
the hearing Cooper bore the brunt of his own case, opened,
submitted a mass of documents that he had collected, and
made two closing speeches. He held a large audience fascinated during six hours of continuous speaking at the final
night session; at its conclusion there was a great burst of
applause, and a hundred people crowded around him. Long
though he had spoken he had not said all that he had wanted

to, and it was perhaps lucky that the lateness of the hour prevented him. Even the friendly correspondent of the Democratic Albany paper, the *Argus*, noted that when he was through with his minute exciting account of the battle and proceeded to a discussion of the libel "a feeling of regret could easily be perceived in the countenance of every one, that he should find himself compelled to turn from a subject so interesting to them to one so unattractive if not odious."

The arbitrators' award directed Stone to pay Cooper $300 (the sum that had been agreed on in advance if he won) and to publish their decision in New York, Albany, and Washington. They agreed unanimously that the *Naval History* was written in a spirit of impartiality and justice and that Duer's review was guilty of personal imputations, misquotations, misstatements, and untruths. One arbitrator, however, irrationally refused to find the review partial and unjust, because he felt that it had been written in defense of a dead friend. More soundly, he suggested that Cooper's duty as a historian necessitated his taking some notice of the controversy over the battle and that it was an error of judgment to write as if Elliott's conduct had been universally approved. He dissented also from the majority finding that Cooper's account of Lake Erie was true in its essential facts. Cooper's triumph on this point is the more remarkable because most later historians disagree with him. Henry Adams, Theodore Roosevelt, Alfred T. Mahan, and George R. Clark are certain that Elliott was at fault in not coming to the aid of Perry. Maclay in his *History of the United States Navy*, like Cooper, follows Perry's official report and makes both men heroes.

During the years of his litigation the greater part of

Cooper's writing was about the sea. Between 1842 and 1845 he sold to *Graham's Magazine* ten short biographies of American naval officers, all but one of which were later published in book form as *Lives of Distinguished American Naval Officers* (1846). He slily reports of Perry that in another case besides Elliott's, he had quarreled with a subordinate and then preferred charges of prior misconduct. Most of the lives are written with a cold formality; the subjects live up to the requirements of naval discipline rather than the standards for a popular hero. In the life of Melancthon Taylor Woolsey, the friend under whom Cooper had served at Oswego in 1809, the author remembers with middle-aged indulgence how at twenty he bedeviled the village doctor to while away a long frontier winter, risking his neck to drop snowballs down the doctor's chimney to cool his mess. Cooper likes the superior officer who permitted such frolics, and there is a struggle, in this life, between the proprieties and the memory of a good-natured friend, which memory wins uneasily: "His familiar association with all the classes that mingle so freely together in border life, had produced a tendency, on his excellent disposition, to relax too much in his ordinary intercourse, perhaps, but his good sense prevented this weakness from proceeding very far. Woolsey rather wanted the grimace than the substance of authority. A better-hearted man never lived."

When Cooper first planned to use English naval history in a novel, it seemed desirable to set his story in the period before the American Revolution, when his country and England were one. Such a setting made it possible for the novelist and the reader to give their full sympathy to one side of the fight; the French Navy is not the villain of *The*

Two Admirals, but that it is "good" to destroy it is assumed without reflection. In *The Wing-and-Wing, or Le Feu-Follet* (1842) Cooper uses English and French ships again, but by pushing the time forward to the wars of the French Revolution he has been able to make a radical change in the distribution of sympathy in the adventure story.

A few ships of Nelson's Mediterranean fleet in 1799 chase and finally sink the *Feu-Follet* (Will-o'-the-Wisp), a privateer of the French Republic, and kill her captain. Our feeling alternates between the parties, between pursuer and pursued, and is at times with both at once so that, as in the poem on the Grecian Urn, we want both capture and escape, consummation and frustration. We should side romantically with the gallant amateur, the French captain Raoul Yvard, who is motivated only by love of country, but Cooper has made us more interested in the professionals. The English are insular, arrogant, devious, unjust, and complicated, which may not be a virtue for the moralist but is a supreme one for the novel of manners.

The best part of the chase is legalistic, the court martial of Raoul for spying on the English fleet at Naples. The nominal question for the judges is Raoul's guilt, the real matter at issue the location of his ship, which they hope to discover either by trick during the questioning or by terror after the sentence of death is imposed. The forms of law, like the rules of a game, merely prescribe the earnest decorum to be observed in attaining the predetermined end. The judges have an equal horror of admitting hearsay evidence to prove Raoul's identity, a fact which they all know, or of admitting to themselves that they believe his romantic tale of a visit in disguise to the girl he loves. They have just enough unawareness of what they are doing to do it with that efficient good faith still the despair of the enemies of England and proof for them of its perfidy.

The senior officer, Captain Cuffe, realizes the enormity of his conduct only when it is apparent that it will not succeed. Raoul will not betray his ship. But Nelson has approved the sentence, and the conscience-stricken captain would rather hang forty Frenchmen than be scolded for neglect of duty. A messenger is sent to Nelson, and during the hours of waiting for the reprieve that comes of course at the last moment the agony we share is not the condemned man's but the captain's.

Nowhere is the distribution of sympathy more unorthodox than in the case of the impressed American seaman, Ithuel Bolt. Courageous and skilful, this victim of injustice should be the hero of the piece. There is something so unpleasant, however, about his slyness, his crude practical mind, his bragging about his native "Granite State" that we share the prejudice of his English captors against "The Yankee," as they frankly call Ithuel, although they have impressed him under the fiction of his being an Englishman. When he escapes and is recaptured, respect for the fiction demands that he be hanged as a deserter, but the necessity that created the fiction, England's desperate need for seamen, is more powerful. Ithuel is spared in much the same spirit as the murderer in "Pudd'nhead Wilson" is pardoned when he turns out to be a slave and valuable property.

The practical need for mercy is cynically covered over by spreading the rumor that Ithuel will not be tried because he has given evidence against his friend Raoul. Cooper protests formally against this wickedness but is fascinated by the ironic reversal of good and evil in his characters: Cuffe by his intellectual fuzziness maintains his human decency in all of his devious conduct; while Ithuel through his too clear perception of the wrong done him is hard, intolerant, and filled with a self-righteous hate of his oppressors that makes him hateful. Ithuel Bolt is obviously the sort of American Cooper disliked; brilliantly representative of the novelist's aversions, Ithuel ends his life as "an active abolitionist, a patron of the temperance cause, teetotally, and a general terror to evil-doers, under the appellation of Deacon Bolt." But surely the man who is unforgivable because he has been so deeply wronged by society is also Fenimore Cooper's creative vision, if not of himself, of his own insoluble dilemma.

In a paragraph near the beginning of *Wing-and-Wing* Cooper has given his clearest public indication, veiled though it is, of his dislike of Washington Irving. His long, one-sided, uneventful enmity with the popular author had begun around the same time as his own flight from popularity in 1832. Before that the two men who had not met had had pleasant relations, and early in Cooper's career, Irving, in London, had tried to find an English publisher for him. In 1832, the incorruptible American learned that the amiable one, while a member of the legation in London, had contributed a few reviews to the anti-American *Quarterly Review*, and had even, at his publisher's request, written for it an anonymous article on one of his own books, for which he was paid. The great dinner given Irving on his return to America, a form of honor which Cooper was to refuse without explanation a year and a half later, brought from him "a burst that was frightful." For years he told the story of Irving's self-reviewing—to Lewis Gaylord Clark, who immediately repeated it in strict confidence to Longfellow; and apparently to Rufus Griswold, who published it in distorted form in October 1842.

Irving on his side was imperturbably friendly to Cooper. In part he had Scott's quality, and in Cooper's damning word was "seemly"; in part he was true to his own ideal of seeing the best. It was a difficult ideal to use directly in defense of the author of *Home as Found,* but it could be used to plead for him with his critics. After the outburst against *Home as Found,* Irving wrote an essay, "Desultory Thoughts on Criticism," deploring the excesses of literary criticism and the sudden changes in literary fame which have dealt so harshly and capriciously with the dead Byron and Scott and the living but unnamed Cooper, who is described as one of the country's greatest geniuses. When Cooper wrote a novel which Irving could like for its own sake and not merely for its author's past, *The Pathfinder,* he campaigned for it vigorously, urged the *Knickerbocker* to do it ample justice, and praised it at length to Bryant, Halleck, and others.

Cooper was unmoved by Irving's efforts. It would be unfair to ask him to think well of his pleasant competitor whose conduct the editors delighted to contrast with his own. Park Benjamin went so far as to compose for Cooper's use a soliloquy in which Cooper in a mood of self-reproach is to compare himself with Irving and ask: "Has Irving . . . made himself as notorious as a ballad-monger's wench?"

The contrast between the two men is almost too pat, not so much in their views of American life as in their conception of their duty to express them. Irving, as well as Cooper, can find an American small town unbearably commonplace, but he sees in it not the subject of a book but of a charming letter to his niece in Paris. When he allows himself an unflattering truth in a phrase like "the almighty dollar," a more universal criticism of his country than Cooper ever attempted, the phrase is slipped in quietly and Irving, unlike Cooper, gaily admits his own guilt; he too is an orthodox worshiper of the dollar. On principle he disbelieves in plain dealing and can write manfully to the editor of *The Plain Dealer*, who had accused him of timidity in changing a line offensive to Englishmen in the English edition of Bryant's poems: ". . . I have at all times almost as strong a repugnance to tell a painful or humiliating truth, *unnecessarily*, as I have to tell an untruth, under any circumstances."

Just as Cooper's unpopularity was for Irving proof of an author's instability (". . . when may an author feel himself secure?" Irving had asked in his "Desultory Thoughts"), so Irving's popularity figured frequently in Cooper's conversation as a shining instance of "the humbuggery of success in this country." When Irving was appointed Minister to Spain early in 1842, Cooper, long accused of being a disappointed office-seeker, was annoyed at the newspaper reports that Irving had not wanted the position; he preferred to believe what he soon heard: that Irving had asked Daniel Webster to remember him if anything good offered. And in *Wing-and-Wing*, he mocks the affectations of governments which care little for literature but feel the need to profess their respect for it by appointing mere men of letters to offices which they are not qualified to hold; his own literary office-holder, the vice-governor of Elba, had in a more simple age "been inducted into his present office without even the sentimental profession of never having asked for it . . .

[and] without a word having been said in the journals of Tuscany of his doubts about accepting it. . . ."

A few days after the publication of *Wing-and-Wing* Cooper was in Ballston to try cases against Thurlow Weed and Horace Greeley arising out of Weed's default at Fonda. Litigation had been costly to Weed if unprofitable to Cooper, and it seemed to the editor that he was being unjustly forced to contribute to the author's support. After his lawyer assured him that he would lose again, Weed agreed to settle the pending suits by publishing a full retraction. He insisted all of his life that he had lost because the law had not permitted the defense of truth in a libel suit; it never seems to have occurred to him that his loose notions of what was true did not come up to the literal and rather dull standards of courts. At his last trial, to prove the charge that Cooper had behaved disgracefully at Fonda, Weed's lawyer—trying to exploit Webb's device in an irrelevant situation—had offered to read *Home as Found* to the jury.

Greeley decided that Weed's trouble was not the law but lawyers, and tried his own case. The verdict against him was for $200. Back in New York he wrote for the *Tribune* a long gay report of his defeat, so popular that it was commented on by over two hundred newspapers and was printed as a pamphlet that circulated much more widely than the favorable accounts of Cooper's success at the *Naval History* arbitration. With good-natured malice Greeley pokes fun at himself and Cooper as the two amateurs, praises Cooper's lawyer, nephew Richard, and gives a picture, which may be false but is certainly convincing, of Fenimore Cooper making a fool of himself.

We see the uncle interrupting constantly with suggestions

and spoiling the nephew's quiet and able opening. In summing up, Cooper further embarrasses Richard "by praises, which though deserved, were horribly out of taste and out of date." Cooper attacks Weed, who had just surrendered unconditionally, for shamming at Fonda, and makes bad jokes about the plague, Asiatic cholera probably, that spread with each report to some new member of the Weed family until all the women were stricken by it. He closes by telling the jury how his own family suffers and his grown daughters are often suffused in tears by the attacks on their father. Greeley effectively uses the newspaper vulgarity, against which Cooper was fighting, to mock his stooping to the lowest tactic of jury-swaying, mawkishness. "We have a different theory as to what the girls were crying for, but we won't state it lest another dose of Supreme Court law be administered to us."

Greeley wrote several editorials on the broad question raised by Cooper's litigation, the relation of the law of libel and freedom of the press. The editor pointed out that the courts do not face the issue honestly. Theoretically they permit a newspaper to publish the truth; practically they curtail the right by imposing absolute liability for all misstatements of fact that defame an individual. As Greeley had learned, an error is not wiped out by later printing the offended party's own version of the facts. Since what an editor publishes is hearsay and not within his own knowledge, the risk of error is tremendous. If he were to take the law seriously, he would be silent on all dangerous topics until a court and jury had carefully sifted the facts, for only then could he write safely. And if he gets by on his facts, the editor still runs the chance of going wrong in his opinions. The right

of fair comment, so celebrated by the courts, is only the right
to draw an inference that a court and jury later agree is one
which a fair-minded man might reasonably draw from the
facts. Freedom of opinion, Greeley argued, if it means anything more than the privilege of saying what everyone believes, involves of necessity the right to express outrageous
opinions and to make unfair comments—to liken Fenimore
Cooper, for example, as Weed and others had done, and
Greeley had not, to an inhuman savage for not granting a
further adjournment at Fonda.

Greeley's views sound extreme because we still pay little
attention to the fundamental split he noted between the law
and the actual standards of society. We do not like to see
the law of libel either questioned or obeyed. Not even judges,
as he pointed out, would read a newspaper conducted in
obedience to their principles.

Greeley tried to keep discussion alive and out of the courts
by offering Cooper a column in the *Tribune* every day for
ten days. The novelist, who was suing the editor again—in
part for his innuendoes in the report of the Ballston trial, in
part for his light-hearted comment a year ago when he
learned of the first suit—did not answer directly. The only
public notice he took of Greeley's arguments was in the
Autobiography of a Pocket Handkerchief, then being serial-
ized in *Graham's Magazine;* an awkward lover's address is
described as "a rigmarole that might have very fairly figured
in an editor's law and logic, after he had been beaten in a
libel-suit."

Autobiography of a Pocket Handkerchief (1843) uses a
juvenile literary form, the first-person narrative by an in-
animate object, to bring within the field of fiction material

that it does not easily deal with, the actual operations of industry and commerce. The handkerchief's history is that of the profit motive in action, of the shabby mean exploitation of the sempstress who makes this grand article of luxury, and of the cheating that accompanies each step of its journey from France to America as it changes hands at a constantly increasing rate of profit the farther it is removed from "the real producer." Its inflated retail price in New York, $100, is its chief element of value. A speculator's daughter is rapturous at the prospect of owning the most expensive handkerchief in America; her father is delighted to buy it for her as a good stroke of business, for his credit is shaky and he must do something magnificent to bolster it. When the crash comes, the speculator's flourish of honesty in insisting on returning the article for which he has not paid gives him such a reputation for virtue that he is able to effect a dishonest settlement with his creditors; he secretly pays the important ones in full while cheating the rest, and avoids the bankruptcy whose horror lies not in poverty but in being pitied.

Cooper's sempstress is not an ordinary worker but an impoverished French noblewoman who has lost her pension after the 1830 revolution. Our fear of snobbishness makes us chary in pity for aristocrats when they become the oppressed, and the novelist's choice is distasteful to us. From his own point of view, which is more anticommercial than prolabor, it is legitimate. His untypical victim furnishes a concentrated instance of the ruthlessness of exploitation. Her employer pays her less than the usual wage, and when she finds this out terror and guilt drive her to work harder than the other girls, for she is in a world where money is the absolute proof of worth.

The process of turning human labor into profitable merchandise is as brutally impersonal in Cooper as in Marx. Its most telling demonstration is the more dramatic because we see it only indirectly and casually as an item in a series of book entries. When the New York merchant takes in the handkerchief he opens an account with it, charging it with all of his expenses, one of which reads:

> To washing and making up.......... 25¢
> (Mem. See if a deduction cannot be made from this charge)

When the handkerchief is sold the entire account is set forth again, showing a profit of $81.39¾, and among the credit items reflected in this profit is:

> By washerwoman's deduction........ 5¢

At almost the same time as these entries are being made, the speculator's daughter is prattling dutifully of the blessings of trade and the distribution of wealth it brings about—the lessons of a political economy that is above all, according to Cooper, the science of concealing men's greed from themselves.

Pocket Handkerchief with its hard facts and figures would be effective as a bitter tract if Cooper had not added to it the conventional satire and inevitable love story of the society novel. The lifeless puppets do well enough as long as the story is about "the resistless power of money"; when, however, we are told that there is a significant difference between the vulgar new rich and the old families of refinement, his usual ineptness with upper-class characters and the force of his facts belie the novelist's point. The titled sempstress, turning up in New York as a governess, is reluctant to marry the wealthy man she loves and is therefore entitled to marry him; American male fortune hunters, because of their eagerness to marry well, are denied the right. The American lover's surprise at a Frenchwoman's refusing him on account of his wealth, and his suspicion of foreign trickery faintly foreshadow Henry James's international theme; and Cooper is daring, for his day, in showing that American young men are willing to marry for money. But when the French girl's uncommercial virtue is solemnly rewarded in the end by the commercially sound marriage, the story's harsh strength is dissipated in sentimentality.

A summary of Cooper's work fails to give an adequate account of how frequently, and often annoyingly, he repeats both in his fiction and nonfiction certain favorite observations on contemporary life, and of how little, as a storyteller, he repeats himself. In a few incidents of the Leather-Stocking Tales the novelist is unprofitably copying what he has already done better. But in general in his other novels when he goes back to old material he works on it afresh, puts it to new uses and in new combinations, presents its meaning more sharply or sometimes as the very opposite of what he had made of it before.

At this period of his career his earlier work was a stronger influence than usual. *Wing-and-Wing* and *Pocket Handkerchief*, related to each other only in time of writing, go back in different ways to the unsuccessful *Water-Witch*. The two sea stories have so marked a resemblance that we can assume the novelist himself was aware of it. Each has an elusive hunted ship whose name symbolizes the pursuit of unreality. The later tale, set in the certified witchery of the Mediterranean and the Bay of Naples, creates the sense of illusion for which the earlier in its mock-Mediterranean setting, the lamentably unbewitched waters of New York harbor, had striven. *Wing-and-Wing* improves on *The Water-Witch* by abandoning its predecessor's bold fantasy and elaborate and rather vulgar magical apparatus for a more modest effect. That life may be a dream is no longer one of the novelist's central suggestions but an adornment of his worldlier wisdom, that men dream it strangely. When the English are certain that they have seen the *Feu-Follet* burn before their eyes and refuse to credit the reality of its reappearance, it is the will to believe that has made the solid world of fact seem unreal.

Having used in *Wing-and-Wing* the mood of *Water-Witch*, Cooper in *Pocket Handkerchief* takes up its theme but in an entirely different mood. The subject in each story is trade—in fact, dealing in contraband; but in the later piece the romantic elements in the earlier one are turned into something flat and dull. Instead of the daring young smuggler's displaying to the alderman's niece at midnight the wares for which he has risked his life, the handkerchief which has been prosaically sneaked into the country without duty is openly shown in the Broadway shop to the speculator's daughter. And for the alderman's frank love of gold, so intense that it is poetic, we have the self-justifying platitudes of political economy. Cooper's opinions of trade had not changed between the two books. Just as in *Notions* one can see presented with love and pride much the same provincial society that appears in *Home as Found*, so commerce is equally lawless and greedy in *Water-Witch* and *Pocket Handkerchief;* but what he had chosen to see as charming in a fantastic eighteenth-century setting he now sees, in the light of the world around him, as ugly because it is respectable.

Cooper's next novel, *Wyandotté* (1843), is about the tragic impact of the American Revolution on a frontier settlement in New York, not far from the site of Cooperstown. Patriotism, which had been unselfish devotion in Harvey Birch, an obsessive madness in old Ralph, has degenerated, if we ignore a few unconvincing and wooden minor characters, into the treachery and self-interest of the demagogue. It is a war without glory. Bunker Hill, a conventionally splendid scene of heroism and carnage in *Lionel Lincoln*, is the subject of a dry factual narrative, told with brutal indifference by an Indian and in a broken English that makes it flat. At the same time that Cooper is depriving the American Revolution of its splendor, he is also—influenced, Clavel suggests, by new realistic works like Robert Montgomery Bird's *Nick of the Woods*—taking away from the Indian the splendor of his rhetoric.

The only fighting that we see directly is a disorderly attack of American irregulars on the house of Hugh Willoughby, the founder of the new settlement. He is in doubt for a long time whether the attackers are Indians or whites in disguise, and whether their excuse is that he sides with the English or with the Americans. Aided by desertions among the defenders, brought about by the local demagogue, Willoughby's overseer, the attackers succeed to the extent of killing Willoughby's wife and daughter, but fail in their main object, the confiscation of his estate. The subordinate incidents of *The Spy* are in *Wyandotté* the visible war, an ignoble social uprising of the crafty and mean-spirited against the wealthy that accompanies the political revolution.

Willoughby is the vague ineffectual man of good will, rational and neutral in a civil war that forces men to take sides irrevocably. A retired British officer, with his permanent home in America, he cannot choose decisively between king and country when what had been a simple single duty splits into two inconsistent conflicting ones. Deploring the English policy, he deplores also its result, the Declaration of Independence; he permits his son to remain in the British army and his daughter to marry an American patriot. He loses the capacity for intelligent action by retaining, after the rest of the world has abandoned it, the desire to live in peace and obey the law. It cannot be done so easily as he thinks, for, as the demagogue reminds him sharply, there is now always the question of which law, the king's or the people's.

Wyandotté, the Indian for whom the story is named, is Magua with a moral problem, and it is, as with Willoughby, the one created by the falling apart of a unitary standard of conduct. This drunken hanger-on of the Willoughby household, known to them as Saucy Nick, hates Willoughby for flogging him (as Munro had flogged Magua) and loves Mrs. Willoughby for saving his life by inoculating him in a small-pox epidemic. The elementary Indian rule, to aid a friend and punish an enemy, has become impossible of application. For years he evades his dilemma by fantasies of scalps, while drinking his enemy's rum. The war makes him the warrior Wyandotté again, and he finds a manlier solution that fulfils with savage literalness both commands of the law: he murders Willoughby and fights bravely in defense of the women, acts of a treachery like Magua's and a chivalry like Uncas', which he never could have performed in his state of degradation.

Nick has lived too long among white men to be happy in the perfection of Indian virtue and is converted to Christianity. Years later he confesses his crime to Willoughby's son, and for the moment once more the savage, offers his life to the English general as unhesitatingly as Lord Jim offers his as a forfeit to his friend, the old chieftain. Nick is forgiven by the younger Willoughby and dies on the spot, from the relief or the burden, we are not sure which, of Christian forgiveness.

The lovers, Willoughby's adopted daughter Maud and his son Bob, are still another instance of the failure of the normal pattern of life to furnish a guide, but the principal emotion that this particular strained relation arouses is false delicacy. The two, reared as if they were brother and sister, find themselves in an equivocal situation when their feelings go beyond the bounds of family affection. Maud, not to betray her love, becomes shy and reserved with Bob; the uncomprehending family queries her worriedly about her coolness and forces her to the old demonstrations of affection that she now feels are unmaidenly and forbidden. Bob fears that his foster-sister will regard his love as incestuous and that he must keep silent all his life.*

* In France Cooper had seen and been shocked by a play with a similar love theme: a girl falls in love with her guardian, whom she believes to be her brother, and marries after the true relationship, or lack of it, is explained. Cooper had a spirited discussion of the play with "a coterie of amiable women" (reported in *Gleanings*). What he said against it then is in large part applicable

The violence that overwhelms the Willoughbys shatters the delicate scruple and brings the lovers together. One feels amid the horror of the catastrophe a ludicrousness in its being put to so trivial a use, but the use is a real one for the story. Bob had come back home disguised, on earnest business (and not in frolic, like Henry Wharton), to offer his father a commission in the British army. His chance of being hanged is not too great, for this is a gentleman's as well as a people's war, and his brother-in-law is well placed among the patriotic gentry. Some of the awkwardness will be removed and the application of influence made easier, Bob explains to Maud, if it seems that he came back to become a bridegroom rather than a spy. The young man with an absurdly high sense of honor and a passion sickly-sweet in its scrupulosity about fancied barriers has turned flagrantly practical in the end and lends himself, as no other Cooper hero has done before him, to an implied deception for the unromantic purpose of saving his neck.

Wyandotté is a remarkably unpleasant book, slow-paced and dragging as an adventure story, remote and unpitying

---

to his own rendering of this ticklish theme, despite the changes he made in adapting it to *Wyandotté:*

"I objected to the probability of a well educated young woman's falling in love with a man old enough to be selected as her guardian when she was an infant, and against whom there existed the trifling objection of his being her own brother. 'But, he was *not* her brother—not even a relative.' 'True, but she *believed* him to be her brother.' 'And nature—do you count nature as nothing —a *secret sentiment* told her he was not her brother.' 'And use, and education, and an *open sentiment*, and all the world, told her he was. Such a woman was guilty of a revolting indelicacy and a heinous crime, and no exaggerated representation of love, a passion of great purity in itself, can ever do away with the shocking realities of such a case.' "

as a tragedy. The only characters whom the author wholeheartedly likes are a few chuckleheaded Willoughby dependents, steadfast and unquestioningly devoted, whose
loyal folly is the occasion of the book's rare flashes of humor.
Some of it is fine extravagant comedy, as when Mr. Woods,
the ex-army Church of England chaplain, explains how he
will rescue Bob from his captors, the supposed Indians: "I
shall take this sprig of laurel in my hand, in lieu of the olive-
branch," said the excited chaplain, "as the symbol of peace.
It is not probable that savages can tell one plant from the
other; and if they could, it will be easy to explain that olives
do not grow in America. . . . I cannot now stop to rehearse
to you the mode of proceeding I shall adopt; but it is all
arranged in my own mind. It will be necessary to call the
Deity the 'Great Spirit' or 'Manitou'—and to use many poetical images; but this can I do, on an emergency. Extempore
preaching is far from agreeable to me, in general; nor do
I look upon it, in this age of the world, as exactly canonical;
nevertheless, it shall be seen I know how to submit even to
that, when there is a suitable necessity."

Among the juxtaposed themes one finds apparently interchangeable fragments. Willoughby's treatment of Wyandotté, contemptuous and humiliating, needlessly referring to
a force that cannot now be applied effectively, assuming a
sort of friendship but never willing to trust it solely, may be
a political parable of England's treatment of America, as
well as a literal instance of the tactlessness of English masters. The contrasting treachery of demagogue and Indian
may have its origin in part in the desire to retaliate on those
contemporary demagogues, the editors; the novelist hurls
back at them their metaphor of his savage inhumanity, refers

bitterly to the current mode of "avenging . . . fancied wrongs, using the dagger of calumny instead of the scalping-knife."

The reader is left with the impression that the various themes point to some larger truth, possess some secret unity, that he cannot name definitely. All are directly or indirectly expressed in the novel, which is full of imagery drawn from family life, in terms of the breach of some familial relation—the colonies overthrowing the authority of the parent country; the settlers rebelling against the patriarchal founder of the settlement; the foster brother and sister in a seemingly incestuous love, declaring it on the day of the father's death and marrying shortly after his funeral; the vagabond Indian murdering the father (even he, after the crime, although he will not speak of the victim as a father, calls the widow his mother).

All these variations in disloyalty to an old tie seem to us, except for the murder, inevitable forms of change and growth. Yet the murder, for all that it is plausibly and realistically disguised as the act of a savage responding to laws different from ours, is the heart of the book, dominating it at the end; in this novel of the birth of a nation, as in some primitive myth of fertility, death is the central fact. The novelist, whose own father, also the founder of a settlement, was murdered, treats with deep respect the savage's ritual need to kill the patriarch. The novel develops this one theme sympathetically, uses it as the basis of spiritual regeneration, while the "natural" manifestations of growth, embodied in the other themes, seem soiled and ugly. Cooper had always been aware of evil, but in this dreary story of sordid betrayals and futile heroism, he is, for the first time, uncertain of the immediate reality of good. He seems to find irrational violent destruction the universal accompaniment of growth, and to have lost faith in the bright American fable of conscious progress toward a milder better world in which men will live by their own reason and not under the compulsion of old myths.

Chapter VIII

I N JANUARY 1843 Fenimore Cooper had received a letter from Edward Myers, an inmate of Sailors' Snug Harbor, asking "whether you are the Mr. Cooper who in 1806 or 1807 was on board the ship *Sterling*, . . . if so whether you recollect the boy *Ned* whose life you saved in London dock, on a Sunday, if so it would give me a great deal of pleasure to see you . . ." The novelist wrote back at once, "I am your old shipmate, Ned." In June Ned visited Otsego Hall and stayed five months. The two men were on the lake together frequently and every morning took a walk in the village, Cooper, as his grandnephew remembered, in the ruddy glow of health at fifty-three, carrying a light whip of a cane, Ned, although a few years younger, hobbling along, leaning on a crooked stick.

Ned had spent most of his life as a common sailor before the mast. He had fought on the Great Lakes in the War of 1812, had run a gambling table while a prisoner of the British, jumped ship sometimes to escape a thrashing, sometimes from caprice, smuggled tobacco into Ireland and opium in China, drunk up his pay on shore. After partial religious conversions and sliding back into drink from reading Tom Paine, he got true religion and became an Episcopalian. Cooper saw a book in Ned, and by November it was published.

In *Ned Myers, or A Life Before the Mast* (1843), "edited by J. Fenimore Cooper," the editor seems to have caught, as both he and Ned insist that he has, Ned's own words, for the book has a limber raciness and easy simplicity quite unlike anything else Cooper wrote. Along with his language, Ned is allowed his own character. He lacks the fundamental trait of a good Cooper sailor, a quiet deep love for his ship. He is the undignified underside of history of which we nowadays record so much more than was deemed proper in Cooper's time. After the victory at York, Canada, Ned is drunk and finds the plundering good fun even if it is at the risk of being flogged through the fleet; still drunk, he helps the dying by giving them rum. And when his ship is boarded, Ned and others of the crew join the victors in their jollification, breaking open barrels of American whiskey to celebrate an English triumph.

When *Two Years Before the Mast* came out in 1840, a copy had been timidly presented to Cooper by young Dana's father, an old acquaintance from the days of Cooper's great success. The subtitle chosen for Ned's story—*A Life Before the Mast*—invites comparison with this famous account of "the life of a common sailor at sea as it really is." Ned, unlike Dana, has the professional's point of view. After a quarter of a century out of sight of land, as he computed it, spent on almost a hundred different ships, he accepts the sea as a simple fact, without grandeur or mystery, and is too casual about its hardships and perils to interest us deeply.*

Ned had himself suffered many more wrongs than Dana had seen on his one cruise, but he has none of the young man's fine indignation. He concedes that a certain amount of flogging seems necessary, merely grumbling mildly that "we might sometimes be treated as men, and no harm follow." Far from believing, as Dana did, that sailors should be taught their rights under the law of the land, he resents legal interference with the customs of the sea. The one time he flares up is when his own traditional privilege of administering physical punishment is infringed, and "a whole pack of quakers" have him fined $60 for striking a saucy black steward who had neglected in bad weather to get him something warm for breakfast. "Well-meaning men often do quite as much harm, in this world, as the evil-disposed. Philanthropists of this school," and here Ned sounds exactly like Cooper, "should not forget that, if color is no sufficient reason why a man should be always wrong, it is no sufficient reason why he should be always right."

Ned is interested not in changing the external conditions of a sailor's life but in inducing his fellow-seamen to reform themselves and become religious men. Ned's views are very close to Cooper's, and his story is in a sense a happy rendering of one of the themes of Cooper's last novel, *Wyandotté*,

---

* Cooper thought otherwise of at least part of this book, which he later praised as generously as if it were solely Ned's and not at all his. A footnote to a revision of the *Naval History* states that some details of the loss of the *Scourge* in a squall were furnished by Ned, and adds: "The account which is given of the loss of the Scourge, in a little sketch of the life of this old salt, and nearly in the words that came from his own mouth, is one of the most interesting, simple and thrilling narratives in the English language."

the conversion of a drunkard. It may be that with another author Ned would have found, or there would have been found for him, a different meaning in his life; he might have been made a hero for his suffering or a coward for fleeing from reality to liquor and religion. But in whatever other way his story might have been told, Ned with his cheerful naive pride in his religion and in his unregenerate past seems very much himself. If, just as Cooper has caught his words, he has caught some of Cooper's ideas, he holds them for the most part in such a simple, unmodulated form as to make them his own. There is throughout a commonplaceness in Ned's outlook that is the book's merit as a social document and its inadequacy as a work of art.

James Watson Webb was tried for a second time, in May 1843, for his review of *Home as Found*, and again the jury disagreed. At his third trial, in November, he was acquitted by a jury that needed only seventeen minutes for its deliberations. Cooper had never done well with juries. In the civil cases, they had been compelled to bring in verdicts for him under the judge's instructions that the offending articles were libelous as a matter of law, but the amount of the verdict, the one thing within the jury's control, had always been small.*

* Cooper expressed privately his disappointment in his verdicts, which ranged from four hundred dollars to much less than a hundred, and blamed the miserable juries. Too many factors enter into libel verdicts to make them comparable, but the following are some of the verdicts against New York editors in earlier cases:
$1400 to the lieutenant-governor for being described as disgustingly drunk while addressing the state Senate. In this case 8 credible witnesses swore that it was true and 10 that he was sober,

In Webb's case the jury had the right to decide the question of defamation for itself, for in a criminal prosecution for libel the jury was the judge of the law as well as of the facts (a result of the struggle in eighteenth-century England between judges and juries over the freedom of the press); and of the thirty-six jurors who had considered the case an overwhelming majority had been for the editor. After all, the editors' trade was to praise majorities, while the author of *Home as Found* had stated that they were not free from fault. To summarize the libel war in the newspaper cant of the day, Cooper the aristocrat won only by the aid of tyrannical judges and was rebuked by juries, the true guardians of liberty and of its sacred palladium, a free press.

Webb was encouraged by his acquittal to insinuate that Cooper had deliberately lied at the trial, and Cooper let this undoubtedly false accusation go by without suit. But no general outbreak by the editors followed Cooper's defeat. The libel war was virtually over. After 1843 only one new case was brought; it was against Thurlow Weed, who in the course of a legal discussion stated casually that everything he had written about Cooper was true and that he had re-

some explaining that the redness of his face was the reflection of the setting sun on the curtains of the Senate Chamber.

$1400 to the Secretary of State of New York for being charged with political corruption.

$1500 to the Federalist editor of the New York *Evening Post* for being charged with treasonable adherence to the side of Great Britain in the disputes before the War of 1812.

$640 to a newspaper editor of whom a much provoked rival had written that he was in an insane asylum and that his paper was being run by an illiterate Irishman; and in this case the judge had suggested to the jury that it bring in a verdict for only nominal damages.

tracted only because the courts would not let him prove it. This case and the second suit against Greeley seem never to have come to trial.

Cooper had silenced his enemies, but they had discovered in silence a powerful weapon against him. Newspapers did not review his books and hardly even mentioned them. The editors always insisted that their vituperation of Cooper was friendly in intention and for his own good. Perhaps there was an odd sincerity in their claim, for they had faith in the value of publicity and not much in the power of words to hurt. (Park Benjamin and a rival editor, George Morris, used to lunch together to plan their attacks on each other.) But whether their libels had been well- or ill-intentioned, their silence was certainly meant to be ruinous.

Cooper in defending himself in the Lake Erie controversy had naturally fallen into the position of defending Elliott and of becoming an opponent of Perry's supporters. After the arbitration proceeding was over, he set to work on a pamphlet attacking them. Tristram Burges, a Rhode Island Whig politician, had delivered a lecture on the battle, celebrating it—Perry was a Rhode Islander—as part of the state's maritime history, and after the *Naval History* was published, Burges had published his lecture. Burges was a remarkable fool; at the time of the removal of the Government deposits from the Bank of the United States he had raved in Congress about a Catilinarian conspiracy for the conflagration of our cities and villages. Cooper's chief enemy was Alexander Slidell Mackenzie, the most literary member of the Perry clan. His books on Spain and England had been mentioned favorably in the *Quarterly*—the one on Spain by Irving, the one on England by Croker in the very review which attacked Cooper's *England* so fiercely. Mackenzie's review of the *Naval History* had not been personally abusive but it had convinced Cooper of the reviewer's bad character. In 1841 Mackenzie brought out a life of Perry and it was accepted for the New York District School Library by John C. Spencer, the Superintendent of the common schools. A few months later, Cooper's abridgment of the *Naval History* was rejected by Spencer on the ground that it was controversial on the subject of Lake Erie. To Cooper, Spencer was a "damned scoundrel," for the whole clamor against the *Naval History* had been raised on account of its refusal to enter into controversy, whereas Mackenzie's book was frankly controversial.

In December 1842, while Cooper was working on his pamphlet, which among other things was to complain of Spencer's partiality to Mackenzie, whatever tie there may have been between these two men was destroyed by a strange and terrible incident. Mackenzie, in command of the brig *Somers* on the high seas, was informed of a plot to mutiny and seize the ship. He had the ringleader, a midshipman, arrested; a few days later, believing that the crew was acting suspiciously, he hanged three men—the midshipman, a seaman, and a boatswain's mate—without trial, but after an investigation by the junior officers. The midshipman was Philip Spencer, the scapegrace son of John C. Spencer, who was no longer a New York State official but the Secretary of War in President Tyler's cabinet.

A pretty story has been told that when Cooper learned of the tragedy on the *Somers* he stopped the printing of the Lake Erie pamphlet, saying of Mackenzie: "The poor fellow will have enough to do to escape the consequences of his own weakness. It is no time to press upon him now." Cooper may have delayed the pamphlet while Mackenzie was being tried by a court martial. In any event, after his acquittal the pamphlet—*The Battle of Lake Erie; or Answers to Messrs. Burges, Duer, and Mackenzie* (1843)—was published, its argument reinforced by several cruel allusions to the tragedy, for to Cooper it was clear that Mackenzie's arbitrary conduct on the *Somers* was of a piece with the way he had pressed facts into his service about Lake Erie. Far from being magnanimous, the pamphlet in criticizing Mackenzie's reliance on rumors circulated after the battle of Lake Erie cites an old rumor about him, that he had assassinated a post-boy in Spain. Of course, the author declares that he doesn't believe it—he is merely illustrating how unreliable rumor can be. But the reader is left wondering—was it intended that he should be?—what might lie at the bottom of this tale of an earlier act of violence. As Cooper himself has said in this very pamphlet, "Calumny may be refuted and rebuked; but it is never wholly effaced."

Cooper, so unfair to Mackenzie as a literary enemy, was at his very best polemically in what he wrote directly of the *Somers*, an eighty-page review of the case that is a masterpiece of quiet sanity ("Proceedings of the Naval Court Martial in the case of Alexander Slidell Mackenzie . . . to which is annexed an Elaborate Review by James Fennimore [sic] Cooper"—1844).*

---

* I am assuming that the anonymous pamphlet, *The Cruise of the Somers: illustrative of the Despotism of the Quarter Deck; and of the Unmanly Conduct of Commander Mackenzie* (1844), sometimes attributed to Cooper, was not written by him. It purports to be by a man who at the time of writing is a professional

The aspect of the sorry business that most interested Cooper was the widespread popular support of Mackenzie. A theorist would assume that in a country of equal rights a strong independent popular opinion would protect the individual and insist that the naval commander prove clearly the absolute necessity of his action. But in fact popular institutions tend "to create so much community-power as almost to annihilate individuality." Two forces worked for Mackenzie, a kind of democratic national pride and the interests of trade, and each operated through a degraded press. The triple hanging was a flattering exhibition of authority. People spoke of how one of *our* officers on one of *our* ships had hanged three villains who had conspired to run off with it. As for trade, "it was supposed that ships and insurers would possess greater security by an oriental administration of justice, than by giving to the citizen a hearing before he was consigned to the gallows." The mercantile class should never be trusted in matters of principle in which its own interests are involved; its fortunes are always at hazard, and it takes the short view. "The magnitude [of their risks] proves too much for poor human nature; and in saying what we do of

---

seaman; and in later editions, in reprinting as an appendix to the pamphlet three letters on the *Somers* written to the Boston *Courier* by a shipmaster, William Sturgis, the author of *The Cruise* states (in a footnote on page 103 of the third edition) that he did not see the Sturgis letters when they first appeared as he was then on a foreign voyage. Cooper was of course not on a foreign voyage, and in fact read Sturgis's letters in the *Courier* and wrote about them at the time (September 17, 1843) both to his wife and to Sturgis. It seems unlikely that Cooper would have used a deliberately misleading and false disguise in attacking Mackenzie, against whom he wrote under his own name in a tone and employing arguments much different from those of the anonymous author of *The Cruise*, who never sounds like Cooper.

this class of men, we are not saying they are any worse than the rest of mankind, but simply that they are no better." Yet these merchants, who should not be listened to, are sure of a hearing in the large cities: "They control most of the leading presses around them, by means of their advertising and other patronage. . . ."

The question for Cooper was not whether there was a conspiracy, but whether Mackenzie was justified in believing in it on the evidence he had, and, if so, whether he had given the accused every opportunity of defense that could be granted them consistent with the safety of his vessel. Mackenzie might have put in at a West Indian port, and it was wicked doctrine, Cooper said, that it was better to hang the men without trial than for a ship-of-war to obtain foreign aid against a mutiny. An American captain should have been proud to explain to the governor of one of the islands that America was a country of laws and that the captain preferred to call on foreign aid for their enforcement rather than to violate them himself.

When Cromwell the boatswain's mate was arrested he might have resisted; but he went along quietly because (Cooper argues) obviously he believed that he would be tried fairly. If men are to be hanged out of hand, as Cromwell was, without even being questioned on their conduct, they will not submit to authority but will fight it. The *Somers* affair must weaken discipline, for discipline depends in the long run not on force but on faith in justice.

The *Somers* affair, as Charles Roberts Anderson has shown, has been used by Melville as well as Cooper. The execution of the three men, for which Melville's cousin, Lt. Guert Gansevoort, was in part responsible as one of

Mackenzie's investigating officers, is one of the sources of Melville's last work, *Billy Budd*. Cooper from his study of the facts arrives at a fine statement—one of his last purely liberal utterances—that as a matter of sheer worldly wisdom and practicality the processes of law must be just if they are to work at all. Melville's fiction seems to move in the very opposite direction from Cooper's rational optimism; to maintain law in this world, a man whom all feel to be innocent must be punished summarily for a formal transgression of the law, and the condemned man himself agrees. Melville, at the very moment that he has won our sympathy for the reluctant yet insistent Captain Vere, cites the *Somers* affair and, without justifying it, suggests that her officers felt the same urgency for their deed.

Melville and Cooper have each used, for their different purposes, one of the most striking incidents on board the *Somers*. Spencer and the seaman Small confessed their guilt. Small, about to die, said to Mackenzie, according to the commander's own report: "You are right, sir; you are doing your duty, and I honor you for it; God bless that flag and prosper it!" From this comes Billy Budd's reverent, "God bless Captain Vere." In *Ned Myers*, Ned, after telling of his service in the Navy, ends up flippantly with: "God bless the flag, I say, and this, too, without the fear of being hanged!"

Cooper's typical crotchets so severely suppressed in his pamphlet on the *Somers* were indulged in his new novel, *Afloat and Ashore, or the Adventures of Miles Wallingford* (1844). He let himself go to such an extent on two of his favorite subjects, his quarrel with his country and his love of the sea, that the novel, twice the usual length, was published in two parts, the second several months after the first.

The two parts have usually been republished with separate titles, *Afloat and Ashore* for the first and *Miles Wallingford* for the second, although they are in fact so much one continuous story that the first part ends in the middle of an incident. The novel is too long in the sense that if Cooper had been a more careful writer he could have created in much fewer words the same illusion of an endless adventure story told by a garrulous old man who can leave nothing out and must tell what he thinks about everything. But we never grudge it its length, for it gets better as it goes on. It becomes an amusing compendium of all of Cooper's notions and a splendid collection of exciting adventures in which action and commentary interrupt each other to their mutual advantage so that we never tire of either.

By making himself the main character Cooper has at last found a way of intruding on the adventure story and making the intrusion a profitable part of the adventure. He is not literally the narrator Miles Wallingford: Miles is almost a decade older than the novelist, of slightly lower social position and from a different part of New York State. (The novelist, one suspects, was not going to repeat the mistake of *Home as Found*.) But Miles holds almost every view that Cooper held, with Cooper's delight in stating it in its most idiosyncratic and annoying form, and the only writer whom he quotes with approval is Fenimore Cooper. He is an idealization of Cooper, not as an elegant gentleman like Edward Effingham, but as a crusty old curmudgeon. If to be Natty Bumppo was, as D. H. Lawrence says, Cooper's innermost wish, we may think of Miles as his superficial dream-life, his fantasy not of being a different person but of having a different career. It is a more rigorous and logical dream than that of a free existence in the woods but a more comfortable one. Miles lives out the adventurous life at sea that Cooper only began, and retains Cooper's dearest privileges: he marries a charming woman who reminds Cooper's biographers of his wife Susan, and he turns everything that happens to him into an occasion to lecture his countrymen on their faults.

Miles's excuse for interrupting himself is that he is a gossiping old man, but all that he can gossip about is the present state of American civilization. When his ship is being boarded and members of the crew are being unjustly impressed by the English in the Napoleonic Wars, the story must stop in the midst of its tension for a disquisition on the right of search on the high seas, in which Miles supports England's current claim to board American ships off Africa in an effort to suppress the piratical slave trade. When his sister is dying and the heavy-hearted Miles is coming down to breakfast, he must pause to denounce "the venerable American custom of swallowing a meal as soon as out of bed," and the bad meals themselves, the pork fried in grease that pervades half the other dishes, the vegetables cooked without any art, the meat done to rags, a subject of the highest importance for "a national character may be formed in the kitchen." At his sister's deathbed he ridicules the belief that liturgy impairs the fervor of prayer. After she dies he comments on the "indecent haste in disposing of the dead." At her funeral he has a new outburst against dissenters and their "semi-conversational addresses to the Almighty over a grave."

As the story nears its climax and the adventure grows more desperate and Cooper more daring, Miles with Peacockian extravagance boasts that when his life was in danger his critical crotchets were not. Alone on a raft in the middle of the ocean, between troubled dreams and waking, he fancies that Lucy, the girl he loves, has married his rival and lives in a handsome new house built in the modern taste; and he adds proudly: "By modern taste I do not mean one of the Grecian-temple school, as I do not think that even all of the vagaries of a diseased imagination, that was suffering under the calamities of shipwreck, could induce me to imagine Lucy Hardinge silly enough to desire to live in such a structure."

Miles exercises an old man's right to like the good old ways, the pleasant forms of life in New York state when he was young and had slaves. He is not opposed to abolition in New York, but rejoices that his former slaves stay on with him in the old friendly relation, refusing wages, and regrets that their children take their freedom literally and move away. Slavery as he knew it in its last days in New York may well have been a mild benevolent domestic arrangement, yet it is odd that it never occurs to him, as it had to Cooper as long ago as the *Notions*, that the form itself is wrong. "It is the deep moral degradation," Cooper had then written, "which no man has a right to entail on another, that forms the essence of its shame."

Miles knows, for all of his love of the past, that the America of his youth was not a truly independent nation. Its political parties were mere pro-English and pro-French factions during the Napoleonic Wars. When Miles is robbed at sea by both the English and the French he is later abused at home by both political parties for trying to tell his story honestly, and soon learned, he tells us a little implausibly, to stop talking about his wrongs and to feel lucky that the whole affair was quickly forgotten. He will not admit that the country has improved at all (except that door-knockers, a vile nuisance, have disappeared) and is certain that things would be just as bad as they ever were if war in Europe were to break out again. In some ways New York is worse in 1844 than in his youth. One of the state's oldest and most peculiar institutions, the long-term farm leases under which land had been owned by the same family for generations and tilled by generations of the same family of tenants, is threatened by the refusal of the tenants to pay rent any longer. Miles is at one moment rebuking English travelers for not realizing how ancient and stable some of the forms of life are in the New World, and at another is rebuking the restless spirit of the times that would do away with them. "God alone knows for what we are reserved," Miles exclaims, "but one thing is certain—there must be a serious movement backward, or the nation is lost." Miles's passing worry, the Anti-Rent War, was to be one of Cooper's main interests for the next few years.

In the late seventeenth and early eighteenth centuries a generous English colonial government, continuing the policy of the Dutch patroon system, had made huge grants of land along and near the Hudson River to a few families. The letters patent, in feudal style, but probably for the practical reason of providing some form of local government, gave the grantees, or lords of the manor as they were called, the right to hold on their land "a court leete and a court baron." With the Revolution this feudal jurisdiction ceased, but the ownership of the land continued undisturbed (except in the case of a few unlucky families who sided with the King and had their holdings confiscated). The old families, unlike newer landholders such as William Cooper, did not want to sell their land, the most honorable form of wealth, but in a new country where labor was scarce they found it impossible to farm it themselves. For the most part they leased it out in small tracts of about a hundred acres each.

The leases usually called for payment in kind, not money, for money too was scarce. A Van Rensselaer lease typically required an annual rent of from 10 to 14 bushels of winter wheat, 4 fat hens, and 1 day's labor of a team of horses and an able-bodied man. The leases varied in duration; all were long to assure the tenant the benefit of his improvements. The Van Rensselaer leases were perpetual, with free rent for the first seven years while the tenant was clearing the wilderness and building his house and barn; those of the Livingstons were for two lives, those of the Schuylers for three. The tenant could sometimes commute his rent to an annual cash payment. He could also sell his lease, but had to turn over a certain portion of the proceeds, usually a quarter, to the landlord. The landlords often reserved to themselves the right of mining and milling, and to cross the tenant's land to cut timber on other parts of the landlords' property.

The leases were generally entered into at a time of high prices for American wheat (such as prevailed during the wars of the French Republic and Napoleon), and when they were made the new land was covered by a rich forest mold. The hopes that were at the bottom of the bargain were bound to be disappointed. The soil was soon exhausted by the unscientific methods of agriculture; the yield per acre declined; and after the opening of the Erie Canal eastern New York

could not compete with the wheat from the new unplun-
dered lands in the West.

When Stephen Van Rensselaer died in 1839, he was owed
over $400,000, much of it by the poorest of his farmers who
held the hilliest lands in the Helderbergs in Albany County.
The "Good Patroon," as he was called, had been forbearing,
and his debtors expected that in his will he would forgive
his claims against them. Instead, his will provided that the
back rents should be collected and put in a trust fund. These
claims became part of his estate along with the splendid
manor of Rensselaerwyck, whose three-quarters of a million
acres covered almost all of Rensselaer and Albany and much
of Columbia County and extended twenty-four miles along
the Hudson and twenty-four miles inland from each side of
the river. His two sons, bound as fiduciaries under the will,
refused to compromise; the farmers refused to pay. The
sheriff and his deputies were driven off when they tried to
serve process. Order was restored in the Helderbergs only
after Governor Seward sent the militia there.

The governor had acted to uphold the law, but he disliked the leases, which he said were oppressive, antirepublican, degrading. Commissioners appointed by the legislature
tried to effect a settlement by having the Van Rensselaers
sell out to the Helderberg farmers. Negotiations failed; the
Van Rensselaers weren't really interested in selling, and the
parties were too far apart in their terms.

With the hard times, low prices, and blighted crops of
the early 1840's the Anti-Rent agitation soon broke out again
and spread from the Helderbergs over most of the land held
on long-term leases. Anti-Rent associations were formed.
Armed men, disguised as Indians, their faces hidden by sheep-

skin or calico masks, their bodies covered by calico dresses, roamed the countryside. (Indian disguise was an old device in American rebellion; it had been used at the Boston Tea Party, and in a tenant riot on the Livingston land in the 1790's "Indians" had killed a sheriff.) The more determined farmers held the more timid in line. Practically no rent was paid. Sheriffs were tarred and feathered and found it impossible to evict tenants. The governor, William Bouck, on the eve of the 1844 election, decided not to antagonize several thousand voters, and saw no occasion to use the troops again. Radical land reformers joined the movement, but on the whole their theories were not accepted by the farmers, who wanted not to attack property in general but to acquire outright for themselves specific parcels of it. The tenants had to find legal reasons to justify their cry, "Down with the rent!" They asserted that their fathers or grandfathers had been defrauded when they signed the leases and that their terms had been misrepresented by the landlords' agents. They even questioned the landlords' title to the land, although some of it, as in the case of the Van Rensselaers and the Livingstons, had been in the same family for from one hundred and fifty to two hundred years, a long time in a raw new world.

Cooper found in the Anti-Rent War, as he had in the 1830 Revolution, a call to consider the structure of society. But now he was against the revolutionary position. He planned a trilogy, the Littlepage Manuscripts, about three generations of landlords; in each novel a member of the Littlepage family would tell the history of the family land in his generation. The loose first-person form, which Cooper had used so well in *Miles Wallingford*, would give him all the room he needed for propaganda. It would also help him make one of his main points, the social value of the relation of landlord and tenant, by allowing each landlord to show himself as a civilized and civilizing character. The series could be, as he stated in the preface to the first novel, a chronicle of manners from the mid-eighteenth century to the present.

Satanstoe (1845), the first of the series, advances Cooper's propaganda purpose very little. Much of the time in this charming book, which George Sand thought one of his best, Cooper is on a holiday from his more strenuous ideas. Taking advantage of his point of view as a pre-Revolutionary New Yorker, he enjoys living in the cozy province that speaks so warmly of England as home and trusts the mother country unhesitatingly, certain of her superior wisdom and ability. Cornelius Littlepage, the narrator, has an unsuspecting good faith in his provincial Toryism which he takes to be the height of worldly wisdom. He is at moments a little too naive—Cooper likes working a joke, even a gentle one, very hard—but Corny's simple-minded political self-abasement gives him a sturdy unaffected self-respect more convincing than that of Cooper's self-consciously independent Americans. Corny's provincialism is the source of his great virtue, a sense of the wonder of life. When he sets out on his travels from the family farm, Satanstoe, in Westchester, and visits New York City he has full eager pleasure in the grand things he is allowed to see there: the Patroon of Albany in his coach-and-four with two outriders; a caged lion at the Pinkster festival of the New York slaves; the elegant British officers who bring the great world to the little city and relieve their boredom by playing Addison's *Cato*, with a slightly drunk young Irish peer as the virtuous Roman matron Marcia.

Corny, fond of his own province and its carefree Episcopalian ways, has a "neighborly antipathy" to New England that is part of his heritage. A Dutch friend warns against sending Corny to Harvard: he will learn how to pray and cheat. But New England cannot be got rid of so easily; Corny is accompanied on many of his adventures by Cooper's most brilliant New Englander, Jason Newcome. This Connecticut Yankee wants the same things in life as Corny—wealth, social position, the good opinion of the community—but he is too eager for them. He is too frankly interested in money, likes it too nakedly for itself to observe the convention of never seeming to speak of it directly. The intensity of his respect for public opinion has given him the Puritan form of the Midas touch that turns everything into sin. When Jason watches the Episcopal clergyman and Corny's mother at a game of cards, he betrays "a sneaking consciousness of crime," and by Corny's standards he is wicked, for "it is clearly impious in man to torture acts that are perfectly innocent *per se*, into formal transgressions of the law of God."

The chief adventures in *Satanstoe* come from Corny's business trip to Mooseridge, his father's new land upstate. He spends a delightful winter in Albany (a town of which Cooper always speaks affectionately from the memory of his schooldays there), has stirring adventures, enjoys good Indian fighting, and marries a wealthy nice girl, Anneke Mordaunt. Herman Mordaunt, Anneke's sensible father, assures Corny that the expense and difficulty of settling tenants on the new Mordaunt land, Ravensnest, are so great that only the payment of rent by future generations of tenants to future generations of landlords will be adequate compensation; Corny agrees gravely and speaks piously of the debt

of gratitude that posterity will owe them. This is mere duti-
ful argument, crammed into a single page as if Cooper suddenly remembered his responsibility to his thesis and wanted
to get it over with. We cannot take it seriously, for the whole
story goes against it: by the canons of romance Corny and
Anneke have their full reward in their adventures and marriage, and Cooper is in *Satanstoe* a skilful enough romancer
to make us accept the rules of the game. Corny is even accompanied on his trip to the new land by his gay friend, Guert
Ten Eyck, who has come along solely for the fun. Guert's
presence makes us realize that future wealth is not the real
motive for the expedition but is only the necessary excuse,
in a world that likes to seem businesslike, for an activity not
financially profitable.

In the adventure story on land (unlike the more realistic
sea tale, where the hero can be frankly engaged in commerce) the love of property is not an honorable basis for
high adventure. Accordingly, Cooper refuses to base his
landlords' rights on the fact that they fight the Indians, and
lets the tenants fight them bravely too. Only Jason, who is
one of the tenants enjoying a rent-free decade, seeks a vulgar
profit from warfare. In the thick of the fighting he ingeniously suggests to Corny that the Indians have conquered
Ravensnest and extinguished the Mordaunt title; if he helps
reconquer it, it will be his own land and he will never have
to pay rent.

While it is mean-spirited of Jason to be so aware of how
war can serve his love of property, Corny, the hero, is allowed to see how it can help him in his courtship of Anneke.
Corny's rival, Major Bulstrode, has two fearful advantages
over him: he is the heir to a baronetcy, and has just been

wounded while gallantly fighting the French at Ticonder-
oga. The sophisticated Englishman, who is friendly to Corny
and a connoisseur of the relation of love and war, discusses
their respective positions on the eve of the Indian attack,
and explains candidly to the young American how the threat
of danger now outweighs his old wound ("It is present valor
against past valor"). Corny takes Bulstrode's disinterested
advice and declares his love to Anneke before the battle.
Poor Jason is not to scheme for Ravensnest, which he loves
for its own sake, yet Corny may scheme successfully for its
heiress. Jason's worldly prospects have scarcely improved at
the end of the tale, while those of the Littlepages are splendid, except that they will have as one of their tenants Jason
Newcome, whose desire to escape paying rent is, we are
sure, an ineradicable and inheritable trait.

In the few months between the publication of *Satanstoe*
and *The Chainbearer* (1845), the second novel of the trilogy,
the rent situation had grown worse. Tenant violence against
sheriffs increased and was met by reckless posses riding over
farmers' lands, ruining crops, terrifying women and children
when they could not find the guilty men. There were rumors
that jails would be attacked to free imprisoned farmers, and
in county seats as well as in the country armed men drilled.
At auction sales of a tenant's livestock for back rent, calico
Indians shot the animals once they were bid in, indemnifying
the original owner. At a sale on a farm in Delaware County
in August 1845, about two hundred armed and disguised
"Indians" surrounded the sheriff, who was in the pasture
with the cattle, and separated him from the three other members of his party, two deputies and a bidder. To bring bidder
and cattle together so as to satisfy legal ceremonial in the

collection of the $64 due for two years' rent, the deputies tried to ride through the Indians and fired their pistols. Indians fired back, and one of the deputies, Osman Steele, was shot to death as his horse was falling. Two men had been killed in earlier incidents, but it had not been certain that they were shot by Anti-Renters. Steele's death stirred New York, perhaps in part because of the disproportions in its circumstances. A few men had faced so many to perform a routine duty that they obviously could not carry out, to collect a trifling sum of money in which principle was but doubtfully involved—for the delinquent farmer had not been a convinced Anti-Renter and that very morning had been about to pay the rent but had been stopped by his more committed foster daughter. Nearly a hundred men were indicted for Steele's murder. The farmers themselves were shocked. Most of them gave up the Indian disguises, but political agitation against the leases continued.

In *The Chainbearer* the pleasant dependent province has become in the critical years just after the American Revolution a tense, unhappy, free world. Corny's son Mordaunt Littlepage, who takes up the family chronicle, has not had his father's sunny youth. War came when he was fourteen; the five years that he has spent alternately between fighting and going to college have made him mature and a little hard. The one thing in which he believes is property. He knows that his own patriotism has its foundation in the Littlepage land and that fine patriotic sentiment unsupported by property is as worthless as the Continental paper with which he has been paid. The chief play of his tight mind at twenty-one is to generalize about his dislikes and to find in all of them a threat to property. The Yankees around Satanstoe have renamed it "Dibbleton"; he sees this squeamish affectation as part of the dangerous new "spirit of improvement," a professed love of liberty that "gives play to malice, envy, covetousness, rapacity, and all the lowest passions of our nature."

Even though we are to take Mordaunt on the whole seriously, the novelist is having his fun in his hero's precocious outburst about the bad new days, for as the reader knows, the Yankee prejudice against the name Satanstoe is not new. Young Jason Newcome had told Corny soon after the two had met that the name was irreligious, profane, ungenteel, vulgar, and only fit to be used in low company. In the third novel, *The Redskins*, we are told casually of a city, Dibbletonborough, that had been founded on a part of Satanstoe during the speculative boom of the 1830's. An ironic suggestion runs through the series that the Yankee spirit of change, supposedly so destructive of tradition, creates its own unconscious pieties and symbolic ties to which men cling for generations, while the conscious love of old ways, which Corny hopes to foster by the family chronicle he has started, never takes hold even of his own descendants. Although they continue the story they do not seem to have read what has gone before. In the very last paragraph of *Satanstoe* Corny thinks it likely that his son Mordaunt, if he writes, will have more to tell of Harry Bulstrode; but Mordaunt knows so little of his father's friend that on the first page of *Chainbearer* he describes him vaguely as a "Sir Something Bulstrode" whom his grandfather Herman was visiting when he died in England.

Mordaunt's trip upstate, unlike his father's, is a serious matter of business. On the sloop going to Albany the young man is already negotiating with prospective settlers and offers them the choice of leasing land at Ravensnest or buying it at Mooseridge. Because all of their wealth is in the packs on their backs, the settlers cannot make the small down payment required on a purchase, and choose leases. For Cooper, the tenants' choice is decisive not only for the profitable rent-free years but for all time. Their descendants must pay rent forever, because the ancestors found it cheaper to begin that way, and in fact could afford no other. There is something chilling but admirable in the forthrightness of Cooper's secular Calvinism that men do not achieve but are predestined to property and poverty.

Mordaunt is rich enough to be a good landlord. He fixes low rents in renewing leases that are expiring; reinvests his money in the land; contributes to building a church. He has the chief virtue of his class, liberality, and will not let it degenerate to the usual fault of indulging tenants carelessly and allowing arrears to accumulate to such an extent that the inevitable day of reckoning is a harsh one.

The tenants at Ravensnest tell Mordaunt that they are satisfied, but one has the sense of a precarious relation. People were disappointed, a tavern-keeper's wife explains, when Mordaunt sided with the colonies; he should have stayed true to the King, as his grandfather would have done, and given them an excuse to seize his lands. ("It is a sweet thing, major, for a tenant to get his farm without paying for it, as you may judge!") This young Revolutionary hero would like to invite his tenantry to an old-fashioned landlord's dinner, but dares not; settlers from New England will put up only with the reality of inequality and not with its signs. Mordaunt's one tie with the tenants is through the leases, but no one believes in their solemn promises in fine print except himself and his illiterate friend Andries Coejemans, the old chainbearer who is marking off his land. According to Jason Newcome, covenants are put in leases much as surveyors put watercourses on maps: they look well there. "Landlords like to have 'em, and tenants a'n't particular."

Jason is witty from desperation. His lease for three lives plus twenty-one years is running out because the three infants whom he greedily chose as measuring lives died almost immediately. Greed intensifies his terror of losing the mill he has built, for he knows what he would do if he were the landlord and all improvements became his property at the end of the lease. Mordaunt will not act like Jason but will not compromise his right to do so. When he finally gives Jason the new lease, he says, ". . . what is conceded is conceded as no right, but as an act of liberality." These words, whether by accident or intention so like Cooper's advertisement about Three Mile Point, arouse no resentment in Jason. With good sense the despicable Yankee accepts the lease once he finds its terms satisfactory, not caring whether it is his by favor or by justice. Mordaunt on his part is proud that he has maintained unimpaired the landlord's legal right, which he never intends to exercise, to gouge a tenant.

What makes *The Chainbearer* a novel of some power and impressiveness, as well as intensely irritating at times, is the uncompromisingness of its propaganda. Cooper will not stoop to prettify property but insists on its rightness in all of its most unattractive aspects. He is offering us a doctrine which, as with one of the sterner truths of theology, we must accept in its full bleakness if we are to understand it at all. It is a purely worldly wisdom, but technically his task is similar to Aldous Huxley's in his later religious novels; Cooper is using the novel, an instrument for the indulgence of our human feelings, to convince us that they are wrong and cannot be trusted. We are to be converted not by our sympathy but despite it. Nothing could be more suitable for Cooper's high purpose than the very title of the book, *The Chainbearer*, or than the chains that Coejemans endlessly drags across the land. These are flaunted before us, with a rhetorical fervor equal to Marx's three years later, as the conventional symbol of slavery; what we must learn, however, is not to rebel against them but to think of them as the necessary restraints to which men must submit if they would be free.

The second half of the novel is a grand debate on the nature of property between the squatter Aaron Thousandacres and his prisoners, Mordaunt and Coejemans, carried on under circumstances which seem calculated to insure that our feelings, however our reason ultimately decides, will be with the wrong side. To bring the debaters together, Mordaunt is made to wander lovesick and hungry in the woods. Seeking out the squatter's family, he breakfasts with them without telling who he is, answers their questions evasively until the others guess his identity and make him their prisoner. The novel's most curious effect is that Mordaunt has become a trespasser on his own land; for a literal mess of pottage he has denied his birthright.

Old Thousandacres is a squatter on principle, more articulate than Ishmael Bush of *The Prairie* and with a sophisticated Puritan conscience to guide him in his lawlessness. He derives his title sanctimoniously from the Bible and practically from his rifle—from the Lord's gift to Adam and his posterity of the possession of the earth, and from his own ability to hold by force what he has taken. These squatters have fought the King's soldiers to be free and will be dependent on no man, particularly a grantee of the King, for the right to earn a living. The boards they have made from the timber they have cut have their own sweat and labor, their flesh and blood, in them. No chainbearer, carrying chains willingly as the servant of the rich to measure the earth, can rob them of what must be theirs because it is part of themselves.

In Thousandacres' arguments Cooper intends to ridicule a few land reformers of his own day who were supporting Anti-Rentism, but their doctrinaire views take on a grim authority when spoken by the rough mean squatter. He is, like Ishmael Bush, man in a state of nature, uglier and more brutal than eighteenth-century philosophy imagined him; the "natural" law of possession which he asserts is obviously a reflection of his own greed. The lawgiver and the law go together; each vouches for the hard reality of the other. The old man and his sons convince us that men can feel in themselves in times of social upheaval the power to choose freely the conventions by which they are to live. It is a power that Cooper abhors, but he makes us believe in its existence. The Littlepages' paper title, so baffling to the virtuous natural man, Mordaunt's Indian friend Susquesus, as well as to the vicious one, Thousandacres, seems absurdly unreal in the uncleared wilderness simply because the squatter will not recognize it, whereas his own possession is an inescapable fact that must be dealt with. The debate ends when one of the squatter's sons kills the chainbearer, and Susquesus kills the old man. Force makes a doubtful arbiter between the two

systems, unless we are to admit that it is at bottom the ultimate sanction of each and that the one which invokes it
most effectively will become the law. We wonder in the end
whether Cooper has not brought about in fiction that union
between radical theory and violent practice which is so
rarely found in American life.

Anti-Rent violence had been suppressed energetically and
punished severely by the end of 1845, but it had been in
large part successful. It had made the state government aware
that a considerable body of voters felt that they had grievances which they were determined to redress. For the first
time both political parties were anxious to pass laws in favor
of tenants and against landlords. The 1846 legislature abol-
ished the landlord's ancient remedy of distraining for rent
—that is, of seizing and selling a delinquent tenant's personal
property without first obtaining a judgment. (It had been
at such a sale that the deputy sheriff Osman Steele had
been killed.) A special tax was imposed on the rents from
long-term leases, in effect subjecting a handful of landlords
and no one else in the state to an income tax. The purpose
of the law was frankly not revenue but to induce the landlords to sell out to their tenants. Under the Federal Constitution the state could not impair the obligations of a
landlord's contract, but legally a good deal could be done
to make him want to get rid of it.

The legislative committee headed by Samuel J. Tilden
suggested one further attack on the leasing system. On a
landlord's death the lease should be valued, and the tenant
given the right to buy the property. The state's power to
control inheritance was believed to be absolute, and this
ingenious and probably constitutional device for getting

around the contracts clause of the Constitution alarmed the landlords and terrified Cooper. Tenants were being invited, he said, to murder their landlord and then help each other get his land cheaply by swearing to a low value for it. The measure failed in the state Senate and never became law. Another land reform, which was adopted in 1846, was attacked by Cooper for its very mildness: the new State Constitution provided that no agricultural lease made after 1846 should be for a longer term than twelve years—a prohibition that could work more hardship on tenants than on landlords since it left unchanged the old rule that improvements to realty became the landlord's property at the end of the lease.

Fast though events were moving, Cooper was almost equally quick in putting them into a book, and in his haste turned out one of his worst novels, *The Redskins, or Indian and Injin* (1846). The story begins well. Mordaunt's grandson Hugh, the last of the Littlepage narrators, is a gay absentee landlord on the grand tour. One night in Paris his Uncle Ro, who has spent half his adult life happily in Europe, tells him what a glorious country America really is. Remembering fondly the good clam-soup of New York and the fine apples grown at Satanstoe, the older man is indulgent of his country's few faults—Pennsylvania's failure to pay the interest on her bonds; the Whig bankruptcy law, repealed after it had been in force just long enough to discharge certain special debts. Ro can afford to be kind, for other men's defaults have been profitable to him; he sold part of Satanstoe for a good sum, mostly cash, and as the mortgage has not been paid he is getting the land back and can keep his money, without obligation to the people who bought lots from the speculators to whom he sold. There is a disposition, Ro admits, to legislate on behalf of the poor and against the rich that makes the relation of debtor and creditor a little insecure, but this is inseparable from democracy and is erring on the right side.

This tolerant mood is broken abruptly the very next morning when the two rich Littlepages learn that New York tenants have risen against the landlords and are being helped by the government to repudiate their obligations. Hugh, faced with the loss of his income from Ravensnest, quickly realizes that repudiation is not a "slight blemish" in the political system but a vice that threatens to ruin it. The rest of *The Redskins* is his struggle, more by his arguments with the reader than by his action in the tale, to save civilization from immediate catastrophe. The frantic young man's tone varies for the most part between a sustained hysterical sneer and pompous indignation. His propaganda is of the sort that convinces only the rabid partisans on his own side. (Significantly, Cooper's most vitriolic enemy among the editors, James Watson Webb, who now denounced tenants as bitterly as he had once assailed Cooper, praised the book: ". . . the very best, practical showing-up of the infamous character of Anti-Rentism. . . . It . . . will go a great way in extenuation of his senseless egotism and never-tiring vanity.") We resist Hugh not because he may not be right but because he can be so tiresomely righteous. If the crisis is as desperate as he insists, how can he find time to strike out as indiscriminately as Miles Wallingford at all of America's other faults: the law exempting a few hundred dollars of property from seizure for debt, which encourages cheating by the poor; the proposal for universal manhood suffrage, which he is sure most of the people secretly oppose; the bad sleeping arrangements at a country inn, which can never be improved because the humblest hamlet believes that it has already attained the highest point of civilization.

Cooper knew that Hugh's tone was wrong, and in a "Note by the Editor" at the end of the book tries to dissociate himself from it. Editor Cooper agrees with all of the Littlepage principles but not with their expression; Hugh has written from a strong sense of grievance and with the ardor of youth. The novelist cannot of course so easily evade responsibility for a foolish, impetuous book by arguing that its tone is natural to its hero; he should have invented a saner narrator, if he could.

Hugh's fundamental principle, which Cooper upholds, is the landlord's right to be intransigent. Government pressure to make a landlord sell, or even persuasion—except in the form of enough money to tempt him—is unlawful. The sanctity of contract is a familiar concept, but no one has stated so starkly and shrilly as Hugh that what is sacred is the greed of the man who wants to keep the bargain and what is wicked is the greed of the one who would break it.

As an advocate for landlords, Hugh believes that all property may be wiped out and all law overthrown by Anti-Rentism. But as a satirist of tenants—and here he does better —he sees shrewdly that they are absurd just because they do not in action live up to the extremity of their rebellious rhetoric and posing. Instead of an uprising by an oppressed peasantry, traditionally the bloodiest and most terrible of social wars, we are shown a rather contemptible jacquerie of voters, safely resorting to law itself and enacting special taxes to bully the oppressor. The oppressed farmers gather armed and disguised not to wage desperate war but to threaten one or two men with tar and feathers or to listen to a "first-rate lecturer on feudal tenures, chickens and days' works" (a form of "feudalism" that does not even exist on the Littlepage land). So powerful are the farmers that Hugh and Ro have to sneak back to Ravensnest disguised as a German organ-grinder and a peddler. But to the Anti-Rent lecturer, Hugh Littlepage is an arrogant aristocrat who "would not put his knife into his mouth, as you and I do, in eating—as all plain, unpretending republicans do—for the world. It would choke him; no, he keeps *silver* forks to touch his anointed lips."

The tenants' favorite argument for not paying rent—appropriately, we hear it first from Jason Newcome's grandson—is that the Littlepages have a canopied pew in the church at Ravensnest. Cooper has always something of the novelist's vision that sees more than it means to, and the pew which starts as the symbol of the tenants' folly ends as proof of the landlords'. The Littlepages themselves admit that the canopy is wrong and has no place in a church, but Hugh cannot take it down while the "turbulent spirit" prevails. A mob throws it into a pigpen one night and everyone is happy. This trivial anachronism which law and order are powerless to deal with (for law and order taken literally, as Hugh insists they must be, are men's promises that nothing will be changed and the future will be like the past) disorder can end decisively.

The only adherents to law are the real Indians who are drawn into the story to shame the calico Indians (or "Injins," as Cooper has to call them to keep the two groups apart). To the novelist who had made Indian virtue world-famous it must have seemed a happy device to contrast the debased imitator with the genuine red man. But Indians in Cooper are always men wrongfully dispossessed, and their presence reminds us that an old wrong is being repeated rather than a new wrong done. Susquesus, so sympathetic to property and landlords, is explicit that "the wicked spirit that drove out the red-man is now about to drive off the pale-face chiefs. It is the same devil, and it is no other. He wanted land then, and he wants land now." Susquesus is telling us of the very "demon of the continent" that D. H. Lawrence was later to find its prime force, "causing . . . the Orestes-like frenzy of restlessness in the Yankee soul, the inner malaise which amounts almost to madness, sometimes." In his search for an unchanging law which will assure continuity, Cooper has discovered an unchanging process which forbids it and demands that the descendant of the original dispossessor must in his turn be himself unjustly dispossessed.

Poor though *The Redskins* is, it has its place in the series as a cranky Götterdämmerung bringing the trilogy to a close. In the beginning of the first book a journey of the Patroon of Albany, with his coach-and-four and outriders, was a grand social event; in the third, a landlord must sneak into his own house, disguised as a wandering alien. The physical world itself seems to have shrunk between *Satanstoe* and *Redskins*. To Corny, everything in the little province was larger than life. To Hugh, Ravensnest, after what he has seen in Europe, appears "diminutive and mean"; for one charming moment, forgetting to be a prig, he is mortified to learn that, although denounced publicly as a great aristocrat, he is really one on so small a scale.

The series ends with Hugh going to Washington to live and to litigate every question connected with his leases. The young man has confidently predicted throughout his book that the courts will sustain his leases and strike down the legislation directed against them. But he is also prepared, should Washington fail him, to move to Florence, "a refugee from republican tyranny."

While *The Redskins* preaches faith in law, it subtly creates doubt. Hugh and Ro comment sneeringly half a dozen times on a recent decision of the state's highest court, the then Court of Errors. They never name the case or the parties, but the stupid judgment to which they refer is one rendered against Cooper in the December 1845 term. In 1842, after the naval arbitration award, William L. Stone wrote with no provocation except his own anger at losing: "Mr. J. Fennimore [*sic*] Cooper need not be so fidgety . . . to finger the cash to be paid by us toward his support. It will be forthcoming on the last day allowed by the award, but we are not disposed to allow him to put it into Wall-street for shaving purposes before that period. Wait patiently. There will be no locksmith necessary to get at the ready." Cooper sued for libel and won. Stone appealed to the Court of Errors, which reversed the judgment and dismissed the suit. The Chancellor as a mere human being who read newspapers knew what the paragraph meant—he cautiously indicated as much—but judicially he was ignorant and could not go behind the written words. Everything was unintelligible except the reference to "shaving" and that was ambiguous. In popular usage "shaving" was exacting usury for money lent, a disgraceful trade; but it also meant buying notes and bonds at a discount, "as the most respectable brokers in Wall-street are in the constant habit of doing. . . ." The milder meaning won. One of the Senators—the state Senate was part of the court—added that courts should not "be found sustaining the effort to multiply the instances in which this action may be brought . . ." nor should they "encourage this remedy, for every trifling assault upon private character." Cooper not only lost his case but was given this hint that he had done the law no good by taking it seriously and resorting to it so frequently.

It was easy for Cooper to make fun of the decision. When two Anti-Renters quarrel, the epithet "damned shaver" is so insulting that they come to blows. Ro never tires of saying ironically that landlords can leave their ancestral lands and shave money in Wall Street; the Court of Errors has made it respectable. It is sad to watch Cooper appealing incongruously from the courts to popular opinion, in a book which is a warning against the excesses of extralegal opinion and a plea to submit to law. He himself had gone to court to protect his reputation, and now the highest court of the state was hurting it.

Hugh's half-wish to leave the country was also Cooper's. In a letter to a fellow-novelist, James K. Paulding, just two months before *Redskins* came out, he is aware how generally unpopular he is with the press and with the people. His publishers have not sold the first edition of *Satanstoe* and *Chainbearer*. The sole use of publishing in America is the convenience of correcting proof sheets. "If I were fifteen years younger, I would certainly go abroad, and never return."

Cooper did not live to see the outcome of the litigation in New York over the manorial leases. All the cases but one were decided ultimately for the landlord, but the law's delays, the unclear language of some of the opinions, the impossibility of collecting rent on thousands of leases by suit rather than by distraint, worked to the tenants' advantage. The highest court held the Van Rensselaer title good, but a lower court had first held it bad because the original grant had been too generous—an argument, the reversing judge drily remarked, which would have been appropriate if addressed to the colonial government a century and a half earlier. The one adverse decision invalidated only the quarter sales provision (that is, the tenant's payment to the landlord of part of the price when he sold the lease). But in the course of the decision the court stated that the perpetual lease was in legal effect a deed of the entire title. This statement made it doubtful whether "rent" could be collected after a sale. It took long years—so many that the controversy was practically over—before the courts clearly held that even if one party was not a landlord and the other not a tenant and the payment not rent, still it could be sued for in the courts just as if it were. A judiciary that took decades to say the last word could not preserve a system daily attacked by an urgent popular movement. Before Cooper died, many of the landlords gave up and sold out. Some of their land was bought by speculators who kept up a bitter and losing struggle for years to collect rent, managing in the end to ruin only themselves and some of the more determined farmers who opposed them.

Chapter IX

"Is this the way
I must return to native dust?"
—Epigraph to *The Ways of the Hour*

FROM COOPER'S own premises his pamphlet on the *Somers* and his trilogy on the Anti-Rent War, which seem to us to be so different in spirit, are each the work of a true democrat concerned with the major problem of political democracy, the achievement of freedom. Democratic freedom is assured not by the universal enforcement of the popular will but by frustrating it in all matters of individual rights with which majorities should not interfere. In our own thinking we agree with Cooper to the extent that we have made "civil liberties" and "minority rights" almost interchangeable terms. It is easy for us to see that no popular vote, however large, could make the hangings on the *Somers* just. But it is hard for us to agree with Cooper that popular will is equally irrelevant when the question is one of the continued enjoyment of traditional property rights by a few individuals favored by the accidents of history. Large aggregates of property are the possession of only a tiny minority, yet it seems to us a play on words to regard them as within the scope of minority rights. For Cooper, the protection of property rather than life had become the prime business of government, not because property was more sacred but because it was more vulnerable; the propertyless many could always be stirred up against the propertied few. From the Anti-Rent War, a specific instance of this danger, he proceeded to a more generalized discussion of it in *The Crater* (1847), the history of the rise and fall of a society compressed into the space of a few years.

Mark Woolston, a first mate and an Episcopalian, and Bob Betts, a common sailor and a Quaker, are the two survivors of a wreck in the South Seas. Their life on a reef which has a volcanic crater is a Robinson Crusoe idyl. They cultivate a garden—Cooper, a devoted gardener, is here in one of his most contented moods—and observe the Sabbath. Bob never forgets the deference he owes to Mark and to his own religion; he pulls off his hat whenever he enters the cabin of the old ship, and puts it on as soon as church services begin. This perfect social arrangement is interrupted when Bob is carried off in a pinnace in a high wind. On his return a year later with Mark's family and friends, the little domain has been conveniently enlarged by an earthquake. More colonists are brought in. Invasions by natives of other islands are fought off. (In this idealized settlement of a new world Cooper has allowed himself the luxury of treating the native as the unprovoked aggressor.) A government is established, the governor, Mark, and his council holding office for life "to prevent the . . . most corrupting influence of politics, viz., the elections, from getting too much sway over the public mind."

A new batch of immigrants brings several agents of unrest into this conservative Utopia: a lawyer, a printer, and four ministers—Methodist, Presbyterian, Baptist, and Quaker— who have been secretly sent for by some of the Craterinos because the Episcopal clergyman, Mr. Hornblower, cannot satisfy their assorted spiritual needs. Mark had never been sympathetic even to Bob's relatively mild complaints against "dressing and undressing in church time" and "praying out of the book," forms which most of the people deem "relics of the 'scarlet woman.' " Convinced that there is but one religious truth and satisfied with Mr. Hornblower's stiff-neckedness in preaching it, Mark had first thought of excluding the four additional clergymen as undesirable immigrants, but unfortunately they are friends of families already settled and have to be admitted. Men soon "began to pray *at* each other, and if Mr. Hornblower was an exception, it was because his admirable liturgy did not furnish him with the means. . . ." The lawyer teaches the people the art of litigation and of lending money on security, the printer establishes the *Crater Truth-Teller*, and the colony is ready for ruin.

The newcomers complain that all of the good land has been distributed and that they have none. The newspaper agitates for majority rights and a new constitution. "To such a height did the fever of liberty rise, that men assumed a right to quarrel with the private habits of the governor and his family, some pronouncing him proud because he did not neglect his teeth, as the majority did. . . . Some even objected to him because he spat in his pocket-handkerchief, and did not blow his nose with his fingers." By a series of local primaries at which only a minority votes, a constitution is proposed which, like the New York Constitution of 1846, makes all offices, even that of judge, elective. It is adopted by a minority, for many of the citizens, believing the entire proceeding illegal, abstain from voting. It is a minority again that actually nominates the new officers who are elected. The people have exchanged responsible choice, made by the governor in his own name, for irresponsible choice made in their name but not by themselves.

Mark, ineligible for office by a trick of the new constitution, is not left in peace as a private citizen. He had retained the crater as his own property and had leased it to the public. A lawsuit is brought against him to attack his title. The jury disagrees and Mark and his family leave the island. Some months later he returns, but in his absence there has been another earthquake, and the entire colony has been destroyed.

Volcanic islands do erupt from the sea and disappear into it, and, as Harold H. Scudder has shown, Cooper may have read about them in Lyell's *Principles of Geology*. But the novelist has not the right, merely because both phenomena occur in nature, to make use of both in his tale. The act of violent creation is a happy invention, enlarging the scene just when more people are about to come on it, and illustrating Cooper's theory of an inscrutable divine will: Mark, simply by being present when the new world becomes visible, falls heir to an unearned providential increment of the earth, so much richer than the little crater-garden over which he has worked so hard. The total destruction also has its convenience, for it helps the novelist to get rid of his invention when he has no more use for it. It helps him, however, to do more—to get rid of mankind. Had he destroyed on his own responsibility and by his own authority, we could accept and even enjoy aesthetically his aggressive misanthropy, as we enjoy Swift's. But we resent the judgment in *The Crater* because it is presented not as the novelist's but as the judgment of the divine will, for the moment no longer inscrutable, passed on mankind when it violates Cooper's laws of the universe.

The violence with which *The Crater* ends is merely intellectual; the destruction of the colony is unseen and unfelt. In *Jack Tier*, which must have been written around the same time (it was published serially in American and English magazines between November 1846 and March 1848, and as a book in 1848), the violence is no longer off-stage nor abstract. The climactic scene of this stirring adventure story is a series of cold-blooded killings, the more horrible because they are the act of a captain of a ship against his own crew and passengers.

Jack Tier seems to be the realistic reworking of an early romance, *Red Rover*, with borrowings from still another romantic tale, *The Water-Witch*. Captain Spike, who secretly sells gunpowder to the enemy during the Mexican War, is the pirate Red Rover, presented as a commonplace low villain instead of as a glamorous gentleman. Spike's relationships are made as close to the Rover's as practicable, and at each point Spike behaves shabbily and meanly where the Rover had been noble. Both have women passengers, an older and a younger woman. While the Rover had conducted himself with punctilious decorum to the women on his ship, Spike is so loutish in love-making that his older passenger, Mrs. Budd, believes that he is proposing marriage to her when he is asking for the hand of her niece. (Mrs. Budd, with her absurd nautical lingo, learned from her dead husband, is a direct copy, as Lounsbury has noted, of the admiral's widow in *Red Rover*.) The Rover is loyal to his crew and gallantly forbearing to his enemies on the cruiser that is pursuing him. Spike, in an overloaded yawl, chased by the cutter from the sloop-of-war, tries to save himself by treacherously killing his own people.

Spike is the sordid truth of romantic fiction nowhere so completely as in this scene. By a recurrence of seeming accidents the surplus human cargo is thrown overboard. When Mrs. Budd's turn comes he takes advantage of her foible and lures her from her seat by silly pseudo-technical jargon to which she replies in kind just as she is being pushed into the sea. Drowning, she clutches the boatswain's hand. " 'Cast off her hand,' said Spike reproachfully, '. . . Cut her fingers off if she won't let go!' . . . The struggle did not last long. The boatswain drew his knife across the wrist of the hand that grasped his own, one shriek was heard, and the boat plunged into the trough of a sea. . . ." There is a surrealist discordance, a grotesqueness added to the horror, in the inappropriateness of the victim—a middle-aged, middle-class woman whose foolish way of talking carries with it always the suggestion of a safe tiresome life, free from danger and reality.

The note of the grotesque is present also in the resolution of the story's main theme, the relation of Captain Spike and Jack Tier. Jack is a sailor, a "little dumpling-looking person, [with a] cracked, dwarfish sort of a voice. . . ." He hails Spike's ship, the *Molly Swash*, at the start of her voyage, claiming to be an old shipmate of Spike's, and is taken on as cabin steward. Jack, aware of Spike's villainy, tries to thwart him in it, but will not desert his captain to whom he is attached. Spike on his side is unobservant and indifferent; he does not remember Jack from the old days. At the end of the story, as Spike is dying, Jack is revealed to be not a man but a woman, Spike's own wife, Molly Swash, whom he abandoned years ago. The dying man on learning that this coarse unattractive creature is his forgotten wife frankly groans, and soon dies, cursing and crying for mercy.

Until this incredible dénouement Jack's relation to Spike has something of the fascination and piquancy, but on a more prosaic level, of Wilder's to Red Rover. The attachment between men is a strong element in Cooper. Indeed, in several of the novels a man speaks as if the bond between men were comparable with a man's affection for a woman. Natty Bumppo, explaining to Jasper his fear that Mabel may find him boring, says absurdly and touchingly in *The Pathfinder:* ". . . if I had to marry you, boy, I should give myself no consarn about my being well looked upon, for you have always shown a disposition to see me and all I do with friendly eyes." Mordaunt Littlepage, in *The Chainbearer*, at his first meeting with the Indian, old Sureflint or Susquesus, thinks at once of the girl his family wants him to marry: "Priscilla Bayard herself, however lovely, graceful, winning, and feminine, had not created a feeling so strong and animated, as that which was awakened within me in behalf of old Sureflint."

When Jack turns out to be a woman the novelist formally denies the very existence of his theme, but the denial serves to emphasize its reality and the intensity of emotional complication in male friendship. For Jack throughout has been plausibly a man, more real as the devoted, jealous, hating and loving friend, than as the spurned wife at the end who has spent years at sea disguised. I do not mean to suggest that Cooper has been dishonest in the last-minute change of sex (as he was in *The Water-Witch*, to save the heroine's respectability) or that he has been afraid to defy contemporary convention. Rather, I would guess that the novelist was himself limited by the conventions of his age and that the only way he could conceive of his subject and work it out in his own imagination was by seeing it himself in terms of his improbable explanation.

False though the dénouement may seem to a modern reader, it does not ruin the story but is consistent with its harsh tone. Jack—instead of being, like the smuggler-into-lady-cousin of *The Water-Witch*, a dashing young man turned into a lovely girl—is always a little ridiculous as a man, with squab figure and waddling gait, and as the woman is ugly and hideous after years at sea. It is as if Cooper, as well as reversing the implications of *Red Rover* with its picture of an attractively lawless life, intended deliberately to put the conventionally titillating device of *The Water-Witch* to an opposite use, and to employ it now to heighten the effect of drabness in ending his grim tale.

The Oak Openings, or The Bee-Hunter (1848), set in Michigan during the War of 1812, is Cooper's last novel about Indians. It starts out as if it were to be a typical story of Indian fighting; tribes paid by the British and stirred up by one of their own chiefs, Scalping Peter, who would exterminate all white men, gather in force to fight. The few Americans, the reader assumes, will escape, join other settlers, and resist. It is only when the story is well on and the fighting has been long delayed that we realize that Cooper's interest is not in a physical but in a spiritual struggle. Scalping Peter and his followers kill a missionary who has preached to them to return good for evil, a contemptible doctrine to the savage warriors. But Peter is troubled because the dying man in his last moments practises his own teaching and prays for the salvation of his murderers. Reluctantly, the Indian, on the road to a religious conversion, gives up his plan for a glorious war to free his people from the white man, and helps the other Americans of the story to flee.

The elaborate preparations at the beginning for a fight that never takes place are deceptive, but these false clues are Cooper's means of leading up with skilful surprise to his central incident, Parson Amen's death, and making it a moving effective scene. The parson is introduced as if he were a comic interlude. He has come among the Indians not only to convert them but to exercise his favorite crotchet. He tries to convince them that they are the lost tribes of Israel and must return to Judea so that prophecy may be fulfilled.

The Indians are shocked to learn that they are related to palefaces of a kind who live apart from the rest, like men with the smallpox. With Indian courtesy, and thinking always of his objective of getting rid of the white man, Peter answers Amen: "Let my brother open his ears very wide, and hear what I have to say. We thank him for letting us know that we are Jews. We believe that he thinks what he says. Still, we think we are red men, and Injins, and not Jews. . . . If the pale-faces believe we have a right to that distant land, which is so rich in good things, we will give it to them, and keep these openings, and prairies, and woods." A blunter and more bewildered chief is indignant: "I am a

Pottawattamie. . . . It is not a tribe of Jews, but a tribe of Injins. It is a great tribe. It never was *lost*. It *cannot* be lost. . . . It is foolish to say you can lose a Pottawattamie. . . . What he says may be true of other tribes, but it is not true of the Pottawattamies. We are not lost; we are not Jews. I have done."

The Indians are righteously certain that they would have been incapable of slaying the Son of the Great Spirit had he come among them. The tidings they have heard, that such a crime was committed among white men, proves the justice of wiping out the entire race. But when they kill the bearer of the tidings, his absurd notion about the Indians takes on a reality connecting them with the universal guilt of which they claim to have no share. We see in their stubborn righteousness an ancient spirit, and in their deed old actors acting out an ancient role. Past and present become confused and one in Peter's mind as he watches the missionary pray for him, and the martyr's death becomes the living proof of the great atonement on which the dying man places all of his hopes. Peter, denying by silence the truth that is being revealed to him, is for the moment at the Crucifixion, of which every martyrdom is in a sense a part. Cooper in this powerful and beautiful scene is using persuasively and dramatically an idea frequently expressed in early theology, about martyrs, the men who bear witness: that it is Christ himself who is present and who suffers in the person of the martyr.

Parson Amen's death, one of Cooper's finest incidents, throws the whole novel out of balance. The novelist can do nothing with his surviving characters except hurry them off the scene in an anticlimactic account of the wiles of flight. To make up for this blank he has added an unsatisfactory epilogue, describing the Indian and the people whom he saved, as they were thirty-six years later when the novelist met them. Cooper had visited Michigan, probably in 1847 before writing *Oak Openings,* and visited it again in 1848 after the main part of his story was written. Local tradition asserts that he met the prototype of his bee-hunting hero and spent hours listening to pioneer history. But Cooper's description, in the epilogue, of his meeting with his characters has details that would be impertinent and too personal if they were actual people, and seems to indicate that they are fictitious. The point of the meeting in the epilogue is not so much to establish the authenticity of the novelist's facts as to drive home inartistically a bad moral to his tale. Peter, smug in his new religion, suggests that the white men were right to dispossess the Indian, or at least that—as the earth is the Lord's —the question of its possession is of no concern to him as a religious man. The white man's conquest and near-extermination of the Indian seem to be viewed by Peter, with Cooper's acquiescence, as they had been by the Spanish conquerors some centuries before—a necessary step in the process of bringing Christianity to the savages of the New World.

Cooper fails in *Oak Openings* because his genuine religious theme embodied in the martyrdom dwarfs everything else and makes even the delightful early passages about Western ways and types insignificant and irrelevant. Cooper's increasing interest in religion is in his next novel, *The Sea Lions* (1849), a minor but bulky excrescence on a competent story of thrilling adventure in the Antarctic and of the life of some nineteenth-century descendants of the Puritans. This time the story has been saved, and it is theology, or Cooper's view of it, that is spoiled for the reader.

The Sea Lions is a study of the meanness of the Yankee spirit on land and of its boldness and bravery at sea. Cooper knew at first hand the Yankees of eastern Long Island (culturally if not geographically New Englanders) in 1819, the date of his story, for at that time he had an interest in a whaler that sailed from Sag Harbor, Long Island's chief whaling port. However much of Cooper's own observation may have gone into this work, the land scenes have the peculiar authority not of directly observed experience but of experience previously recorded in a long series of books. The miserly pious deacon, torn between the fear of losing what he has and the desire for more wealth; the dying sailor who tantalizes the miser with the tale of a secret fortune (a tropical island with pirate gold and an uncharted antarctic island abounding in seals); the relatives and dependents crowding around the deacon's own deathbed, seeking to figure in his will, their greedy hopes expressed obliquely in the whispered censure of the greed of others who would rob a dying man—all of these are as old as the comedy of manners. They have the credibility of the completely familiar; by the sheer power of long-established literary convention we recognize them at once in all of their exaggeration as absolutely true.

This conventional greed is presented with the sharp exactness of a genre picture on a small scale; it is a deadly sin practised for modest ends. Deacon Pratt, the local magnate from whom so many expect a legacy, is worth from thirty to forty thousand dollars at the most. The pirate gold that he clutches as he dies, forgetting God and salvation, is a scant two thousand dollars more. The worldly needs that have corrupted Parson Whittle are pitifully small—a new horse-shed for the meeting-house, new shingles for the parsonage—and for these, which he never gets, he toadies and abases himself before the wealthy deacon.

Greed is the driving force of the entire action. The deacon builds a schooner on which he sends the hero, Roswell Gardiner, to find the seal island and the pirate treasure. One of the dead sailor's relatives, Daggett, knowing something of the secret, builds an identical schooner to follow Gardiner on his search. Daggett, the spy trying to get at Gardiner's secret, must play the part of the unselfish friend. He helps Gardiner in a storm; he gives up his right to a whale, which both claim under the laws of whaling. "In all this there was a strange and characteristic admixture of neighborly and Christian kindness, blended with a keen regard of the main chance." The hypocrisy of virtue, whatever its motives, becomes indistinguishable from virtue itself when Daggett, his ship disabled, releases Gardiner from all claims and generously urges him to sail off before the coming of winter. Of course Gardiner must stay. (The terrible antarctic winter, of which Cooper had been reading in accounts of recent explorers, is one of the best parts of the book.) After his fine gesture, Daggett's greed reasserts itself. Hoping to save his wrecked ship and his cargo, he refuses Gardiner's suggestion to use the ship for fuel for the common good of all; instead of taking his crew to safety with Gardiner's men, Daggett remains on his own property, where he and his men freeze to death.

It is in the depth of this winter that Gardiner resolves his theological doubts about the Trinity, which had kept Mary, the deacon's niece, from marrying him. Cooper had used religious differences as a device to keep lovers apart in *Wing-and-Wing*, where the hero's devout atheistic Jacobinism and the heroine's devout Catholicism suggest a real incompatibility. Raoul has at moments traces of the intolerance and condescension of the enlightened to the benighted, and the reader is certain that it will be easier for the heroine to cherish his love after his untimely death than it would have been after marriage. In *The Sea Lions* the difference is much narrower. Roswell is a religious man, who believes that Jesus was crucified for man's redemption and that the atonement was acceptable before God, but he cannot understand and does not believe in "the crucifixion of one who made a part of the Godhead itself."

There is logic, if of a dangerous kind, in Mary's argument with him: ". . . you commit the, to me inexplicable, mistake of believing a part of a mystery, while you hesitate about believing all. Were you to deny the merits of the atonement altogether, your position would be much stronger than it is in believing what you do." But it does seem unfair of Mary to insist that his inability to believe what he cannot understand is a form of worship of his own reason, "idolatry of the worst character," and to refuse to marry an idolater.

Roswell, supposedly so foolishly and wickedly proud of his own mind, listens meekly through the long winter to the prosing of an old sailor who urges with arrogant self-conscious humility that Roswell imitate him and abandon reason for faith. For all that Stephen admits that the revealed truth goes against the truth of nature, as we know it, he has enough vanity to press his own argument based on human nature: it is improbable that the apostles would have invented a doctrine "which would seem to be opposed to all men's notions and prejudices." In worldly matters Cooper had long acted as if the fact that a doctrine was unacceptable by popular standards were itself evidence of its truth; and Roswell is enough like Cooper at bottom that it is this argument of Stephen's which first moves him toward accepting the Christian mystery in its entirety. After Roswell's conversion and successful return to Long Island, "the moist, rosy hand of our Mary," as Melville put it in his contemporary review of *The Sea Lions*, "is the reward of his orthodoxy. Somewhat in the pleasant spirit of the Mahometan, this; who rewards all the believers with a houri."

In concluding his brief review Melville erred on the side of generosity in appraising Cooper's latest novel: "Upon the whole, we warmly recommend the Sea Lions; and even those who more for fashion's sake than anything else, have of late joined in decrying our national novelist, will in this last work, perhaps, recognise one of his happiest."

Cooper was as usual in need of money, and when he was in New York to put *The Sea Lions* through the press, he tried also to sell some of the pictures he had bought in Europe. *The Sea Lions* had a fairly good sale for late Cooper, and he found a new and enthusiastic publisher, George Palmer Putnam. Putnam was reviving interest in Irving, whose sales had fallen off completely, and offered to bring out a good edition of Cooper's best works. The novels had been frequently republished in America, and Cooper's English publisher, Bentley, regularly included them, usually with new prefaces and occasionally with some revision of the text, in his library of Standard Novels. But until Putnam's venture Cooper had not had a satisfactory uniform edition of his own, and the Leather-Stocking Tales had not even been brought together as a series.

Putnam republished eleven of the novels during Cooper's lifetime: *The Spy, The Pilot, Red Rover*, the five Leather-Stocking Tales, *Wing-and-Wing, The Two Admirals*, and *The Water-Witch*. It was a good selection, certainly a safe one. On the surface none of the works chosen was controversial or unpleasant, and the prefaces used in the new edition were, with a few conspicuous exceptions, generally mild.

In the past Cooper had tended when his stories were unobjectionable to pick a quarrel in his preface. As far back as *The Pioneers*, his sunniest book, the author made fun of his critics, who had each found some different fault in *The Spy;* he proclaimed exuberantly how little he cared about them and how much about sales. By the time of *The Deerslayer*, when sales were poor, the scope of insult had been enlarged to take in most of his American readers, and the tone had changed from amusement to defiant sarcasm. The original preface to this novel about the eighteenth century patiently explains to the literal-minded that if anyone has the Christian name or color of hair of any of the characters this should be regarded solely as a coincidence; the novelist knows, however, that in a republican country only a minority will understand that a novel is a work of fiction and is to be read as such. While these two pugnacious prefaces were replaced by milder ones in the Putnam edition, Cooper revised the preface of *Red Rover* so as to attack a new enemy, the Rhode Island Historical Society, whose enmity had been incurred in the protracted course of an old controversy, that over Lake Erie.

Commodore Elliott, grateful to Cooper, had caused a

medal to be struck in his honor and distributed widely—to
the President and heads of departments, ex-Presidents and
their widows or eldest child, American ambassadors abroad,
and foreign ministers in Washington. John Quincy Adams
undertook to send it to learned societies in various states.
The Rhode Island Historical Society debated through most
of 1845 how to reject its copy and returned it after passing
a resolution uncomplimentary to Cooper. He cared very
little about such opinions, he said, but found it necessary to
parade his indifference—by referring in the course of *Oak
Openings*, when his characters reach Lake Erie, to the blun-
ders of "a renowned annalist . . . sustained by the collected wisdom of a State Historical Society"; and by revising
the preface to *Red Rover*. Part of the action of that tale
takes place in Newport's famous stone tower, whose origin
was being discussed in Cooper's day as it still is now. Cooper
was positive that the structure was only a seventeenth-century mill and not, as the society thought, a pre-Columbian
fortress. The revised preface linked the society's inflated
notion of this local antiquity with its distortions about Lake
Erie. "Little institutions, like little men, very naturally have
a desire to get on stilts. . . . We prefer the truth and com-
monsense to any other mode of reasoning, not having the
honor to be an Historical Society at all."

In some of the additions to the prefaces to the Putnam
edition one can see how much Cooper's social views have
changed and merged with his religious beliefs. In *The Pilot*,
the preface written for Bentley in 1831 had ended with the
hope that through the numerous sea tales following Cooper's
"an interest has been awakened in behalf of . . . a sort of
proscribed class of men, that may directly tend to a meliora-

tion of their condition." In 1849, while letting the old passage stand, he is, in the new matter added, fighting one of
the reforms currently proposed, the abolition of flogging in
the Navy. To the high-sounding argument that American
citizens are too good to be brought under the lash on the
high seas, he answers that there are thousands on shore who
would be benefited by a little judicious flogging. It is better
to trust to experience than to impulsive experiments. Peace
Societies, Temperance and Moral Reform Societies—man's
substitutes for a divinely established church—mistakenly try
"to get the fruits of the Christian Faith, without troubling
themselves about the Faith itself." Christian philanthropy
is the only rational method of reform; first the sailor must
be improved morally, and then the lash can be laid aside as
unnecessary.

Putnam brought out one new novel by Cooper, his last,
The Ways of the Hour (1850). It is a disordered, fascinating book, an improbable murder mystery that remains mysterious for hundreds of pages only because Mary Monson,
the rich woman who has been unjustly accused, refuses to
tell the facts which she knows and which would clear her;
it is her insane whim to be acquitted by the jury solely on the
ground that the evidence against her is insufficient. In part
Mary is literally insane; in part she is the victim of the ways
of the hour: the new-fangled Married Women's Property
Act, which spoils wives by giving them control over their
own property; the prospect of easy divorce in some Western
state, encouraging their disobedience; the press, whose
great fault is "making a trade of news . . . as soon as the
money-getting principle is applied to it, facts become articles
for the market, and go up and down, much as do other com-

modities . . ."; the direct election of judges, which makes
them hesitant in enforcing the law when it goes against the
popular will; and above all trial by jury, the great instrument
for nullifying the law and for deciding cases by rumor and
prejudice rather than evidence and reason.

Cooper of course will not forgo any chance for comment
on many of his old grievances and on his new ones, which
are surprising in their number and their freshness. His views,
when he does not give them himself, are stated in deliberately outrageous form by Mary's Wall Street lawyer, a
crusty bachelor of sixty (which happens to be Cooper's age).
Dunscomb is deeply engaged in his client's cause, to save
her life, but he is so intractable that he would see her hang
rather than appeal to humanitarian sentiment against the
gallows.

Dunscomb's high-minded cocksureness, which turns us
against him as Cooper's mouthpiece, has its function as part
of the drama, because for once Cooper's formal ideas about
contemporary life are integrated into the action of a contemporary tale. Dunscomb is interested in justice and in
saving an innocent woman's life. The two interests, apparently one, are inconsistent and in conflict under the American system of jury trial. The ethical lawyer maintains a
superficial harmony between them by turning over to unscrupulous junior counsel the dirty work which he suspects
must be done: the prejudicing of the potential jurors in
advance of trial, the spreading of false reports, the distribution of money.

It is Cooper's thesis that a fact will not submit to democracy, cannot be ascertained by counting noses, and that our
noble concept of justice democratically administered through

trial by jury is in practice a shabby fraud. "The American tradition . . . contemplates," as the United States Supreme Court said a few years ago, "an impartial jury drawn from a cross-section of the community," or in Tocqueville's phrase, "a certain number of citizens chosen by lot and invested with a temporary right of judging." But this same tradition, as Cooper shows, leaves too much of the selection of the twelve disinterested jurors to the interested lawyers. The conflicting desire of each for men prejudiced to his side is supposed to result in a fair-minded choice, just as from the conflict of two partial and distorted versions of the facts the truth is somehow to emerge. Mary gets not a neutral jury but one with a secret partisan, an advocate who is formidable because he is undisclosed and does not himself know that he is taking sides; he easily wins over the others, who true to the law's requirements for a good juror "stand indifferent between the people of the State of New York and . . . the prisoner at the bar."

Classically, the jury system is viewed as a means of educating the citizen in the sober exercise of power, and the publicity of judicial proceedings is deemed to be both educational and a check on possible abuses. The system did not always work as it should even in Cooper's day. In 1844 a woman named Mary Bodine was accused, on circumstantial evidence, of stealing her brother's property, murdering his wife and child, and then setting fire to the house to hide her crime. Mary's alibi, her lawyer suggested, was that at the time of the fire she was visiting an abortionist. She was tried three times before she was acquitted, but each trial had to be held in a different place, for after each it was impossible to get an impartial jury in the same county. In New York

City, in the attempt to hold another trial there, out of some four thousand jurors challenged all but ten were set aside, and the District Attorney agreed with Mary's lawyer that two more fit jurors could probably not be found. The full examination of jurors to assure a fair trial seemed to defeat its purpose; the bias against Mary increased during its course.

Mary Bodine's supposed crime was, I believe, one of the starting points of Cooper's elaborate plot in *The Ways of the Hour*. In the novel as in the actual case, there has apparently been a double murder by violent blows, an effort to conceal it by arson, and a general belief that a hoard of coins has been stolen. Each Mary is a married woman separated from her husband. But here the major superficial resemblances end. Cooper has not merely discarded the sordid facts of Mary Bodine's life, which were not suitable material for him; he has significantly turned them around. His Mary, instead of being a poor outcast violating the code of sexual morality, is a rich woman brazenly displaying her wealth and refinement. The display of the very wealth that takes away any motive for the crime with which she is nominally charged is the chief proof of Mary's guilt, for the display is her real offense against the community. She must be punished for being different from the people in the small town in which she has been living temporarily. Her life is in danger because she will not, while she is in prison, give up her "hanging ways": she speaks French, reads foreign books, has a maid, plays the harp, and refuses to show herself at the prison window to the neighborhood loafers.

Cooper, while denouncing jury trials for their appeal to our baser emotions, as a novelist exploits shamelessly the emotional theatrical atmosphere of a trial; lecturing us that judgment should be unimpassioned, he makes us excited spectators at the game that should not be played at all. He has a right to his contradictory methods, for the contradiction between the psychological reality and the intellectual pretense is his subject. A jury trial is dangerous because it is fascinating; the corruption that we see is the more evil because we like it. When Timms, the junior counsel, talks to Dunscomb about the "out-door work" in a jury case, we enjoy the talk because we know that the younger man, under the guise of describing his opponents' tactics, is indicating what he is prepared to do. Cooper himself, although he believed that he had been the victim of these practices in his libel cases, takes pleasure in his knowing command of the terms used to describe them—"horse-shedding" (discussing a case with a juror when he has left the courtroom to look after his horse), "pillowing" (planting a few outsiders in the bedroom at the inn in which the jury sleeps).

Our faith in Timms perhaps shows our own ambivalent attitude toward money—it can accomplish anything, even wipe out the prejudice that it creates. Timms disappoints us when, under Mary's instructions, he circulates rumors that can only damage her. Yet in this absurdity the implausible story is striving for its deepest truth. Majority opinion is so strong that it carries a certain conviction against all logic; even Dunscomb, the spokesman for property, has his moments of doubts about his wealthy client's innocence. The rich, like any other minority, somewhere below the level of consciousness share the majority's prejudice against them. It is with this basic problem that Mary in her wild way is grappling, and she cannot be content with an easy victory. She has, in exaggerated form, that strange futile desire of the rich to be loved only for themselves, and spends money extravagantly to accomplish this. The deliverance which she seeks and which must come freely from society itself, she never gets, for in the end it is by her own acts in the courtroom that she is freed.

The novel's supreme failure is that Cooper does not dare to keep up with Mary in her longing to be forgiven her differences and accepted for herself as she is. He withdraws too far from her dilemma, which is so like his own, and makes it so special that it becomes meaningless, when he reveals in the dénouement that Mary is literally suffering from some hereditary insanity. In our anger at this irresponsible solution, just as through our irritation at the repetitious argument that impedes the story, it is easy to lose sight of the story's fitful merit and of Cooper's brilliant glimpses of truth about a supposedly sane world.

The Ways of the Hour failed in America, and Cooper had to go through a humiliating experience to get it published in England. Cooper's prices for his English rights had fallen constantly since the high point of *The Bravo*. For *The Ways of the Hour* Bentley offered only £100. His avowed reason for the new low price was the uncertainty of copyright. The Court of Exchequer had just held, contrary to prior lower court decisions and to the general understanding which had prevailed about the English law, that a nonresident foreigner did not secure a valid copyright by first publishing in England. Ultimately this new view unfavorable to Americans was sustained by England's highest court, the House of Lords (in 1854, after Cooper's death); but Cooper, with too much faith in the law and too little in men, was positive that Bentley was exaggerating the importance of the Exchequer decision and was using it unfairly to cheapen his price. Cooper asked Putnam to help him find another English publisher, and the book was offered to Murray, who refused it on any terms. Cooper was now willing to take Bentley's £100 but unwilling to write directly and "expose himself to the mortification of a possible refusal." He had to appeal to a young novelist, Richard B. Kimball, who had been published with great success by both Putnam and Bentley, to intercede for him. Bentley wrote Kimball that he would certainly lose whatever he paid for the new book but that he had made too much money from Cooper in the past to drop him for the sake of £100. Cooper had to accept Bentley's terms and around the same time told his wife that he would write no more novels.

He had no intention of giving up writing; he was only abandoning the form that had made him famous and that had become unprofitable. During the last two years of his life, despite increasing illness and the time spent on the Putnam edition, he did a considerable amount of miscellaneous work.

Upside Down, or Philosophy in Petticoats, a comedy of which only one scene has been published, was produced in June 1850 and ran for three or four nights in New York. The novels of adventure were natural material for the theater and beginning with *The Spy* had been successfully dramatized by others; but according to the *Literary World* Cooper's own play was an undramatic lecture on "the follies of the time." To this reviewer, with whom the *Albion* in effect agreed, the leading character, the gouty old bachelor who rescues his nephew from socialism, is obviously Cooper; "the only wonder is, how he should have been able to have presented such another caricature of himself, as he appears in his later novels, without seeming to be aware that he was doing so." The *Express* was kinder and found the scene in which the bachelor is "wooed by a she-Socialist . . . screamingly delectable."

Cooper, if never really like his irascible bachelors, had created the expectation that he would behave like them about his grievances. Putnam was nervous when his two great authors, Cooper and Irving, met one day by accident at their publisher's office. Cooper had persistently kept aloof from Irving for years but to Putnam's relief was friendly. The two writers chatted pleasantly for an hour and parted with cordial good wishes. The meeting, which made Irving happy, is one of several incidents of Cooper's last years that make him seem personally more mellow while in his writing he kept true to his unpopular course.

Cooper's friends in New York—he had many from his days in the Navy and his successful New York and European years—planned again, as they had almost twenty years before, to give a public dinner in his honor, but again it was not held, this time perhaps because of his illness. His unpopularity had lost with the years some of its sharp edge, but he was so used to being unpopular that he was always being surprised by proof of how much he was liked. When he wired to reserve a hotel room, the telegraphers who relayed the message sent him complimentary messages of their own. At one of Fanny Kemble's Shakespearean readings he found himself among old acquaintances in an old-fashioned New York assembly and delightedly reported to his wife that heads were bobbing at him all evening and a great many callers came the next day; he was, he believed, a sort of lion himself because he was so seldom seen.

His social position was naturally more ambiguous in Cooperstown than in New York. Cooper took some part in the community life of his village. He gave a Gothic oak screen to Christ Church; addressed the local group that was raising money for the relief of Ireland during the famine of 1847; debated the slavery question with the philanthropist and reformer Gerrit Smith, arguing for African colonization and against immediate abolition; lectured on naval battles and also on hypnotism. (His early interest in "magnetic trances" was connected with the occult, and some time after attending a seance of the Fox sisters, around 1850 in New York, he came to believe in spiritualism.) He was even willing to enter into the general evening discussions in the hardware store, at least when his friend Judge Nelson of the United States Supreme Court, the village's second most distinguished citizen, was present.

Despite these activities, the antipathy between Cooper and many of his fellow townsmen persisted. It had more fundamental causes than Three Mile Point. His trade was different from anyone else's; it made him famous but hardly respectable. According to a tradition recorded in Ralph Birdsall's engaging *Story of Cooperstown*, a very old lady who sat at her window said to Cooper whenever he passed, "James, why don't you stop wasting your time writing those silly novels, and try to make something of yourself!" Yet, as a world-famous man it was incumbent on him in a democratic village to be affable to everyone. "In this part of the world," as Cooper said, "it is thought aristocratic not to frequent taverns and lounge at corners, squirting tobacco juice. . . ." Friends might explain that when he walked through the streets not recognizing people who thought that they knew him he was abstracted and thinking of his current tale, but many people took it as proof of deliberate aloofness.

Cooper's habits, in fact, kept him apart from much of the routine of the village. Almost daily in summer—and often in winter as well—after his morning stint of writing he drove with his wife to the Chalet, his pretty and unprofitable farm on a hill rising from the east shore of the lake and with a fine view of the countryside. In the evening he played chess with his wife (they had played on their wedding day after the ceremony while waiting for supper), and in the last of his few surviving diaries his winning and losing are recorded as faithfully as his Bible reading and the weather. Cooper visited less in Cooperstown than in New York, and he himself noted that during a whole winter he had not been in a single house in the village other than his relatives'. There were enough younger Coopers to make the Hall gay, and the close family circle was for years unthreatened by marriage.

In Paris Cooper had refused the proposal of a Frenchman of noble family and good fortune to marry his oldest daughter, Susan; the Coopers were to remain Americans. He considered reports of Morse's attachment to her absurd; Morse was too old. Susan was probably his favorite child—it became his odd joke to speak as if he were her suitor. The young woman, who had danced once in a great Parisian house to waltzes played by Chopin and Liszt while the hired musicians were at supper, settled down to a spinster's life of good works and ladylike writing.

Elinor Wyllys (1846), a novel by Amabel Penfeather, "edited by J. Fenimore Cooper" and with a preface by him, is, as Robert E. Spiller has shown, Susan's work. Her *Rural Hours*, a naturalist's notebook in journal form, was brought out by Putnam in 1850. Cooper's letters are more concerned with it than with his own work: everyone praises Susan's book; Bryant chides him for not valuing it highly enough; Cooper carries a copy of the fine edition on his visits in the city and can be induced to sell it—the price was $7—to a friend.

Cooper so took for granted the pleasure of grown unmarried daughters that he was shocked when Caroline, his second child, asked his permission to marry Henry Frederick Phinney. The Phinneys, Cooperstown printers and publishers whom Cooper occasionally used, were unexceptionable; his doubts seem to have been about marriage itself. But in the midst of the alarmed tender anxiety of his letter to Caroline asking her to do nothing hasty or rash there breaks through the more tender assurance, conveyed pompously but so warmly, that she will in the end of course have her way and be loved for it. A few years after Caroline's marriage, Maria Frances, the youngest of the four daughters, married the novelist's nephew Richard, a widower with seven children. Paul, Cooper's youngest child and only son, soon married too.

His life was not deeply changed by his children's marriages, for the wife of his unchanging love was still with him. We know of their happiness together from his letters to her when they were apart. These letters are not great or even good, but they are the letters of a happy man, untroubled, at his ease, and above all never on his guard. Their unaware assumption that he cannot possibly be misunder-

stood tells us even more of love than do the sweet messages
with which they abound. He can repeat scandal heartily
without pretending to be edifying (his letters bubble with
high spirits as he recounts how frequently and variously
Bishop Onderdonk has indecently fondled clergymen's
wives). He can discuss everything, politics, divorces,
money, his publishing hopes and disappointments, can move
easily from one to the other, from a diocesan convention to
October peaches, without explanation or apology, for
everything that interests him is an interest shared with her.

For a miscellany Cooper wrote a very feeble short piece,
"The Lake Gun" (1850) for which he received $100, a
price satisfactory to him. It is a legend about an Indian demagogue, See-wise, who induces the young men of the tribe to
violate the laws of the Manitou and fish in Seneca Lake out
of season. He is punished by being turned into a tree that
must float a thousand years on the lake; the sound like the
explosion of heavy artillery that is still heard on the lake is
the voice of the Manitou forbidding him to fish. Cooper's
interest was not in legendary Indian demagogues but in his
own contemporaries, and Robert E. Spiller has ingeniously
suggested that See-wise is William H. Seward, who as governor had been sympathetic to the Anti-Renters. The educated Indian who tells Cooper the tale sees a resemblance
between it and present-day conditions. "The man or the
people that trust in God," he concludes, "will find a lake
for every See-wise."

Putnam was planning a book on "the picturesque beauties
of American landscape," a handsome presentation volume
with steel engravings "from pictures by eminent artists"

accompanying a series of essays by American writers. Among the more famous contributors were Irving, Bryant, Cooper, and N. P. Willis, and among the less well known was Cooper's own daughter Susan, who wrote on autumn and autumnal thoughts. *The Home Book of the Picturesque*, or *Home Authors and Home Artists*, for it bore a double title, did not appear until 1852, after Cooper's death.

Cooper's contribution, "American and European Scenery Compared," written apparently in 1851, seems to be his last piece of finished work. On this dangerous subject he wrote mildly. He retracted nothing of what he had ever said in favor of the Old World and against the New, but even on the inferiority of New York harbor to the Bay of Naples he expresses himself gently. He is perhaps too frank in preferring a medieval town and its one imposing church to an American village with its "half a dozen ill-shaped, and yet pretending cupolas" and its most aspiring roof that of a tavern. But his major criticism of the meaning underlying the straggling scene is muffled in irony: "No one of ordinary liberality would wish to interfere with freedom of conscience, in order to obtain fine landscapes; but this is one of the hundred instances in which the thoughtful man finds reason to regret that the church, as it exists among us, is not really more Catholic."

"Idealizing the magnificent scenery of America" was, as Balzac said, one of Cooper's finest faculties; he was the great literary landscape-painter. ("If Cooper had succeeded in the painting of character to the same extent that he did in the painting of the phenomena of nature, he would have uttered the last word of our art.") Yet in his one formal essay on the scenery of his native land, in a book undertaken to reveal its picturesqueness, he delivers a series of cool judgments and is primarily concerned with the social significance he can find in his subject. His theme, a comparison between Europe and America, may in part be responsible, for after his return to America Cooper had an almost diseased fear of pandering to his countrymen's insatiable desire to be told that everything here was better than abroad. But in a larger view the essayist and the novelist are consistent. Cooper had never been seriously interested in nature for its own sake, and lacked the naturalist's capacity to surrender to it. He had always used it as an accessory to the novel. The accessory, it is true, is overwhelming in the Leather-Stocking Tales, but this is not merely because Cooper did better with nature than with men. Their grand settings are but another form of the same moralistic effort to teach a lesson of humility from nature; as Balzac put it, ". . . the characters become what they really are, of little importance, in the midst of this majestic scene. . . ."

Up to a very short time before his death Cooper was working on a book to be called *The Towns of Manhattan*, which it seems was to describe the past, present, and future of New York. After his death, his daughter Susan intended to bring out the unfinished work, an introduction and at least eight chapters, but most of it was lost in a fire in a printer's office. Only the introduction has been published. It first appeared during the Civil War in a magazine issued in connection with the New York City fair held for the benefit of the Sanitary Commission, a precursor to the Red Cross. It has since been reprinted under the title *New York*.

In *New York* Cooper is almost respectful to the city which he had once described, in the *England,* as "a perfect rag-fair, in which the tawdry finery of ladies of easy virtue, is exposed, in the same stall, and in close proximity to the greasy vestments of the pauper." By the end of the century New York will take its place among the capitals of the first rank. It may take longer "to collect the accessories of a first-class place," but even now the new buildings that are being erected are fit for a great city. New York will be at the head of a great commercial civilization, and it is the immediate and distant prospects of this civilization which Cooper briefly surveys in his introduction.

Writing in the false security born of the Compromise of 1850, Cooper is certain that the slavery dispute is not very serious and that disunion is not a great risk. "The slave interest is now making its final effort for supremacy, and men are deceived by the throes of a departing power. The institution of domestic slavery cannot last. It is opposed to the spirit of the age. . . ." (The same conclusion about the manorial leases had made him angry.) Calhoun's doctrines, of states' rights extending even into the territories, and of a balance of power between North and South guaranteed by the Constitution, are refuted in a quiet, authoritative tone, as if logic could put an end to the dispute. Cooper's only anger is against the abolitionists and "dissolute politicians, who care only for the success of parties, and who make a stalking-horse of philanthropy. . . ." But for their agitation well-intentioned Southerners might "be induced to adopt a wiser mode of procedure. . . ."

Cooper, concluding from his clear-sighted evaluation of the relative strength of the opposing forces that they are not likely to fight, makes the common-sense mistake of not reckoning sufficiently on the possibilities of madness in human action. But there is also in his calm analysis some of the peculiar sanity of the man with a fixed idea. He can see clearly that other men's fears are baseless, for the only one that is real is the one that he insistently proclaims. The true threat to the nation comes from demagogues, from the factions that govern in the name of the people, from the innovations being made "on not only the most venerable principles . . . but on the divine law. . . ." He speaks darkly of a possible time "when the class of the needy become formidable from its numbers, and they who had no other stake in society than their naked assistance, could combine to transfer the fruits of the labors of the more industrious and successful to themselves by a simple recurrence to the use of the ballot box." The only specific instance which Cooper mentions of the evil tendency he fears is the legislation attempted in the Anti-Rent War, to give the tenant the right of purchase on the death of the landlord.

He sees but three possible solutions: "the bayonet, a return to the true principles of the original government, or the sway of money." Cooper refuses to predict which choice will be made, but he seems fairly sure that whatever happens, money will be the master. "Trade issues its own edicts, and they are ordinarily found to be too powerful for resistance. . . ."

Cooper has not so much changed his opinion about commerce as he has about the mass of the people. He still sees commerce motivated by its selfish interests. But contrary to the usual assumptions of American political thought, he finds the large-scale greed of combined wealth less dangerous than the small-scale greed of the virtuous farmer. There will be much to mitigate the selfishness of commerce: it will at least be national in spirit, and the magnitude of its interests must place it on the side of the laws, at least of property. Yet Cooper never asserts that the rule of commerce will be good; he accepts it as the lesser of two evils. Liberty has already disappeared unnoticed: "The people have yet to discover that the seeming throes of liberty are nothing but the breath of their masters, the demagogues. . . ." What Cooper is celebrating is a future change of masters. Much though he has suffered from demagoguery, there is something displeasing in his looking forward with satisfaction to its defeat by a force that will carry out none of his early high hopes for America.

Over the years, as Cooper's faith in his countrymen's virtue was dissipated, a faith in Providence took its place. He recognized the logical force of the doctrine that if human history is a department of Providence, man, while he has every right to hope for the best, has none to predict what that unknown best will be. But it was a difficult doctrine for Cooper to adhere to strictly, for he had very positive views on the conduct of human affairs and at times uses religion chiefly as an additional sanction to enforce them. *New York* is a compromise between Cooper's temperament and his formal belief. He cannot abandon prophecy, but because it is the characteristic of national destiny to be unknowable, at crucial moments he speaks unclearly. His very refusal to be outspoken gives his warnings a greater power and saves them from the despair of certainty. With all of its doubts for the future, there is a vigor in *New York* of an intensity that is itself an act of faith and asserts the worth of human action.

Although Cooper had long been a warden of Christ

Church in Cooperstown and had been frequently a delegate to Episcopal diocesan conventions in New York, it was not until July 1851, and during the course of his last illness, that he was confirmed by his wife's brother, Bishop De Lancey. Through this illness Cooper continued at his work as long as he could. After he had been forbidden to write, his mind still dwelt on his unfinished book, and he looked forward to marking the map that was to illustrate it. By the end of August his doctor told him that there was but little hope for his recovery. His oldest friend, William Jay, who had been his schoolmate at Albany half a century before and who had thirty years ago read his first novel and encouraged him to go on, wrote him a letter of farewell, tender and formal, in a style that was already passing. For years it had been Cooper's practice, before separating from his wife even for a short business trip, to say with her the prayer in the marriage service. On the last morning of his life, September 14, 1851, she added this prayer to their morning prayers. Some hours later he died, just one day before he would have been sixty-two years old. His wife, to whom he had been married for forty years, survived him by only a few months.

American literature was still so new that Cooper's was the first death of an American writer internationally famous solely as a man of letters. The literary community felt that the unprecedented occasion demanded special forms and observances. Within a few days a meeting was held at City Hall in New York at which Washington Irving presided; a committee was formed which laid plans to set up in New York a colossal statue of the dead novelist and to hold a great public meeting in his honor. The Cooper Monument Association never succeeded in raising enough money, and after years of effort turned over its funds to a group in Cooperstown, which added to them and erected a charming small shaft with a statue of Leather-Stocking, in Lakewood Cemetery outside the village.

The public meeting, first planned for December 1851 and then postponed because New York was busy celebrating the arrival of the Hungarian patriot, Louis Kossuth, was finally held in February 1852. Letters were read from Emerson, Melville, Hawthorne, Longfellow, Parkman, and others. The great Whig orator, Daniel Webster, presided, and spoke grandiosely of literature and patronizingly of Cooper's work.

The one notable event of the evening was Bryant's "Discourse on the Life, Genius and Writings of James Fenimore Cooper," a splendid critical study of the novels and an honest attempt to narrate the strange career of the novelist. Its highest felicity is that, in its scrupulous regard for the decorum of an official eulogy, it does not suppress unpleasant aspects of the truth but states them with fitting tenderness. We see Cooper, as his friend saw him, an unflinching hero, and his faults as the price paid for the very virtue of uncompromising independence of which he was so proud. "He never thought of disguising his opinions, and he abhorred all disguises in others; he did not even deign to use that show of regard towards those of whom he did not think well, which the world tolerates, and almost demands." By this gentle approach to the truth, which Cooper seldom used, a kinder but not necessarily narrower vision has been attained than by its forthright pursuit.

Cooper's literary career, beginning haphazardly without conscious preparation or plan and advancing rapidly to world fame, in its apparently eccentric course from the time of the European experience onward touches on almost every situation that can confront the American writer or that criticism insists on confronting him with. The questions so often argued since are thoroughly argued in Cooper's work and in contemporary criticism of it: whether an American writer expatriates himself and loses touch with his own country by living abroad; whether it is dangerous for his development to write on "foreign" subjects; the extent to which he should be influenced by popular opinion and, conversely, should try to influence it; his role in American civilization, and his duty both to represent and to create it.

Stated bluntly the questions seem unprofitable and unreal, but they have a historical reality. They are as old as American literature, and in fact largely preceded it. Before there was a national literature a critical attitude toward it, an anxious parental expectation of what it was to achieve, had been developed. The questions are significant not for the answers that we may give them now but for what they reveal about the demands that the nation was making of the American writer, and the strained relation that in consequence of these demands was to exist between him and his country.

In Cooper's day and for long afterward every question about American culture involved Europe, and it was the European trip that made Cooper self-consciously aware of the great American questions. The length of the trip itself presented a problem. Jefferson had said that an American could safely live abroad only five years. Cooper meant to stay away for no more than the allotted period but overstayed his leave. He returned out of step with his country; he doubted, however, that he had fallen behind, as Jefferson said an American would, and suggested brashly that he had gone too far ahead alone. This may be a way of admitting that Europe had unfitted him for life in America, but he never regretted his European adventure. To the end of his life he defended the American artist's right of access to Europe as part of his heritage. It was a "provincial absurdity" for Americans to say that Thomas Cole's painting or even Washington Irving's writing had lost in originality after their European years. He insisted always that his own *Bravo*, which had analyzed European aristocracy, was in spirit the most American book he ever wrote.

Europe had made Cooper feel the need to write about the American democratic ideal and to adopt new forms for this purpose—the treatise, the pamphlet, the propaganda novel with the direct and often intrusive exposition of ideas. Cooper's theme in Europe, the superiority of American principles, became, after his return, the inferiority of American life. His countrymen failed to live up to the high standards which he had proclaimed were theirs. In defense of the ideal he denounced the actual as a fraud. The newspapers, largely under the control of the Bank of the United States, the self-appointed leaders of small-town life calling and manipulating "public" meetings, the provincial rich in the cities, were not the real America. He attacked them as usurpers who spoke in the country's name; but the usurpation was so broad that he frequently sounded as if he were attacking all American opinion and ultimately came close to doing so. The manufacture of public opinion by the few was no less undemocratic merely because it succeeded and brought the many around to their views; success only made the tyranny of opinion more complete. The liberalism of the 1830's during which he asserted the soundness of the great mass of the people gave way in his conservative last years to a struggle for democracy carried on against the people. According to Cooper, it was the masses and not he who had abandoned the democratic faith.

Cooper saw as a fundamental problem of democracy his own right to be different and on his own terms. It is hard to describe his position with any exactness, for in its defeat the very word that would most accurately define the difference that he asserted, "gentleman," has been erased from the language as a meaningful term. American democracy has at times gone about solving the problems of the various kinds of difference by glossing over them. In Cooper's own day, as he gleefully noted, such frank terms as "master" and "servant" were disappearing and their place was being taken by "boss" (the Dutch word for master) and "help" (surely a euphemistic understatement of the amount of work expected from the worker). The right of a gentleman to be different has been denied by denying the existence of gentlemen as a special class, just as, by much the same device, the rights of racial and religious minorities have been defended chiefly by denying that they are really different from the rest of the community.

Cooper was writing about American class manners and attitudes in the very period in which they were undergoing a profound change. The traditional rights of social position were being reduced to mere perquisites that might be gracefully offered to a man but which it was unbecoming for him to demand. The political revolution of Jacksonian democracy had brought about a revolution in social tone, more thoroughgoing in politics than elsewhere. The discovery was made—but not by the Jacksonians—that in the era of the common man it was politically astute for his leaders to appear to be common men. At almost the same time that Whig editors were attacking Cooper as an aristocrat who aped the style of an English lord and looked down on his fellow-townsmen as peasants, the Whig party was inveighing against Martin Van Buren as the little aristocrat who drank champagne and used finger cups amid the royal splendor of the President's palace; its own candidate, William Henry Harrison, who it was hoped would restore the Bank of the United States, was presented successfully in 1840 as a simple man, happy in a log cabin with a barrel of hard cider. This triumph of "democratic" manners was for Cooper the triumph of the worst elements of the commercial classes. The honest observance of class distinctions and the honest description of social classes might help preserve political sanity and the distinction between true democracy and the bastard democracy of the demagogue. In the Anti-Rent novels Cooper seems nearly as indignant at the inaccurate description of the landlords as feudal aristocrats as he does at the attempt to take away their property. He was not a large landholder himself, but both he and they were victims of the same loose rhetoric. In his hatred, if not in his love, he was still guided by what he had always thought the standards of the true democrat.

The Whig myth of Fenimore Cooper—Dorothy Waples' happy phrase for the editors' composite picture of their adversary as a morbidly sensitive, embittered failure—is, as Miss Waples insisted, a gross distortion. Yet, normal though it was for Cooper to resent the attacks on him, there is something disconcerting in the elaborate publicness of his resentment, in his going so thoroughly into the minutiae of his quarrels, as if bent on immortalizing each moment of his anger. The genteel and the democratic tradition both agree—the one in the name of dignity, the other in that of good fellowship—that a man attacked, stoutly though he may defend himself, must pretend not to mind too much or too long.

Cooper was too obviously really hurt. He was a literal patriot, and beneath the excellent formal logic of the political philosopher and novelist of ideas there is always the illogic of love. Half a dozen Whig editors were not the country—this is his political point—but his personal one is that his country, speaking through them, has rejected him. While he is discoursing on his country's faults and on the distance to be kept between himself and his countrymen, his aggrieved tone reveals his need for their affection.

There is nothing remarkable in the fact that the writer who denounces demands admiration. It was bound, however, to be denied Cooper for reasons which he himself had indicated: Americans of his day were accustomed to flattery from their fellow-Americans; and in a society that strove so hard to seem homogeneous, there was no place for an opposition from within—it was not the recognized function of a democrat to harry democracy.

Because his right to speak out was questioned, he insisted not only on the substance but on the appearance of opposition. He became as absorbed in the denunciatory role as in denunciation, but too frequently is not frank enough about it; only as Miles Wallingford does he generously give himself away and admit his honest pleasure as a self-appointed censor. The role which he typically assumed, often to the disadvantage of his modulated thought, may be described as that of the plain dealer, that blunt foe of hypocritical cant and friend of disagreeable truths. It is not too far from the editors' myth by which the warm, eager, social, hopelessly domestic Fenimore Cooper of private life, fond of his friends and good talk, had been transformed, for his contemporaries, into the legendary isolated misanthrope. Misanthropy and plain dealing are close to each other and can be taken as rough equivalents (as we can see by the fact that Molière's *Misanthrope* became *The Plain Dealer* on its adaptation into English by Wycherley). And at times Cooper seems to be almost cooperating with the editors in myth-making, to show that their version of his role is accurate. In refusing to join the Copyright Club, although believing in its objective, international copyright, he wrote to the club's secretary that he desired to do nothing for his country beyond his inescapable duty, paying his taxes.

Cooper was not withdrawing from American life in actuality; the letter to the Copyright Club may represent a moment of churlishness, and his true adherence is demonstrated by his continuing to write. But the subject of his writing was more and more his withdrawal in his imagination, his estrangement from the world he knows and in which he feels increasingly insecure. When, in his last wholly successful novel, *Satanstoe*, he imagines a hero secure in all of his relations to the world and certain of its affection, he has made him not an American like himself struggling between two worlds but a dependent colonial for whom there is but one. Cooper has not in his old age become the conventional conservative loving the past for its own sake as inevitably superior to the present. He has moved Corny back in time to escape not only the American present but America itself. In terms of national existence, past and present are remarkably alike. A grey disenchantment hangs over the beginnings of the nation in *Wyandotté* and *The Chainbearer;* if Cooper has become too disillusioned to see Utopia in the American future, he refuses with equal steadfastness to see it in the purely American past.

The instability and impermanence of American life, which Cooper in the last half of his career sees as endangering the gentleman's right to his rational enjoyments, the landowner's right to his property, and finally, in his last novel, the literal right to life itself, had been one of his themes in the years of his untroubled beginnings. His first worth-while novel, *The Spy*, is about a revolution, and his next, *The Pioneers*, is about the destruction of an older way of life by the coming of civilization. Even in his early works Cooper's finest awareness is of the victims of change and of the cruelty of the process. But he is not yet committed to seeing as evil the irresistible forces that make for change, and it is this uncommitted insight, which sees no more than the mere inevitability of life, that makes the persecuted and exiled Natty so great. With his most famous class of the dispossessed, his good Indians, Cooper succeeds not by sympathetic identification but by a pathetic fallacy which endows them with his own ability to accept their dispossession philosophically; and it is this capacity for acceptance that gives them their haunting improbable charm.

Cooper's untroubled detachment—so remarkable because he was himself one of the victims of American instability and his writing career was begun just after, perhaps because of, the loss of the family fortune which left him burdened with family debts—gives way to personal involvement only when he feels himself unjustly victimized. He may have been wrong in his feeling, may in fact have created the conspiracy against himself which he discovered and which soon by his efforts took on an objective reality. He was not, however, turning aside from his work. His creative energy burst forth amid his fiercest quarrels with the press. For all of its nagging byways, small folly is his own road, at once difficult and self-indulgent, to inaccessible truths. The sense of betrayal, so unbecoming in him personally, enriches the meaning of his work. It gives him, while he seems perversely bent on taking his stand against time itself, his sudden tragic glimpses that every present moment of living is in some form a treachery to the past.

He never found a wholly adequate symbol in which to concentrate his tragic vision, perhaps because in the depths of his nature his heart was cheerful, and the bitterness was on the surface, for all the world to see, in his mind. The vision remains scattered and fragmentary, distributed not quite impartially, among his best and his poorest works, for his best, the Leather-Stocking Tales by which he was content to be remembered, do not have their full share. But to know his best well and to enjoy it fully, his other work, his very failures, must also be taken into the reckoning; for the gusto and enjoyment of life of which the best are so full are all the finer for a knowledge of their bitter price.

Bibliographical Note

BIBLIOGRAPHY

A Descriptive Bibliography of the Writings of James Fenimore Cooper, by Robert E. Spiller and Philip C. Blackburn (New York: Bowker, 1934), is detailed and complete. *James Fenimore Cooper: Representative Selections, with Introduction, Bibliography, and Notes*, by Robert E. Spiller (New York: American Book Company, 1936), has a good critical bibliography of both biographical and critical writings about Cooper. Later material may be found in *Articles on American Literature Appearing in Current Periodicals: 1920-1945*, by Lewis Leary (Durham, N. C.: Duke University Press, 1947), pages 44-47, and in the bibliography in volume 3 of the *Literary History of the United States* (New York: Macmillan, 1948).

WORKS

Of the numerous nineteenth-century collected editions of the novels none is in print in its entirety. *Cooper's Novels*, 32 volumes, illustrated from drawings by F. O. C. Darley

(New York: Townsend, 1859-1861), is one of the leading editions, and many later sets, using the Darley illustrations, were based on it. *J. Fenimore Cooper's Works*, Household edition, 32 volumes (New York and Boston: Hurd & Houghton, later Houghton, Mifflin, 1876-1884), has prefaces by the novelist's daughter Susan Fenimore Cooper to 15 of the novels. The last edition, *The Works of James Fenimore Cooper*, 33 volumes, usually known as the Mohawk edition (New York: Putnam's, 1895-1900), includes *Ned Myers*, and seems to be the only collected edition some of whose volumes are still in print.

Of the numerous reprints of The Leather-Stocking Tales and of *The Spy* and *The Pilot* very few are now in print. *Satanstoe* has been published with an interesting introduction by Robert E. Spiller and Joseph D. Coppock (New York: American Book Company, 1937). The most useful introduction to *The Spy* is by Tremaine McDowell (New York: Scribner's, 1931). *Autobiography of a Pocket Handkerchief*, never included in any of the collected editions, has been published in a limited edition (Chapel Hill, N. C.: George F. Horner and Raymond Adams, 1949) and was previously brought out with an introduction by Walter Lee Brown (Evanston, Ill., The Golden-Booke Press, 1897).

There has never been a collected edition of Cooper's nonfiction, and many of his contributions to magazines and letters to newspapers have never been published in book form. Among the more important reprints of the nonfiction are: *The American Democrat* (New York: Knopf, 1931) with a lively introduction by H. L. Mencken, written in part from the point of view of the "liberalism" of the

Prohibition era; *Gleanings in Europe*, 2 volumes (New York: Oxford University Press, 1928 and 1930)—the *France* and the *England*, both with introductions by Mr. Spiller, the one to the *England* being particularly felicitous in its picture of Cooper in London; *New York* (New York: William Farquhar Payson, 1930) with an introduction by Dixon Ryan Fox analyzing Cooper's views on Federal Constitutional history and on the Anti-Rent War. *The Chronicles of Cooperstown* has been reprinted and continued in the following histories of the town: *A Condensed History of Cooperstown* . . . , by S. T. Livermore (Albany: J. Munsell, 1862); *A Centennial Offering* . . . , edited by S. M. Shaw (Cooperstown: Freeman's Journal, 1886); *A History of Cooperstown* . . . , by Walter R. Littel (Cooperstown: Freeman's Journal, 1929). Mr. Spiller's *Representative Selections* consists entirely of excerpts from the nonfiction and shows it at its best.

Correspondence of James Fenimore-Cooper, edited by his grandson James Fenimore Cooper, 2 volumes (New Haven: Yale University Press, 1922), has only some of Cooper's letters, and, as the editor notes, where part of a letter is omitted the omission is not indicated. It contains also a great many letters to Cooper (in fact, almost as many as those by him), his last diary (January-May 1848), and "Small Family Memories"—the recollections (to 1828) of the novelist's daughter Susan, written in 1883 for her nephews and nieces. The novelist's grandson also turned over a great mass of Cooper's correspondence, manuscripts, and other papers to the Yale University Library, which has the most extensive collection of Cooper material.

Unpublished letters of Cooper can be found also at the

New York State Historical Association, Fenimore House, Cooperstown (which has as well an important collection of clippings relating to Cooper and files of the *Freeman's Journal* and *Otsego Republican*); in the Berg Collection and the Manuscript Collection of the New York Public Library; in the New-York Historical Society; and in Houghton Library of Harvard University.

BIOGRAPHY AND CRITICISM

Memorial of James Fenimore Cooper (New York: Putnam's, 1852) has Bryant's Discourse and speeches and letters by others, including Dr. John W. Francis who had known Cooper for thirty years. Bryant's Discourse appears also in *Orations and Addresses*, by William Cullen Bryant (New York: Putnam's, 1873) and in *Precaution* in the Townsend-Darley edition and in other editions based on it. *James Fenimore Cooper*, by Thomas R. Lounsbury (Boston: Houghton, Mifflin, 1882), written for the old American Men of Letters Series, is the first full-length biography. Scholarly, witty, urbane, it is the genteel tradition at its best, and is remarkably accurate in view of the fact that the biographer was not given access to the family papers. The biographer performs the difficult feat of being unsympathetic with his subject but not unfair to it; the reader is always made sufficiently aware of Lounsbury's tacit assumption that the novelist should not have interested himself so intensely in politics and controversy. *James Fenimore Cooper*, by W. B. Shubrick Clymer (Boston: Small, Maynard, 1900), also written for a series, the Beacon Biographies of Eminent Americans, is much shorter and more sympathetic, a pleasant account but not so distinguished as its predecessor. *James Fenimore Cooper*, by Mary E. Phillips (New York: John Lane, 1913) is charmingly illustrated and sweetly written but inadequate and at times inaccurate. *The "Effingham" Libels on Cooper . . .* , by Ethel R. Outland (Madison: University of Wisconsin Studies in Language and Literature, Number 28, 1929) is a well-documented history of the libel suits, the only attempt at full presentation of this complicated subject. *James Fenimore Cooper*, by Henry Walcott Boynton (New York: Century, 1931) is the most complete narrative of the novelist's whole life; Mr. Boynton was the first writer given access to the mass of family letters and documents many of which had never been seen by anyone outside of the Cooper family. *Fenimore Cooper, Critic of his Times*, by Robert E. Spiller (New York: Minton, Balch, 1931), is a biography of Cooper emphasizing primarily his social and political thought and is the first and the leading study of the novelist as a social and political critic; it is supplemented by Mr. Spiller's introduction to his *Representative Selections*. In this field there is also a monograph, *The Social Criticism of Fenimore Cooper*, by John F. Ross (Berkeley, Calif.: University of California Press, 1933); and Dorothy Waples' *The Whig Myth of Fenimore Cooper* (New Haven: Yale University Press, 1938), a study of Cooper as a good party-man and loyal Democrat attacked by the Whig press solely for party reasons. *Fenimore Cooper: Sa vie et son œuvre: La jeunesse (1789-1826)*, by Marcel Clavel (Aix-en-Provence: Imprimerie Universitaire de Provence, 1938), a doctoral thesis, is the most detailed biographical work on Cooper yet produced, with respect to both his life and his writings, up to the time he sailed to

Europe. M. Clavel's book is on a monumental scale and with meticulous scholarship corrects even slight errors of its predecessors, at times somewhat severely. A useful companion-piece is M. Clavel's *Fenimore Cooper and his Critics* (same publisher and year), a series of excerpts and summaries of American, British, and French criticism of the first six novels from their publication through 1933.

Susan Fenimore Cooper's notes to *Pages and Pictures from the Writings of James Fenimore Cooper* (New York: Townsend, 1861) have a considerable amount of biographical information as well as occasionally sprightly criticism. She also wrote two articles for the *Atlantic Monthly* (February and October 1887), "A Glance Backward," about the writing of *Precaution* and *The Spy*, and "A Second Glance Backward," which is about the European years and contains what seems to be Cooper's only surviving poem, an elegy in a Leghorn cemetery at the grave of a naval friend. Miss Cooper would perhaps have been a devoted and excellent official biographer had she not been prevented by her father's injunction, but her reminiscences scattered over more than a quarter of a century are sometimes inconsistent and give the impression of being carelessly written, as if her respect for her father's wish made it impossible to take the problems of biography seriously.

The bibliographies of writings about Cooper which I have mentioned list books and articles that contain Cooper letters not found in the *Correspondence* or that have biographical information about him. To these can be added: *A Memoir of George Palmer Putnam*, by George Haven Putnam, 2 volumes (New York: Putnam's, 1903); *A Biography of William Cullen Bryant* . . . , by Parke Godwin, 2 volumes (New York: Appleton, 1883); "J. Fenimore Cooper," by Richard B. Kimball in *Frank Leslie's Popular Monthly*, June 1881; *The Letters of Willis Gaylord Clark and Lewis Gaylord Clark*, edited by Leslie W. Dunlap (New York: New York Public Library, 1940); "Editor's Table" in the *Knickerbocker*, February 1860, clearly by Lewis Gaylord Clark; and "James Fenimore Cooper" in *Lippincott's Magazine*, December 1871, later recollections by Lewis Gaylord Clark, conflicting in some details with his anonymous article in the *Knickerbocker*.

Some of the most interesting criticism of Cooper, for the general reader, is by writers of great fiction: Balzac's article on the publication of *The Pathfinder*, "Fenimore Cooper et Walter Scott" (*Oeuvres Complètes*, volume XXIII, Paris: Calmann-Lévy, 1879; translated by Katharine Prescott Wormeley in *The Personal Opinions of Honoré de Balzac*, Boston: Little Brown, 1908); and his conversation about Cooper (*Balzac en pantoufles*, by Léon Gozlan, Paris, Michel Lévy frères, 1856; translated in *Balzac in Slippers*, New York: McBride, 1929); Poe's unfavorable review of *Wyandotté* (*Graham's Magazine*, November 1843, and reprinted in the Stedman-Woodberry edition of Poe's works and also in the Richard Henry Stoddard edition); Melville's review of *The Sea Lions* (*The Literary World*, April 28, 1849); Mark Twain's gay and devastating essay "Fenimore Cooper's Literary Offenses" (*North American Review*, July 1895; reprinted in any full edition of his works and in such anthologies as *A Subtreasury of American Humor*, edited by E. B. White and Katharine S. White, New York: Coward-McCann, 1941, and *The Shock of Recognition*, edited by Edmund Wilson, New York: Doubleday, Doran, 1943). A previously unpublished part of Mark Twain's attack, not so funny as the original, has appeared as "Fenimore Cooper's Further Literary Offenses" in *The New England Quarterly*, September 1946. Joseph Conrad's brief appreciation of Cooper and Marryat, "Tales of the Sea," is published in his *Notes on Life and Letters* (New York: Doubleday, Page, 1921). D. H. Lawrence's provoking, willfully subjective, impressionistic masterpiece, *Studies in Classic American Literature* (New York: Seltzer, 1923; also in *The Shock of Recognition*), has fine chapters on Cooper, rewarding even when false to fact, as in the suggestion of a wealthy Cooper writing all of the Leather-Stocking Tales in a Paris boudoir.

The political background of the New York of Cooper's early years is well presented in *The Decline of Aristocracy in the Politics of New York*, by Dixon Ryan Fox (New York: Columbia University, 1919). *The Age of Jackson*, by Arthur M. Schlesinger, Jr. (Boston: Little, Brown, 1945), is a brilliant study of the intellectual basis of Jacksonian democracy and has a good brief description of Cooper's political views. *Tin Horns and Calico*, by Henry Christman (New York: Holt, 1945), a fascinating and vivid history of the Anti-Rent War as a significant political movement, is written with a warm sympathy for the farmers and reformers whom Cooper hated. An excellent supplement to it for the underlying economic facts is *Landlords and Farmers in the Hudson-Mohawk Region, 1789-1850*, by David Maldwyn Ellis (New York: Cornell University Press, 1946).

For the Mary Bodine case, see *The People* v. *Mary Bodine* in *Reports of Select Cases decided in the Courts of New York . . .* , by John W. Edmonds (New York: Diossy, 1868), volume I at page 36 *et seq.*, Judge Edmonds's report of the trial at which he presided in March 1845 and of the attempt in November to hold another trial in New York City.

ENGLISH TITLES

In England some of Cooper's books were brought out under titles quite different from those used in the United States. Some of the more important differences are:

AMERICAN TITLE	ENGLISH TITLE
The Wept of Wish-ton-Wish	*The Borderers* (also *The Heathcotes*)
Gleanings in Europe (the book about France)	*Recollections of Europe*
Gleanings in Europe: England	*England; with Sketches of Society in the Metropolis*
Gleanings in Europe: Italy	*Excursions in Italy*
Sketches of Switzerland	*Excursions in Switzerland*
Sketches of Switzerland: Part Second	*A Residence in France, with an Excursion up the Rhine, and a Second Visit to Switzerland*
Home as Found	*Eve Effingham*
Autobiography of a Pocket Handkerchief	*The French Governess*
Miles Wallingford	*Lucy Hardinge*
The Redskins	*Ravensnest*
Jack Tier	*Captain Spike*
The Crater	*Mark's Reef*
The Oak Openings	*The Bee Hunter*

Index

Index

Jays, the, 11
Jefferson, Pres. Thomas, 12, 257
Johnson, Dr. Samuel, 55
Journal des Débats, 87
July Revolution, 75, 76
juries, 239-42

Kemble, Fanny, 245
Kent, Chancellor James, 39, 50
Kimball, Richard B., 244
King, Charles, 50
King Philip's War, 68
Knickerbocker, 124, 126, 166
Kossuth, Louis, 256

Lafayette, Marquis de, 53, 59-60, 66, 75, 85, 89
landlords and tenants, 199-219, 253, 260
Lawrence, D. H., 29, 30, 117, 194, 216
leases in the Hudson Valley, 198, 207-208, 211-12, 218-19, 252
Leather-Stocking statue, Cooperstown, 256
libel, 169-70, 186-88, 217
libel cases, verdicts in, 186n.
Literary World, 244
Livingston, Edward, 89
Livingston leases, 198
Livingstons, the, 11, 200
Lockhart, John Gibson, 98, 124-30, 131
Life of Scott, 124-30
Longfellow, H. W., 166, 256
Louis Philippe, King, 53, 75
Lounsbury, Thomas R., *James Fenimore Cooper*, 3, 226
loyalists, 16
"Lunch, The," 39
Lyell's *Principles of Geology*, 224
Lyons consulate, 49-50

Mackenzie, Alexander Slidell, 140, 188-93
Maclay, *History of the United States Navy*, 161
Mahan, Alfred T., 161
Married Women's Property Act, 238
Marx, Karl, 209
Melville, Herman, 144, 192-93, 235, 256
Billy Budd, 193
Mexican War, 225
Mickiewicz, Adam, 75
Molière, *Le Misanthrope*, 262
Monarchy vs. republic, 76, 85
Monk, Maria, 89
Montauk packet, 115-16
Montcalm, General, 43
Montgomery County, 152
"Morgan, Jane," *see* JFC's Works: *Tales for Fifteen*
Morning Courier and New York Enquirer, 131
Morris, George, 188
Morse, S. F. B., 39, 87, 88-90, 133, 247
Murray, John, 244
Myers, Edward, 183-86

Naples, Bay of, 71, 174, 250
Napoleon Bonaparte, 86
Napoleonic Wars, 196, 198
Nelson, Judge R. R., 246
Newport, stone tower at, 237
New York American, 50, 86
New York Commercial Advertiser, 135, 140, 141
New York *Evening Post*, 136n., 186n.
New York *Evening Signal*, 151
New York harbor, 71, 250
New York *Herald*, 154
New York *New World*, 152

Index